DEFEASIBILITY IN PHILOSOPHY

Grazer Philosophische Studien

INTERNATIONAL JOURNAL FOR ANALYTIC PHILOSOPHY

FOUNDED BY

Rudolf Haller

EDITED BY

Johannes L. Brandl

Marian David

Maria E. Reicher

Leopold Stubenberg

VOL 87 - 2013

Rodopi

Amsterdam - New York, NY 2013

DEFEASIBILITY IN PHILOSOPHY

KNOWLEDGE, AGENCY, RESPONSIBILITY, AND THE LAW

Edited by

CLAUDIA BLÖSER, MIKAEL JANVID,
HANNES OLE MATTHIESSEN & MARCUS WILLASCHEK

Die Herausgabe der GPS erfolgt mit Unterstützung des *Instituts für Philosophie der Universität Graz*, der *Forschungsstelle für Österreichische Philosophie, Graz*, und wird von folgenden Institutionen gefördert:

Bundesministerium für Bildung, Wissenschaft und Kultur, Wien
Abteilung für Wissenschaft und Forschung des Amtes der Steiermärkischen Landesregierung, Graz
Kulturreferat der Stadt Graz

The paper on which this book is printed meets the requirements of "ISO 9706:1994, Information and documentation - Paper for documents - Requirements for permanence".

Lay out: Thomas Binder, Graz
ISBN: 978-90-420-3761-8
E-book ISBN: 978-94-012-1011-9
ISSN: 0165-9227
E-ISSN: 1875-6735

Printed in The Netherlands

TABLE OF CONTENTS

Preface v

Claudia BLÖSER, Mikael JANVID, Hannes Ole MATTHIESSEN & Marcus WILLASCHEK: Introduction 1

Michael WILLIAMS: Knowledge, Ascriptivism and Defeasible Concepts 9

Klemens KAPPEL: Knowledge, Defeasibility, and the Gettier Problem 37

Mikael JANVID: The Challenges of Traveling without Itinerary: The Overriding Case 59

Hannes Ole MATTHIESSEN: Entitlement and Public Accessibility of Epistemic Status 75

Marcus WILLASCHEK: Strawsonian Epistemology. What Epistemologists Can Learn from "Freedom and Resentment" 99

Claudia BLÖSER: The Defeasible Structure of Ascriptions of Responsibility 129

R. Jay WALLACE: Comment on Claudia Blöser "The Defeasible Structure of Ascriptions of Responsibility" 151

Claudia BLÖSER: Reply to Wallace 157

Katarzyna PAPRZYCKA: Can a Spasm Cause an Action? An Argument for Responsibilist Theories of Action 161

Michael QUANTE: Autonomous by Default. Assessing "Non-Alienation" in John Christman's Conception of Personal Autonomy 177

Frederick SCHAUER: On the Open Texture of Law 197

Michel de ARAUJO KURTH: Selected Thematic Bibliography of Work on Defeasibility in Philosophy and Related Disciplines 217

PREFACE

This volume grew out of a conference on defeasibility in ethics, epistemology, law, and logic held at the Goethe-Universität Frankfurt am Main in September 2010. We are grateful to Klemens Kappel, Michael Quante, R. Jay Wallace, and Michael Williams for their contributions to both the conference and to this volume, as well as to Katarzyna Paprzycka and Frederick Schauer, who did not participate in the conference, for contributing to the volume. Thanks also to Michel de Araujo Kurth for updating his bibliography on defeasibility.

The conference on defeasibility itself grew out of a three-year research project, funded from 2007 to 2010 by the Deutsche Forschungsgemeinsschaft (DFG), on "Defeasibility and Discourse Dependence" ("Anfechtbare Zuschreibungsbegriffe"). Claudia Blöser, Hannes Ole Matthiessen and Mikael Janvid were the researchers employed in the project, Marcus Willaschek the project leader. The scope of the papers in this volume reflects the scope of our research project, which aimed at investigating defeasibility on both the "theoretical" and the "practical" side—primarily in epistemology (perception, epistemic justification, a priori knowledge) and in action theory (free will, responsibility, imputation). We are extremely grateful to the DFG for their funding of both the project and the conference. Additional funding for the conference was provided by the Verein von Freunden und Förderern der Johann Wolfgang Goethe-Universität, whom we would also like to thank.

Between 2007 and 2010, distinguished guests came to Frankfurt for various workshops and provided our work on defeasibility with important input and feedback: Albert Casullo, Fred Detske, Kathrin Gluer, Terry Horgan, and Michael Williams. Among colleagues from Frankfurt, Klaus Günther and André Fuhrmann participated in these workshops. We would like to thank all of them.

Many people have helped us with our research-project and with the conference. We would like to thank Michel de Araujo Kurth, Andreas Maier, Andreas Müller, and Maria Russo. Special thanks are due to Claudia Cuadra Carbajal, who supported the project as a student assistant from beginning to end with much enthusiasm—and with her camera.

Claudia BLÖSER
Mikael JANVID
Hannes Ole MATTHIESSEN
Marcus WILLASCHEK

Grazer Philosophische Studien
87 (2013), 1–8.

INTRODUCTION

Claudia BLÖSER, Johann Wolfgang Goethe-Universität
Mikael JANVID, Stockholm University
Hannes Ole MATTHIESSEN, Université de Fribourg
Marcus WILLASCHEK, Johann Wolfgang Goethe-Universität

Although defeasible reasoning, defeasible rules, defeasible concepts, and defeasible normative statuses play a role in many different philosophically relevant human practices, the term "defeasibility" has been introduced into philosophy only recently. Today, the concept of defeasibility is employed in many different areas of philosophy, some of which are represented in the present volume. We find epistemologists discussing defeasible warrant, justification, and entitlement (cf. the contributions to this volume by Mikael Janvid, Klemens Kappel, Hannes Ole Matthiessen, Marcus Willaschek and Michael Williams); legal philosophers arguing for and against the defeasible character of legal rules (cf. the contribution of Frederick Schauer); and philosophers working on agency, autonomy and responsibility debating whether or not these concepts exhibit a defeasible structure (cf. the contributions by Claudia Blöser, R. Jay Wallace, Michael Quante and Katarzyna Paprzycka; for more applications of the concept of defeasibility in these and other areas of philosophy, cf. the extensive bibliography by Michael de Araujo Kurth at the end of this volume). In this brief introduction, we want to outline some mainly structural aspects of defeasibility that are relevant for the current discussion. We will not offer an overview of the contents of this volume; instead, a brief abstract can be found at the beginning of each contribution.

In his 1949 paper "The Ascription of Responsibility and Rights", H.L.A. Hart claims that central legal concepts do not follow the logic of necessary and sufficient conditions. The concept of a contract, for example, is applicable as soon as certain initial conditions—"i.e. at least two *parties*, an *offer* by one, *acceptance* by the other, a *memorandum* in writing in some cases and *consideration*" (Hart 1949, 148)—are fulfilled, whereas we can no longer apply the concept once it turns out that "other circumstances are present which brings the case under some recognized head of exception" (Hart 1949, 147f.). Hart remarks that "[t]his characteristic of legal concepts is one for which no word exists in ordinary English. The words 'conditional' and 'negative' have the wrong implications, but the law has a word which with some hesitation I borrow and extend: this is the word '*defeasible*', used of a legal interest in property which is subject to termination or '*defeat*' in a number of different contingencies but remains intact if no such contingencies mature. In this sense, then, contract is a defeasible concept" (Hart 1949, 148).

Defeasible concepts in Hart's sense are thus concepts that are applied according to the schema: "***If*** *x satisfies conditions* A_1*–*A_n, ***then*** *x is F,* ***unless*** *some defeating condition* B_1 *or* B_2 *or* B_3 *or … obtains.*" Hart takes the presence of an "unless-clause" to be the distinctive characteristic of defeasible concepts. Since what is defeasible (what is followed by an unless-clause) need not always be (the application of) a concept, it is helpful to regard Hart's account of defeasible concepts as a special case of a more general schema of the form "*If A then B unless C*". This "Hart-Schema" contains the logical core of Hart's account of defeasibility.

Not all applications of defeasibility in philosophy do conform to the Hart-schema, though. Whereas defeasibility according to Hart involves a set of conditions A for its being the case that B (unless C), some treatments of defeasibility focus mainly on the element of revisability (that is, the *unless-clause*) without committing themselves to any specific view about the initial conditions (A). One might label these two classes of theoretical approaches *one-pronged* versus *two-pronged.*

For instance, theories that highlight the corrigibility or fallibility of certain kinds of statements, and thereby the defeasibility of our entitlements to hold certain beliefs (beliefs about the empirical world, the future, the past, other minds, and so on) involve a one-pronged conception of defeasibility. They usually do not recognize *special* conditions for the obtaining of the state of affairs that is defeasible, since they argue that all kinds of conditions are on a par since none of them can give us certainty. Another example of an application of one-pronged defeasibility is at work in the linguistic thesis that, due to the *open texture* of language, all statements are defeasible because we can never exclude cases in which we *don't know what to say.*

Two-pronged conceptions of defeasibility may seem more philosophically challenging insofar as they pick out a phenomenon that is not as widespread as fallibility. The Hart-schema ("If A then B unless C") is the classical model for such a two-pronged approach to defeasibility, since it contains both the initial conditions for the obtaining of the state of affairs, and the conditions of defeat. These have to be clearly distinguished. The first set of conditions ("A" in the schema)—the initial conditions that are responsible for the obtaining of the defeasible state of affairs in the first place —is normally also sufficient for the state of affairs B to obtain. Without them, there would be no entitlement in the first place. Consider the following examples:

S looks at a bouquet of daffodils in broad daylight—so, defeasibly—S is entitled to believe that there is a bouquet of daffodils.

A promised B to help—so, defeasibly—A is obliged to help B.

S knows that Tweety is a bird—so, defeasibly—S is entitled to infer that Tweety can fly.

The second set of conditions ("C" in the schema) are the *conditions of defeat.* If one of them is present, then the state of affairs does not obtain even though the initial conditions obtain. Consider:

S does not know what daffodils are (or is unable to distinguish them from tulips); S is looking at a bouquet (if one may say so) of artificial flowers.

A is a small child; A was coerced into making the promise.

Tweety is a penguin.

These are conditions under which the prima facie entitlement to believe that there are daffodils, the prima facie duty to help someone, and the inference to the conclusion that an individual can fly, are defeated.

Two-pronged conceptions of defeasibility contain a number of structural peculiarities. Whereas the initial conditions are *normally* (i.e. in the absence of a defeater) *sufficient* for the state of affairs in question to hold, they need not be *necessary* in all cases. Sometimes, there is another route to the defeasible state of affairs, such that a specific set of conditions may be absent and yet the state of affairs obtains. Someone may know, for example, that there is a bouquet of daffodils in the room without having looked in its direction recently. She might, e.g., remember having put it on the shelf an hour ago. So looking at (or having recently looked at) a bouquet of daffodils is not necessary for an entitlement to believe that there are daffodils in the room. The case of a contract, on the other hand, is an example of an entitlement that requires the fulfilment of the entitlement conferring conditions. Without two parties, offer by one, acceptance by the other and consideration, there can be no binding contract.

Another vital feature of two-pronged defeasibility is the asymmetry between the *normal case* and the *exceptional case* of defeat. In the normal (or privileged) case, the fulfilment of the initial condition is sufficient for the entitlement to obtain (in the Hart-schema: A implies B). *Normally,* S is entitled to believe that there is a bouquet of daffodils in the room just by looking at it. The case of defeat where the entitlement conferring condition obtains and yet there is no entitlement because a condition of defeat is also present (in the Hart-schema: A, but not B because of C) is *exceptional.* This exceptional character of defeat can be cached out in various ways, depending on the subject matter in question. In law, for example, it is manifest in the claimant-challenger asymmetry: The party who claims a contract before court is only required to show that the initial conditions are satisfied. It is not her duty to rule out possible conditions of defeat. Rather, it is the party who challenges the claim to a contract who has to show that such a condition is present. In epistemology the asymmetry between normal and exceptional cases has sometimes been formulated in deontological terms in a similar fashion: Once you are in conditions that entitle you to a belief, you are not required to rule out *possible* circumstances that *could* defeat your entitlement. Unless you have some reason to suppose that things are other than they seem, you behave epistemically rationally if you silently assume that everything is going well. Generally speaking, then, the exceptional case is one that requires some sort of explanation, argument, or evidence. Where in the normal case we can simply infer B from A, in the exceptional case ("A, but not B because of C") the specific circumstances C that defeat the inference to B in this particular case must be mentioned in order to claim defeat.

Note that the distinction between normal case and exception is not a statistical one: Sometimes the privileged normal case is not the most common and yet the exception is what needs explanation. Take, e.g., the defeasible generalization "other things being equal, fish eggs develop into fish". Here, for many species of fish at least, it is in fact only a small percentage of eggs that actually make it. So there is nothing exceptional, *statistically speaking*, in a fish egg not developing into a fish . Nevertheless, those cases in which a fish develops out of an egg are normal, and require no explanation, insofar as eggs develop into fish unless something else (predators, disease) intervenes, whereas every story of a fish egg not developing into a fish is incomplete unless it mentions what it was *this time* that prevented the normal course of nature (cf. Lance and Little 2004, 441f.).

The asymmetry between normal and exceptional cases has an important effect on the rational requirements that hold according to a two-pronged conception of defeasibility: Typically, the obtaining of the state of affairs in question, B, does not need to be argued for once the initial conditions A are in place. So wherever the initial conditions for the obtaining of a state of affairs are in place, its obtaining is the *default*. Things are different with defeaters: In order to defeat a state of affairs you need to be able to point out that a defeating condition obtains. The act of putting into question a state of affairs by considering or showing that a defeater is present is commonly called a challenge. Whereas defeat is a success-verb (because a state of affairs is only defeated if there is a condition incompatible with it), challenges may sometimes be legitimate even in the absence of actual defeaters: Evidence to the effect that there *might be* a defeater is often sufficient. If it turns out that actually there was no defeater, the challenge has been rebutted.

Challenges, as we just said, do not come for free. In order to be successful the challenger has to show that there is some reason to suppose that a defeater might be present. Challenges that are not backed up by such a reason – so-called "naked" challenges– are dialectically inefficacious. Just saying "I doubt that this contract is valid" or "I think you don't know that these are daffodils" is not normally sufficient to undermine a claim to contract or knowledge.

Given the Hart-schema "If A then B, unless C", different readings of the impact that a defeating condition has on the state of affairs B are possible. In particular, we can distinguish between a temporal and a non-temporal reading. According to the *non-temporal* reading, the occurrence of a defeater is incompatible with the obtaining of the state of affairs *tout court*: If B is defeated at some point of time by C, then B in fact never held true. Defeasible states of affairs in this sense, then, are states of affairs that obtain *unless* a defeater exists. According to a *temporal* reading, on the other hand, the state of affairs may hold *until* it is defeated. The result of the challenge, in this case, is merely that B *no longer* obtains.

Whether the temporal or the non-temporal reading of defeaters is more suitable will depend on the specifics of the case at hand. H.L.A. Hart

(Hart 1949, 149f.), e.g., remarks that the content of the defeater determines whether its occurrence renders a claim, e.g. a claim to a contract, "void ab initio" (such that the exceptional circumstances show that in fact there never was a contract) or merely "voidable" (such that the contract can be nullified from then on). In epistemology, also, both options may have applications: If it turns out that a given true belief could easily have been false, some epistemologists will take this to show that the belief *never* qualified as knowledge. But the same epistemologists can admit that the person holding the belief may well have been entitled to do so *until* she became aware of the challenge in question.

In some areas at least, two kinds of challenges can be distinguished. On the one hand, a defeasible status can be challenged by pointing out that a defeating condition is (or appears to be) present in the actual case. Although the initial conditions obtain, the state of affairs in question does not, because the defeating condition undermines it. According to the Hart-schema, these challenges have the logical structure "Not-B (although A) because of C".

On the other hand, a challenge can be raised without reference to a defeating condition, namely if it turns out (or seems likely) that the entitlement conferring conditions were not fulfilled in the first place. Hart notes that these so-called "joinders of issue" form a part of the legal practice. Sometimes a claim to a contract fails because one of the initial conditions for a contract was (contrary to first appearances) not satisfied. The joinder of issue has the logical form "Not-B because not-A". Of course the inference from "A implies B" to "Non-A implies non-B" is not logically valid. Joinders of issue are primarily effective in contexts where the entitlement conferring conditions are *necessary* for the entitlement in question (as, e.g., in the law of contract). In other contexts, the challenge may, however, bring about a shift in the burden of proof: Once the initial conditions A are proven to be absent, the obtaining of state B can no longer be assumed by default, but rather stands in need of argument. Note, however, that joinders of issue can occur in cases of states of affairs that are not defeasible in any interesting sense. Take the entitlement to draw the inference from "Number n is divisible by 2 and by 3" to "Number n is divisible by 6". There are no conditions of defeat such that your entitlement to draw an inference of this type can be defeated in case n can be divided by 2 and by 3 – *every* number that is divisible by 2 and 3 is also divisible by 6. However, a joinder of issue can be raised against instances of "number n is divisible by 6 because it is both divisible by 2 and by 3", namely in case it turns out that n is in fact not divisible by 2 and 3. This would be a case of defeasibility only insofar as claims of the form "number n is divisible by 6 because it is both divisible by 2 and by 3" are fallible.

Conceptions of defeasibility are confronted with two main lines of criticism: On the one hand, one may doubt that defeasible concepts, rules, or entitlements are substantially different from their non-defeasible alternatives. After all, as Hart already remarked, it is *in principle* always possible to regard the absence of defeating conditions as a necessary condition for the obtaining of the state of affairs. So the logical structure of the Hart-schema "If A then B, unless C" may turn out to be merely superficial if it can also be expressed in terms of necessary and sufficient conditions: "If A and non-C, then B". The reason why this approach does not work in the case of the law, according to Hart, is simply that there are often very many and divers defeating conditions. So the attempt to get rid of the defeasible structure would result in legal definitions that contain dozens or hundreds of necessary conditions for their application. These would be of no practical use whatsoever. Moreover, the set of recognized defeating conditions may be subject to change—new exceptions can be added in the course of time. This would have the consequence that legal concepts are constantly changing their content—an at least unwelcome consequence. It is, however, not clear from the outset that this line of argument works for all possible examples of defeasible structures. Where the conditions of defeat are few and temporally stable it may indeed be possible to replace the defeasible logic with a deductive logic. This is a question that has to be answered case by case.

A related criticism concerns defeasible concepts the content of which may not fully depend on the rule-governed use we make of them. Think, for example, of default and challenge-conceptions of epistemic status, autonomy, or moral responsibility (cf. Hannes Ole Matthiessen's, Michael Quante's and Claudia Blöser's contributions to this volume). Here one might wonder whether defeasibility may not be a merely pragmatic, surface phenomenon. While our ascriptions of knowledge, autonomy, or responsibility may indeed follow a default- and-challenge pattern, it might be held that whether someone *really* knows something, is autonomous, or responsible depends on factors (e.g. reliability, freedom of the will) that are quite independent from the criteria we use in our practice of attributing knowledge, autonomy, and responsibility.

The impact that both kinds of criticism actually have depends, partly, on the philosophical framework in which defeasibility is studied. If one regards the logic of default and challenge as a robust alternative to competing conceptions, one has to deny the possibility of a deductive alternative that captures the same phenomena adequately. Hart, for example, surely thought that many legal concepts could not play their role in the legal practice if they were reformulated in terms of necessary and sufficient conditions. It is, however, also possible to take a more relaxed approach. Even if one remains agnostic about the possibility of formulating necessary and sufficient conditions for certain concepts, one may still employ the dialectics of default and challenge to reach an understanding of how these concepts are embedded in human practices. This, after all, seems to be a philosophically promising enterprise.

Grazer Philosophische Studien
87 (2013), 9–36.

KNOWLEDGE, ASCRIPTIVISM AND DEFEASIBLE CONCEPTS

Michael WILLIAMS
Johns Hopkins University

Summary

In "The Ascription of Responsibilities and Rights," H. L. A. Hart introduces two ideas, which he takes to be importantly related: ascriptive sentences and defeasible concepts. Hart's purpose is to dispel certain confusions that he finds in the philosophy of action; but I argue that Hart's ideas are equally pertinent to epistemology. Knowledge is a matter of epistemic authority; and authority is a matter of rights and responsibilities. But Hart's "ascriptivism" has attracted serious criticism and stands in need of clarification, elaboration and even correction. The overall aim of the paper is to present a form of epistemic ascriptivism, in which justification emerges as a defeasible concept in Hart's sense.

Introduction

In his seminal paper, "The Ascription of Responsibilities and Rights," H. L. A. Hart attempts to dispel the confusion that he finds in the philosophy of action. (Hart 1948-49) Hart traces the confusion to a failure to appreciate the semantic character of certain sentences and concepts. First, the real function of sentences that seem to *describe* an act as voluntary is *to ascribe* responsibility to the actor. Second, the concept "voluntary" belongs to a family of concepts that Hart calls "defeasible," borrowing an extending the application of a term from the law of contract. Although such a concept may entail positive conditions for its proper application, they do not exhaust its meaning, since there are also *defeating* conditions in which the concept would not apply. Since these conditions need not have much, if anything, in common, Hart argues that we should not expect an analysis of a defeasible concept in terms of some compact set of necessary and sufficient conditions.

Hart's "ascriptivism" has attracted serious criticism and will not do as it stands. It needs clarification, elaboration and even correction. My first task is to provide this. Then I will turn to knowledge and justification. For me, this is a natural move, for I take knowledge to be a matter of epistemic authority, and authority to be a matter of rights and responsibilities: Hart's original topic. My overall aim, then, is to present a form of epistemic ascriptivism, in which justification emerges as a defeasible concept in Hart's sense. Hart's ideas, introduced to illuminate the concept of action, are equally pertinent to that of knowledge.

1. *Ascriptive sentences and defeasible concepts*

Hart thinks that failure to appreciate the ascriptive character of certain sentences has been a major obstacle to giving a correct philosophical analysis of the concept of human action. As he says, his "main purpose" is

> to suggest that the philosophical analysis of the concept of a human action has been inadequate and confusing, at least in part because sentences of the form "He did it" have been traditionally regarded as primarily descriptive whereas their principal function is what I venture to call *ascriptive*, being quite literally to ascribe responsibility for actions much as the principal function of sentences of the form "This is his" is to ascribe rights in property. (Hart, 1948-49, 171)

Hart insists on a sharp contrast between sentences that are *ascriptive* and those that are *descriptive*. The vital point is that ascriptive sentences are not true or false. Thus:

> Since the judge is literally deciding that on the facts before him a contract does or does not exist, and to do this is neither to describe the facts nor to make deductive nor inductive inferences from the statement of facts, what he does may be either a *right* or a *wrong* decision or a good or a bad judgment and can be either *affirmed* or *reversed* ..., [w]hat cannot be said of it is that it is either *true* or *false* ... (Hart 1948-49, 182)

To say "This is mine" is to give voice to a *performative* utterance, akin to "I promise." In this purely ascriptive context, I employ the words "This is mine" not to *say* but to *do* something: to claim a proprietary right. The same goes for "S did A voluntarily." The primary use of such sentences is not to *de*scribe S's action but to *a*scribe responsibility to S: to hold him liable or accountable for what he did. In both cases, while something significant is done, *nothing* is said. Since no proposition expressed, there is nothing to take a truth value. If Hart is right, philosophers who have assumed that the task of the philosophy of action is to identify—and perhaps to demystify—the property in virtue of which an action is (properly described as) voluntary have gone badly wrong. If sentences like "He did it on purpose" are ascriptive *rather than* descriptive, there is no such property.

Of course, it is far from obvious that Hart *is* right. As Geach famously pointed out, so-called ascriptive sentences can be embedded in truth-functionally complex sentences: for example, as the antecedents of conditionals. But when I say, "If S did A voluntarily, he deserves to be punished," I do not ascribe responsibility to S. According to Geach, this objection shows that Hart's whole way of thinking is confused, conflating judgment with predication. The sentences Hart counts as ascriptive involve predicating a property of a subject, and are thus descriptive, whatever further speech-act may be performed by giving voice to such a sentence. (Geach 1960, 221–5)

It must be said in fairness that Hart himself is reluctant to insist on a sharp distinction between ascriptive and descriptive sentences. As he says, although "This is mine" can be uttered ascriptively to claim a property right, the very same words can be used descriptively, as when (in Hart's example) I am taking a visitor around my estate, pointing out the land that belongs to it. Hart suggests that there is a "sliding scale" from the purely ascriptive to the purely descriptive, with result that there are sentences that are difficult to classify. But while Hart's view is nuanced, the nuances raise more questions than they answer. To begin with, it seems clear that Hart should not have spoken of ascriptive sentences but rather of ascriptive uses of sentences. However, had he done so, questions would have arisen concerning the relation between a sentence's ascriptive *use* (in some contexts) with its descriptive *meaning* (in others). I shall come back to this. But for now, let us continue with Hart.

Hart does more than call attention to ascriptive sentences: he offers to explain their non-descriptive character in terms of the "logical peculiarities" of the concepts that figure in them, arguing that we can learn useful lessons from an examination of certain legal concepts. Thus:

> ascriptive sentences, though they may form only a small part of our ordinary language, resemble in some important respects the formal statements of claim, the indictments, the admissions, the judgments, and the verdicts which constitute so large and so important a part of the language of lawyers; and the logical peculiarities which distinguish these kinds of sentences from descriptive sentences or rather from the theoretical model of descriptive sentences

> with which philosophers often work can best be grasped by considering certain characteristic of legal concepts, as the appear in the practice and procedure of the law … (Hart 1948-49, 171f.)

The logical peculiarities arise from the presence of defeasible concepts, an idea Hart explains with the example of "contract." Although there are positive conditions—notably, the acceptance of an offer—that must be met for a contract to be in place, the meaning of "contract" cannot be given by a set of necessary and sufficient conditions; for when the student has learnt about the positive conditions, "he has still to learn what can defeat a claim that there is a valid contract, even though all these conditions are satisfied." (Hart 1948f., 174f.) The signing of an appropriate document will constitute, or authorize a judge to affirm, the existence of a contract, but only in the absence of certain defeating conditions. A concept is "defeasible" when its application is subject to this kind of defeat.

Now even waiving Geach's objection, we may feel that simply recognizing that certain sentences apparently predicating voluntariness of an action are primarily ascriptions of responsibility to an agent will not dispel the air of mystery surrounding the concept or property of voluntariness (or freedom). After all, ascriptions of responsibility have grounds, so there must be something about an action or actor that makes such ascriptions appropriate, and what is that? But as Hart has shown, there is no set of positive conditions, necessary and sufficient for calling an act "voluntary." Perhaps there are some necessary conditions for ascribing responsibility; but once they are met, a person is properly held responsible for what he has done unless the ascription of responsibility is defeated—unless responsibility is removed or mitigated—by some excusing factor. Notice that the defeating conditions need not have much in common. Presumably, in the case of contact, the rationale for defeating conditions is the general purposes served by the institution. In cases like this, seeking a standard "analysis" of the concept in terms of necessary and sufficient conditions can only breed confusion.

Whether used ascriptively or descriptively, then, defeasible concepts have *no* exhaustively specifiable positive meaning. However, once we understand how defeasible concepts work, we can see that there is no mystery about this. We will not waste our time looking for necessary and sufficient conditions where there are none to be found. Nor will failure to find them leave us puzzled by the "nature" of voluntariness.

Recognizing the existence of defeasible concepts is a major step forward. Less clear, however, is the connection between defeasible concepts and the ascriptive character of judgments involving them. Hart is not as explicit about this matter as we could wish, but I take his thought to run along the following lines. In the case of a descriptive judgment, meaning must determine the judgment's truth-conditions. Ideally, then, when a judgment involves a concept that we would naturally take to be "analyzable," an explanation of that concept's meaning would take the form of a set of necessary and sufficient conditions for the truth of atomic sentences involving it. Thus if "S did A voluntarily" were descriptive in character, we should be able to state necessary and conditions for its being true that S did A voluntarily. However, since the concept of voluntary action is defeasible, no such conditions can be given. Accordingly, the meaning of "S did A voluntarily" is not determined truth conditionally, which means that the meaning of "S did A" is not descriptive.

If this is Hart's argument, it moves far too quickly. Even if we grant that the impossibility of giving necessary and sufficient conditions for the truth of an unembedded sentence involving a defeasible concept shows that the meaning of such a sentence is not to be explained in a simple truth-conditional way, we cannot immediately conclude that the sentence—or even the ascriptive use of the sentence—is non-descriptive.

One reason for challenging a dualism of ascriptive and descriptive sentences—or of uses of sentences—is suggested by Hart's own discussion. Although Hart does not put the point quite this way, I take him to suggest that an essential feature of defeasible concepts is that they enter into (uses of) sentences with a distinctive *epistemic* character. The fact that a certain action was performed—say, signing a document—provides only a *prima facie* reason for judging that a contract has been made. It is through this association of defeasibility with *prima facie* reasons that John Pollock introduced the term "defeasible" into general epistemology: specifically, with respect to the idea of defeasible reasoning. But it may be that the meaning of some—or even all—descriptive sentences is constituted in whole or in part by their justification conditions. This was Pollock's view, and it is not a view to be lightly dismissed. (Pollock 1967, 28–60)

Again, Hart's discussion is qualified but in an unhelpful way. If defeasible concepts are to illuminate that of ascriptive sentences, the presence of a defeasible concept should explain a sentence's non-descriptive—that is, non truth-apt—character. But Hart tells us that that the presence in certain sentences of defeasible concepts does not distinguish "these kinds of sentences from descriptive sentences" so much as from "the theoretical model of descriptive sentences with which philosophers often work."(Hart

1948–49, 171f.) If this is so, the presence in a sentence of a defeasible concept is no reason for supposing that the sentence is non-descriptive. If some theoretical models cannot account for how the sentence's descriptive meaning is constituted, that is an objection to the models.

Summing up, there does not seem to be a dualism of descriptive and ascriptive sentences. Further, the postulation of such a dualism gains no support from the idea of defeasible concepts. It is therefore tempting to conclude that the ascriptive character of certain uses of sentences like "This is mine" or "He did it on purpose" cannot play a fundamental role in constituting their meaning, which appears to be descriptive. But this would be a mistake.

2. *Meaning and use*

In contemporary analytic philosophy, there is a broad current of thought that can reasonably be called "neo-Pragmatist." For present purposes, this contemporary version of pragmatism can be characterized in the terms offered by David Macarthur and Huw Price:

> *PRAGMATISM* =
> *LINGUISTIC PRIORITY* + *ANTI-REPRESENTATIONALISM.*
>
> The Macarthur-Price equation does not mention what is often taken to be the hallmark of Pragmatism: an instrumental (or epistemic) conception of truth. This is all to the good. One of contemporary neo-pragmatism's main advances it to have adopted a *deflationary* (e.g. disquotational or Minimal) account of truth, in contrast to the instrumentalist or epistemic accounts typical of its classical forebear. (Macarthur & Price 2011, 211)
>
> Linguistic Priority is a methodological commitment. It counsels us, when dealing with forms of discourse thought to raise metaphysical problems, not to start by asking about the nature of what we seem to be talking about, but by inquiring into the character of the form of discourse—the vocabulary-genre—in question. For example, in the case of moral discourse, don't court metaphysical puzzlement by asking about the nature of values: investigate the distinctive character—the "logical peculiarities"—of moral vocabulary. It may turn out that such language is not best understood in referential terms at all, but in terms of its expressive function. If so, there will be no problematic ontological commitments to worry about.

If we conclude that moral vocabulary is best understood in broadly "expressivist" terms, we shall have become (in Price's terminology) *local* expressivists: local, because we may still think that a referential or other "representational" approach to meaning remains appropriate for other kinds of discourse, such as scientific discourse or descriptive talk generally. But Anti-Representationalism counsels us that *no* form of discourse should be understood this way. Indeed, a deflationary approach to truth already requires as much since, for deflationists, truth-talk is not fitted to bear this kind of explanatory weight. For pragmatists, some variant of what expressivists attempt locally should be attempted across the board. In a slogan, meaning (including reference) must be explained in terms of *use*. (Macarthur & Price 2011, op. cit.)

Does global expressivism (Price's term) invite a global version of Geach's objection to ascriptivism? No. We must remember that neo-pragmatism combines a non-representationalist approach to meaning with a deflationary approach to truth, so that truth-aptness will lie wherever we find the logical syntax of assertoric discourse. It may be that the global anti-representationalist faces a problem of distinguishing, in non-representational terms, between those forms of discourse that appear to be distinctively "expressive" in character and those that seem "prosaically descriptive." But this is not Geach's problem; and if it is a problem at all, there is no reason to suppose that it is insoluble.[1]

Hart's methodology has evident affinities with the pragmatism of Macarthur and Price. Following the maxim of Linguistic Priority, Hart investigates the character of sentences like "S did S voluntarily," which are not assumed to be straightforwardly descriptive. This leads him to explain the distinctive semantic character of such sentences in non-representational terms, assigning them an ascriptive function. Hart is thus at least a *local* ascriptivist, though his suggestion that the existence of defeasible concepts calls in question a prevalent "theoretical model" of *descriptive* judgments suggests that he would have been open to a more generalized non-representational approach to meaning.

If Geach's objection need not trouble the global non-representationalist, it need not trouble Hart either. But to nail down this claim, I need to explain how the ascriptive uses of certain sentences can play a distinguished role in explaining their conceptual (descriptive) content. To do this, I must say more about what is involved in giving an explanation of meaning in

1. For further discussion, see my (Williams 2013).

terms of use: an EMU. It will be best to begin with a concrete example. I shall take Paul Horwich's Minimal Theory of truth, which Horwich himself treats as a paradigm of his use-based approach to meaning. Horwich's theory of truth, or better (given Linguistic Priority) of truth-talk, can be broken down into four claims:

(1) "true" means what it does to us in virtue of the fact that the law governing its use is that we are prepared to provisionally accept any instance of the schema

(MT): <p> is true ↔ p.

("<p>" is to be read as "the proposition that p.")

(2) Since this law is a meaning constituting acceptance property, the disposition to accept instances of the schema is cognitively fundamental.

(3) These use-facts given by (1) and (2) are "the source of *everything else* we do with the truth predicate."

(4) As a device for semantic ascent and descent, "true" permits new ways of generalizing, allowing us to endorse propositions that we cannot simply list: for example, we can say that every proposition of the form 'p or not-p' is true. (Horwich 2001, 149)

The account is strongly anti-metaphysical. Truth has no interesting nature. For example, it is not explained in terms of reference. As a result, there is no problem of explaining how the relation of reference can be "naturalized." This is very much in the spirit of Hart's treatment of "voluntary." But while much in sympathy with Horwich's general approach, I have two critical observations.

The first is that Horwich's notion of use is strictly "regularist": his acceptance-properties are empirical laws. However, MT contains a logical connective (the biconditional). But if, following Brandom, we understand logical as well as semantic vocabulary in terms of its expressive function, we will hold that MT makes explicit inferential commitments that we could otherwise only exhibit in practice. (Brandom 1994, chs. 2, 5) In effect, MT gives an introduction and elimination rule for "true". This leads me to suggest that the use properties that give meaning to "true" are best understood not as concerning underived *de facto* acceptance of certain sentences, but rather as delineating a class of material-inferential commitments regarded as primitively *acceptable*. Horwich's regularist EMU should be rewritten in normative-inferentialist terms.

My second observation is that, like deflationists generally, Horwich does not limit himself to giving truth-talk's characteristic *inferential proprieties* (or as he would prefer, acceptance *properties*): he also calls attention to its *expressive function*. This means that the EMU for "true" involves *more than one notion of use*.

In the light of these observations, I propose rewriting the EMU for "true." There are still four clauses, but their character is changed and clarified. The first states certain material-inferential proprieties; the second gives the epistemic character of those proprieties; and the third and fourth bring out the functional significance—expressive-performative role and utility--of a word with the use-characteristics just given. Thus:

(1) (Inf/True). Excepting sentences that generate paradox, the inference from "Snow is white" to "It is true that snow is white", and vice-versa, is always good; the inference from "Grass is green to "It is true that grass is green", and vice-versa, is always good, and so on…
(2) (Epist/True). Such inferences are *primitively* acceptable (*a priori*). They are "free" moves in the discursive game.
(3) (EPF/True). As a generalizing device, truth-talk allows us to endorse or repudiate claims that, for whatever reason, we cannot explicitly state.
(4) (U/True). The generalizing power accorded by "true" allows us to make explicit inferential or general assertional commitments and epistemic norms, which can then become objects of critical discussion.

Generalizing from this rewriting yields a meta-theoretical analysis, according to which an EMU involves four components, falling into two sub-groups.

A. Content-determining clauses:
   1. (Inf.) Material-inferential (intra-linguistic) role.
   2. (Epist.) Epistemic character of those inferential commitments.

These content determining (CD) clauses give a word's content-determining use-proprieties (CDPs). CDPs characterize use as **usage**: *how* a word is to be used. In so doing, they explain conceptual content: *what we are saying* in deploying the word in question.

B. Functional Clauses:
   3. (EPF.) Expressive/performative function.
   4. (U.) Practical significance/utility.

These clauses concern use as **function**: what we are *doing* in saying such-and-such; and what we gain by being able to do that.

An important feature of this meta-theoretical analysis is that it brings out how explanation runs in both directions. The CDPs for "true" explain its functional significance in the sense that conforming to them *enables* truth-talk's functional role. They are not laws explaining speech-behavior but rational requirements on talk with a certain functional significance: proprieties that must be observed if truth-talk is to do the things we use it to do. But the functional clauses in an EMU explain its CD clauses in the sense that they *rationalize* them, bringing out why we possess and retain a concept constituted by just those CDPs. As Horwich himself remarks, we have the concept of truth because of a certain "logical need": the need to endorse or repudiate propositions that we cannot list. (Horwich 1998, 3) The explanatory relation running from content to function is many-one, since there could be other ways of talking (in the case of truth-talk, substitutional quantification into sentence-position) that would serve the same expressive function.[2] That from function to content is one-many: there is good reason to have *some* way of doing what we use truth-talk to do. Summing up, usage enables function; function constrains usage. But although in the manner indicated explanation runs in both directions, a pragmatic approach to meaning is "function first." The one-many explanatory relation is fundamental.

We can draw two lessons. The first is that, with the two notions of use clearly distinguished, there is no need to contrast doing and saying. Both are involved in the constitution of "meaning." What we are doing explains what we are saying; and what we are able to say allows us to do things we otherwise couldn't. Second, the speech-act function that is one dimension of "use" is not confined to "expression" or "performativity" as normally understood. This is clear in the case of "true": we are able to do something—issue generalized endorsements or repudiations—precisely by virtue of having something new to say: that all statements in a certain class are true (or false). But sometimes, sentences have no *special* expressive use beyond enabling us to say—for example *report*—on how things are. Such sentences are prosaically descriptive.

2. Thanks to Steven Gross for making me appreciate this point.

3. *Knowledge*

Because the concept of truth is "thin" in the way that logical concepts are thin, we can give an account of the meaning of "true" that is both simple and exhaustive. We should not expect all EMUs to be like this.

Consider Hart's target case: "voluntary." It is easy enough to indicate the general character of each of the four components. The functional clauses are straightforward. Any form of social life will depend on some system of incentives and sanctions, and will therefore need some way of marking cases in which it is appropriate to apply them: some way of ascribing responsibility. This foregrounds the expressive-performative function of calling actions voluntary, and is very much in the spirit of Hart's pioneering work. We can also see that responsibility for one's actions and at least their more immediate consequences will be the rule. However there will be circumstances in which rewards and punishments are ineffective, and this gives us reason to make "voluntary" defeasible. Its defeasible character will be reflected in various material-inferential proprieties, such as an action's being voluntary entailing that it was not reflexive or coerced. With respect to their epistemic character, these material-inferential relations, like their counterparts for "true," will reflect standing inferential entitlements, not normally requiring justification. However, unlike those for "true," they will be expandable and revisable in the light of our developing understanding of human psychology and social interactions, and taking into account the point of the practice of ascribing responsibility. Further, the EMU's epistemic component will have to take account of what entitles us to consider actions voluntary in particular cases. Because the concept is defeasible, the relevant clause will specify, perhaps with some qualifications, that we are entitled to consider a person's movements a voluntary action unless we have reason to think that some defeating condition (mentioned in the material-inferential component) is met. But although they will be more complex, the functional clauses for "voluntary" will stand in the bi-directional explanatory relations to the terms' CDPs that we identified in the case of the EMU for "true."

An EMU for "know" is likely to be even more complex and schematic than one for "voluntary." Our full range of knowledge-ascriptions may well involve analogical extensions from a prototypical case. Nevertheless, we can hope to isolate central CDPs that are intelligible in the light of core functions.

Edward Craig offers an interesting thought experiment; and while I don't propose to defend or endorse all the details, I do find it a useful way to think about how an EMU for "know" could go. Craig invites us to imagine a group of humans in a "state of nature." They have needs and capacities that are recognizably human, but lack complicated institutions. More particularly, they lack explicit epistemic vocabulary, and so have no word corresponding to our word "knowledge." What would they get by adding such a word? Craig's answer begins with the observation that their need for information exceeds their individual capacities for gathering it. In the primitive (prototypical situation) the function of information is to answer a practical question: what we want to determine is *whether* p. Craig therefore proposes that the original function of knowledge-attributions is to *tag potentially good informants*: people who can be counted on to settle a question. (Craig 1990, esp. chs. I–II)

Craig's genealogy is avowedly fictional. Klemens Kappel suggests understanding it as an exercise in "practical explication." (Kappel 2010) I take practical explication to be what I have called the "function first" approach to meaning-analysis. In effect, Craig is engaged in tracing the contours of the concept of knowledge—including the concept's demonstrated capacity to spark controversy—to its functional significance. More precisely, in terms of my meta-theoretical analysis, Craig's suggestion concerning the original point of knowledge-ascriptions corresponds to the clauses for the utility and expressive-performative function of "know" in freestanding knowledge-attributions.

A complementary account of the expressive-performative function of "know," in the context of a practice of information-sharing, can be found in Brandom's pragmatic recasting of the "justified, true belief" (JTB) analysis of knowledge. According to Brandom:

> (1) "In taking someone to be a knower, one *attributes a commitment, attributes entitlement* to that commitment, and *acknowledges commitment* to that same content oneself ... These correspond ... to taking to believe, taking to be justified in that belief, and taking the belief to be true." (MIE.)
> (2) Knowledge is a complex, hybrid deontic status. The *attributor* acknowledges commitment on the *claimant's* authority. (Brandom 1994, 202f.)

Brandom's version of the JTB analysis provides a more detailed clause corresponding to (EPF/Know): it specifies what we are doing when we tag a good informant by characterizing him as knowledgeable. Of course, much remains to be said. The authority in question is *epistemic* rather than (say) political, so the EMU must be developed to take account of this.

The distinctive character of epistemic authority should be revealed by the content-determining clauses. So the way forward is to look for inferential/epistemic constraints appropriate to the functional significance of knowledge-ascriptions. It is uncontroversial that knowledge entails true belief. The function-first account, centered on the need to keep track of good informants, obviously demands this entailment. But possessing a true belief is not sufficient grounds for epistemic authority. I might have a belief that happens to be true, but hold it for bad reasons. It is not even clearly necessary. I may have authority, even though (through no fault of mine) what I believe is false. Epistemic authority is just another way of talking about justification.

Craig argues that one primary desideratum is that a good informant must be reliable. The rationale for demanding reliability is that our information regarding our situation is typically (even always) incomplete: to put it another way, there can be some question as to exactly what situation we are in. This being so, we want an informant who can be counted on to provide correct information across a range of possible situations. We don't want an informant's ability to get things right to be overly sensitive to chancy factors. The reliability in question will be expressed by some modal condition. For present purposes, there is no need to go into details. Something along the lines of Sosa's "safety" is a plausible candidate: we want an informant who could not easily have gone wrong. (Sosa 1999) But while the function first approach leads us to make reliability a condition on epistemic authority, it does not encourage pure externalist reliabilism.

In attributing knowledge, we are tagging not just *good* informants but good *informants*. An informant is not just an information-source. A thermometer is an information-source for those who understand how to read it; and it is possible to treat a person the way we treat a thermometer. Given suitable collateral information, I can treat someone's reactions (including verbal performances) as evidence for whether or not p. I may know that uttering certain sentences co-varies reliably with some further fact. But to infer that-p from someone's *saying* that-p is not the same as being told that-p. There must be more to epistemic authority than reliable covariance involving speech dispositions and environmental circumstances.

Craig emphasizes our need to recognize good informants, if we are to tag them. One important way of identifying a good informant—good with respect to settling a particular question in a particular communicative context—is by recognizing that he is better placed than I am (by situation, visual acuity, whatever) to determine whether p.[3] Some of these will have to do with the informant's situation: for example, does he have a better view than I do? But others will have to do with him. Has he taken steps to get a good view? Is he sharp-sighted? Would he give a confident answer to the question of whether p even if he hadn't or wasn't? Now some of these considerations will not clearly take us beyond the reliable co-variance of utterance with situation that does not distinguish an informant from an information-source. But others will. There are two kinds. One kind involves treating the informant as an active gatherer of information, and not just a passive recipient or channel. After all, informant-potential need not always be immediately recognizable. In many cases, we will have some previous acquaintance with a proposed informant, or at least have paid some attention to his conduct in the current context. Either way, we will have some ideas regarding how he goes about settling questions, or at least how he is currently going about determining whether p. Does he usually take, or is he now taking, sufficient care (given the stakes, difficulty of the question, etc.? This brings us to a second kind of consideration: would he be willing to answer my question, even if I would regard him as a shortcomer in his way of settling questions? Both kinds of consideration introduce an explicitly *deontic* element into our account, for we are asking whether our informant is duly diligent in collecting or passing on information. Is he the kind of person who recognizes and lives up to his epistemic responsibilities?

If this is right, some degree of epistemic self-awareness is built into the practice of knowledge-ascription on the ground floor.[4] In fact, epistemic self-awareness is what distinguishes informants from mere information sources. This points to a further way of dealing with the recognition problem. Given some grasp of what makes for such informant-potential we can seek reassurance by asking our informant why he answered as he did.

---

3. Recognizing that p is factive: indeed, a way of coming to know that p. But this can begin as implicit-in-practice reliance (on particular persons, in particular situations). It does not presuppose a mastery of explicit epistemic vocabulary. Such vocabulary brings to self-consciousness aspects of practical skills that it presupposes. I am treating epistemic vocabulary in the way that Brandom treats logical and semantic vocabulary in (Brandom 1994).

4. This is the position advanced by Sellars, though without much defence or elaboration. See Sellars 1997, Section VIII. Interestingly, in the Study Notes Brandom suggests that, by insisting that a reliable reporter recognize his own reliability, Sellars "perhaps goes too far" in an internalist direction. See p. 157f. For a defence of Sellars, see (de Vries & Triplett 2000, 82f).

And he must be able to answer. If informants are necessarily possessed for some grasp, rudimentary and practical as may be, it is not an accidental feature of informants that they can questioned, challenged, or asked to explain themselves. This is an important point, for it connects the status of possessing authority—*being justified*—with the *capacity to justify*. Indeed, I think that a central function of epistemic vocabulary is not just to *tag* good informants but to *question* them, which is often our best option for assuring ourselves that they are what we need them to be.

At this point, we have the general outlines of a use-theoretic approach to epistemic vocabulary: in particular, to "know." We have seen what we are doing, and why, in ascribing knowledge. From this, we have derived the standard content-determining implications of knowledge: justified, true belief. Regarding epistemic authority—justification and assertional entitlement—knowledge entails *both* reliability and responsibility (in the sense of recognizing and conforming to standards of due diligence). If we equate reliability with safety, knowledge is true belief, safely and responsibly held. This gives us a sketch of a clause for (Inf/Know) and, by extension, the beginning of a clause for (Epist/Know), since the implications of knowledge indicate what we must look out for when ascribing it.

The important feature of this account is that knowledge can fail either through unreliability or irresponsibility. Since irresponsibility is culpable, when unreliability results from irresponsibility it will be culpable too. However, unreliability *need* not arise from irresponsibility, and can therefore be non-culpable. We can do our best in trying to determining whether p, but our method may be unreliable: we may be stuck with misleading evidence, which we have nor reason to think misleading. Reliance on an unreliable method can be a matter of sheer bad luck. These features of knowledge are the source of familiar anxieties concerning the relation between knowledge and justification. Non-culpable unreliability, coupled with a compensating stroke of good luck leading to a true belief anyway, yields a typical Gettier case. The near-universal reaction to early Gettier cases—that they showed the possibility of justified true belief without knowledge—confirms the suggestion that epistemic authority is evaluated in two dimensions: reliability and responsibility. Typically, we expect the two to go together. But when they fall apart, and a person responsibly but unsafely comes to believe that-p, we think that he is justified in believing that-p because he has lived up to normal epistemic obligations but nevertheless we are reluctant to say that he is knows that-p.

This reaction, though once common, is not mandatory. We could say that someone in a Gettier situation is justified *in a way*, but in another way not. He has handled his reasons well; but through no fault of his own, they are not good reasons. Gettier cases do not compel us to say that there is justified, true belief without knowledge. Indeed, I suspect that Alston is correct then he says that there is no single, pre-theoretical conception of justification, which (unlike "knowledge") is an epistemologist's term of art, covering more than one epistemic desideratum. (Alston 1993)

None of this is meant to suggest that my EMU for "know" yields a Gettier-proof analysis. Rather, as Craig argues, a function first approach can explain why the Gettier problem comes up and why it may be less interesting than many have supposed. Two comments are in order. First, Gettier cases are rare and peculiar. The attributor *shares* the claimant's commitment, but not on the claimant's authority. That is because, s Robert Fogelin emphasizes, he already occupies an informationally superior position. (Fogelin 1994, ch. 1) Second, in tagging good informants, we have an interest in repeatable performances. Getting true beliefs by luck fails to indicate repeatability, though responsibility might suggest future reliance. It is not surprising that we are ambivalent about such cases. Beyond this, there is little to learn from considering them.

4. *Three kinds of responsibility*

I suggested at the outset that epistemic concepts should be understood in deontological terms. Knowledge (and justification), imply epistemic authority, which is a matter of rights and duties. I can elaborate the point by saying that epistemic authority involves epistemic responsibility, in three senses of "responsibility."

We are responsible (epistemically responsible_1) *for* our beliefs in much the way that we are responsible for our actions. This is responsibility as *accountability*. Being an epistemic subject *just is* being accountable for what one believes, in the way that being an agent *is* being accountable for what one does. But we are accountable for our beliefs because we are required to be responsible (epistemically responsible_2) in our management and use *of* them. This is responsibility as due diligence—living up to one epistemic obligations (or as we also say, responsibilities), and it is what I had in mind in speaking of epistemic responsibility as a means to and indicator of truth-reliability. The antonym of 'responsible_2' is 'irresponsible.' Finally, we further must distinguish responsibility$_1$ (accountability) as a general condition from *liability*: being held responsible, thus subject to sanction, in a particular case. This is the sense of "responsible" (label it "responsible$_3$") that Hart has in mind in claiming that the point of characterizing an act as voluntary is to ascribe responsibility for (at least some of) its consequences to the actor.

The three kinds of responsibility are related in obvious ways. Only beings that are responsible$_1$—subjects and actors—can be (or fail to be) responsible$_3$ for believing or acting in regrettable ways. In plainer terms, only *accountable* beings can be held *liable* for what they believe or do. However, when it comes to the relation between liability and due diligence (responsibility$_3$ and resonsibility$_2$), the parallel between belief and action partially breaks down.

Agents are always accountable (apt to be held to account) for their actions: in one sense of responsible, "responsible agent" is a pleonasm. But agents are not always *liable* for or *culpable* in respect of their consequences. This is Hart's point in calling attention to the "defeasible" character of the concept of voluntariness. In the case of responsibility for actions, the *liability structure* is a defeasibility structure: given certain conditions, we are presumed "responsible," thus praiseworthy or culpable, unless we have an excuse that cancels or mitigates our degree of responsibility. Epistemic accountability works differently, because epistemic authority is compromised by unreliability *even in the absence of irresponsibility*. There is a legal analogy here. In the case of epistemic accountability, the liability structure is one of *strict* liability. Brought to light, epistemic shortcomings cancel entitlement (thus exact penalties) even when non-culpable. We are subject to epistemic sanction—loss of assertional entitlement—even when we have *done* nothing wrong. It is of course true that, once a non-culpable shortcoming has been pointed out, it would be irresponsible to *continue* to pretend to epistemic authority. But given evidence of unreliability in the epistemic procedure that led to or sustained a particular belief, we retrospectively re-evaluate. We don't say that we used to know and now we don't: we say that we only *thought* we knew.

Suppose that we non-culpably came to believe that p *via* some defective method: though we lacked knowledge, were we nevertheless justified in believing that p? This is not a good question, or at least not one with a definite answer. Where believing involves some non-culpable shortcoming, we are justified *in a way*, but not *unqualifiedly*. "Justification," as it figures in current epistemologists' talk, is not an everyday word but a semi-technical term of art. This is why, in the situation of non-culpable but flawed belief-management, we are uncertain what to say. The same ambivalence haunts comparably semi-technical talk of epistemic entitlement. Before the shortcoming is suspected, we were entitled in a way; but our entitlement was defective even if we had no reason to think it so. So we could say that we were never *really* entitled: just entitled to take ourselves to be entitled. However, in both instances, we are legislating rather than making explicit a settled meaning. The main point is to be aware of the possibility of confusion or merely verbal disagreement, the better to avoid them.

5. *Justification as a defeasible concept*

A consequence of a deontological approach to epistemic concepts is that that human knowledge—knowledge in the full sense—differs from animal cognition in the way that human action differs from animal behavior. I am not bothered by this. The view I am defending does not entail that all talk of animal knowledge is illegitimate or confused. I have already allowed for ways of talking about knowledge that involve analogical extensions of the word's primary or prototypical use. The extension may depend on deletions as well as similarities.

A more pressing objection is that the deontological approach, like internalist approaches to knowledge generally, offers a seriously over-intellectualized conception even of human knowledge.[5] I think this charge is misplaced.

Much philosophical thinking about the role of reasons and evidence in underwriting knowledge has been shaped—in my view distorted—by concern with skepticism: or perhaps it would be better to say, by commitment to confronting skepticism in too direct a fashion. The form of skepticism I have principally in mind is Agrippan (or "regress") skepticism.

The Agrippan argument can usefully be presented in the form of a dialogue (which I could have with myself). So suppose that I make a claim. The skeptic asks "How do you know?" I explain. The skeptic re-iterates his question: "How do you know *that*?" There seem to be three possibilities. I can:

---

5. Goldman 1999. For critical discussion of Goldman's anti-internalist argument see my (Williams forthcoming 2).

(i) keep responding by finding something new to say, in which case I embark on a vicious infinite regress, or
(ii) at some point, refuse to answer, in which case my "knowledge" rests on a mere assumption; or
(iii) recur to something I have already said, in which case my reasoning is circular.

In no case do I explain how I know; and since there is no fourth option, it seems that knowledge is impossible.

If we find the skeptical conclusion unacceptable, as we must, it may seem that we have to put a better face on one of the skeptic's options. If we agree, as most philosophers have, that an infinite regress of justifiers would be vicious, we are left with two options. One option is to espouse some kind of foundations theory, according to which demands for justification are brought to an end by terminating judgments or basic beliefs. The other option is to go holistic, claiming that a belief is justified neither by being self-evidencing nor inferentially traceable to beliefs that are but by being a member of a sufficiently coherent total system: a system whose members stand to each other in various logical, inductive and explanatory relations.

Now although I won't develop the argument in detail here, I think that anyone familiar with these traditional theories will agree that they have more than a suspicion of over-intellectualization. Further, this over-intellectualization seems a direct consequence of their "internalist" character. Not only do they make justification at large depend on complex inferential relations, they demand "cognitive access" to these relations. It is not enough that there be basic beliefs that *in fact* stand in appropriate evidence-conferring relations to non-basic beliefs. We have to have some kind of awareness of the full array of our foundational beliefs, together with their epistemic relations to the vast structure that depends on them. Similarly with traditional coherence theories. The claim is not that we will have justified beliefs if our belief-system is *in fact* coherent: we have to have some awareness of how and why.

Reflecting on the extremity of these demands for epistemic self-consciousness, we can easily persuade ourselves that the only way to see how knowledge is *humanly* possible is to understand it in externalist-reliabilist terms. Such an understanding allows for basic beliefs: they will be beliefs that are the product of some truth-reliable cognitive process not taking beliefs as input. Since such beliefs are not supported by reasons, the regress is cut off. Further, the link between basic and non-basic beliefs need not be—and generally is not—self-conscious inference or the following of principles. Inference can itself involve further truth-reliable process: a process that tends to yield true beliefs as output, given true beliefs as input. (Goldman 1976, section II) Since we do not have to be aware of the reliability of our cognitive processes—either with respect to basic or non-basic beliefs—there is no threat of epistemic circularity, so once more the skeptical argument is short-circuited. Externalism thus invites us to resolve the skeptical problem while sidestepping the problematic features of both traditional foundationalism and the coherence theory. However, I treat knowledge as requiring *both* reliability and epistemic responsibility (responsibility$_2$ or due diligence); and I have argued that the kind of justification that arises from duly diligent epistemic conduct is essentially connected with both the capacity to justify one's beliefs and the possession of reliability-knowledge. For all its attractions, the externalist option is foreclosed.

Epistemically responsible$_2$ belief-management gives rise to what is sometimes called *personal* justification. But I have said little about what such management requires. Two questions:

(1) With respect to knowing that p, what is the role played by the ability to justify believing that p in the sense of being able to give reasons for p?
(2) With respect to claiming or attributing knowledge, what entitles us to claim or attribute responsibility and/or reliability?

The answer to the first question shows how to answer the second.

Epistemic questions—Do I know? Should I believe--are questions about permissions and obligations. How such permissions and obligations are incurred, lost and discharged determines the deontic structure, or more precisely the *entitlement structure*, of the space of reasons. In my view, the regress problem arises from a misrepresentation of this structure. It is perfectly obvious that we don't usually tolerate the persistent questioning that the Agrippan skeptic goes in for. So the question to ask is, who or what gives the skeptic *the right* to interrogate me like this? The skeptic has an answer: I do. If I merely express an opinion, the skeptic has nothing to say to me. But if I represent myself as knowledgeable, I lay claim to epistemic authority. It is perfectly reasonable for the skeptic to ask where my authority came from. This is the Founding Intuition of the Agrippan Problem.

Although on first encounter the Founding Intuition may seem reasonable enough, it should be resisted, for it imposes a **severe** *claimant-questioner asymmetry* with respect to the right to challenge (or question) and the obligation to respond. More precisely:

> (CQA) If I represent myself as knowing that P, there is nothing you have to do, no way that things have to be, or no special position you have to be in, in order for you to have the right to raise an epistemic question (i.e. to ask me how I know).

But our ordinary practice of giving and asking for reasons shows no such asymmetry. Questions are themselves open to question. A claimant may respond to "How do you know?" by asking the interlocutor to be more specific: e.g. to explain why or how he thinks the claimant may be going wrong or lack entitlement to his claim. *Blank* questions are typically and properly *dismissed*. Indeed, in cases when I say something that anyone, including my interlocutor, can see to be the case, such a question does not even *make sense*.

Now the skeptic (and some traditional epistemologists) will reply that all this shows is ordinary questions about knowledge and justification are local. For a local epistemic question, an answer will do if it is dialectically acceptable: the question will be taken to have been answered satisfactorily if the claimant comes up with a something that the questioner is not inclined to doubt. However, in epistemology we ask questions about justification in a more general and systematic way, and this is how the claimant-questioner asymmetry arises.

This reply already involves a significant concession. It is no longer clear that the skeptic is engaging in a natural extension of our ordinary practice of epistemic questioning. Rather, he seems to be asking a special kind of "philosophical" question: how are we justified in believing anything whatsoever? He had better be sure that the very attempt to ask this question does not *itself* distort the entitlement structure of our everyday practices of epistemic assessment.

I think that it does. Claimant-questioner asymmetry assumes that the entitlement structure of the space of reasons is a *Prior Grounding Structure.* On this view, it is epistemically irresponsible of me to represent myself as knowing that p unless I possess and make proper use of good reasons for believing that p. My counter-suggestion is that the entitlement structure of the space of reasons is *Default and Query.*

> (DQS) In some contexts and with respect to some claims, claimants possess and are properly granted default epistemic assertional entitlement: entitlement that does not depend on the claimant's doing or having done any *specific evidential work* or possessing any *citable reasons* for his commitment. Default entitlement is *situationally* unearned and imposes no *standing* defence requirement.

Default entitlement is often (though far from invariably) defeasible, lapsing in the face of a *contextually appropriate query* to which the claimant lacks an adequate response.

We have come back to Hart. I noted previously that one way of understanding Hart's claim that defeasible concepts pose a challenge to a certain theoretical model of descriptive sentences is to take him to be claiming that we can understand the semantic character of defeasible concepts by seeing how they enter into judgments with a distinctive epistemic character: for example, the fact that I signed a document provides only a *prima facie* reason for judging that I have entered into a contract. Another way of bringing out the epistemic character of defeasible concepts is to say that, with respect to making a contract, signing the document has the *default status* of *acceptance* of an *offer* unless certain defeating conditions, such as fraudulent misrepresentation or duress, are in play, in which case no valid offer was made or accepted. Judgments regarding the existence of contracts are embedded in a *contextually circumscribed default and query structure.* This is what makes "contract" a defeasible concept. "Personal justification" is a defeasible concept in just the same way.

In the case of the concept of contract, Hart notes that there are certain positive conditions that need to be met. So we might ask whether there are positive conditions for a someone's being personally justified in claiming or believing that p. Naturally, these conditions cannot involve his having done specific evidential work: to insist on that would be to undermine the very idea of a default and query structure. But there are conditions, just not of that kind.

In discussing the three kinds of epistemic responsibility, I noted that the requirement of due diligence can only be imposed on epistemic subjects: beings that can be held accountable for their beliefs and epistemic conduct. So one source of conditions on default personal justification can be found in the conditions for epistemic accountability.

At the risk of belaboring the obvious, only beings capable of making claims and holding beliefs can be held accountable for them. It would be too large an undertaking to discuss everything entailed by the capacity for making claims or holding beliefs. However, let me mention some implications that are relevant to the simple cases of knowledge-attribution envisaged in Craig's thought-experiment: cases where a potential informant is better placed than an inquirer to determine whether p because the informant, but not the inquirer, can see what is going on.

Holding beliefs requires the mastery of concepts; and I shall assume without defense that the development of conceptual mastery goes hand in hand with acquiring a language. Now neo-pragmatist approach to linguistic meaning is broadly use-theoretic. In the sample EMUs discussed in previous sections, conceptual content was traced to material-inferential proprieties, not ignoring their epistemic character. For example, in the EMU for "true," the fundamental inferential proprieties were treated as epistemically primitive. But it seems clear that, epistemically speaking, not all concepts can be like the concept of truth. If language is to hook up with the world, there must be concepts with an observational use: concepts that are deployed on particular occasions on the basis of appropriately reliable recognitional capacities. So I take it that reliability with respect to some range of non-inferential observational judgments is a precondition of having any beliefs at all. It follows that if one has beliefs at all, one is already on the road to being a potential informant in the primitive case that is the starting point for Craig's function-first approach to the concept of knowledge.

Let me now turn to implications more immediately related to accountability. As noted, we cannot be held accountable for failure to live up to norms we do not recognize. It is therefore not sufficient for our being accountable that we possess the sort of reliable recognitional capacities that go with being a believer at all: we must also recognize, to some degree, how reliable we are and in what circumstances. Only given such knowledge will we be able to recognize the demands of epistemic responsibility with respect to putative perceptual knowledge. Only given such knowledge will we be able to recognize appropriate epistemic questions and appropriate responses to them. And only if we meet these conditions can we be held accountable. (Of course, some level of practical logical competence must also be presupposed.) Here we have returned to the distinction between informants and mere information-sources.

If this is right, an epistemic subject must have, and recognize himself as having, a range of reliable recognitional capacities, together with some grasp of the situations in which they are reliably exercised. Accordingly, an epistemic subject will enjoy a range of beliefs such that the very fact of his holding them is at least a *prima facie* reason (and in many case a conclusive reason) for their being true. For such beliefs, epistemic authority does not need to be earned by specific evidential work: it is the default condition, as that condition is defined by (DQS). To be sure, a degree of reliability knowledge is a necessary condition for *possessing* authority. But such knowledge, as a general condition of epistemic accountability, does not provide justifying reasons in particular cases. For one thing, such knowledge is typically no more certain than particular perceptually-based beliefs, and may well often be less so. With respect to such beliefs, the positive conditions for *claiming* or *attributing* authority, then, are not that the claimant has specific reasons for holding a belief, but simply that he is an epistemic subject.

In the simple cases of perceptual knowledge under consideration, then, the implications of being a subject give the positive conditions for *both* possessing and attributing authority. There is, of course, also an essential negative condition: there must be nothing in the situation of belief-acquisition to arouse suspicions of unreliability. Putting these points together, we can say that the home of default personal justification is a *Prototypical Communicative Context*. This is a context involving the communication of information that (relative to the mutually-recognized background knowledge and cognitive capacities of the interlocutors) is not notably exotic or surprising, either in itself or with respect to the claimant's access to it. In such a context, epistemic queries are generally inappropriate. And when they are appropriate, the grounds for their appropriateness need not be apparent. In this case, it will be reasonable for a claimant to ask for some explanation: what exactly does the questioner want to know?

Following Brandom, I used to call the structure I have been sketching "Default and Challenge." (Brandom 1994, 204f.) However, "challenge" suggests that "How do you know?" is asked *pointedly*, the implication being that perhaps you *don't* know (Austin 1961), whereas this question may simply be a request for an explanation.[6] I now think that the latter is its *usual* force. In asking "How do you know that p" I concede that you do know that p: I just want to know how you know. I want an explanation,

---

6. Ram Neta, personal communication. Austin writes (Austin 1961, 46): "Either question, 'How do you know/' or 'Why do you believe?' may be asked out of respectful curiosity, from a genuine desire to learn. But again, they may both be asked as pointed questions." Maybe; but I think that "Why do you believe' is the more normal—because more obviously non-committal—way of implying doubt about one's interlocutor's epistemic authority.

not a justification. (Perhaps I want to find out more for myself.) The more usual form of a pointed query is "Why do you believe ...?" Here I concede that you *do* believe, but imply that I am dubious, or at least agnostic, as to whether you *should*. I therefore now reserve "challenge" for hostile questions. I call non-hostile queries "epistemic questions." When properly entered, challenges have a strong tendency to suspend entitlement. Epistemic questions need not have such a tendency. However, personal justification can be impugned by failure to respond to queries of either type. An epistemic question may (though it need not) prepare the ground for a challenge; or it may become the functional equivalent of a challenge if not properly answered. However, the appropriateness conditions for challenges and epistemic questions may (probably do) differ.

Although default entitlement allows for personal justification without prior validation of the reliability of one's epistemic procedure. But knowledge (unqualified justification or authority) requires responsibility *and* reliability. For this reason, default entitlement carries forward-looking *reliability commitments*. Reason to suppose that reliability conditions, either general or situation-specific—have not been met is a standard route to a contextually appropriate query. Still, because they are (at least sometimes) open to question and laden with defense commitments, default-entitled claims are fully within the space of reasons: fully incorporated into the practice of justifying and being able to justify what one says. The important point is that "being able to justify" means "being able to justify *when required*." When unquestioned, they are available to justify other things.

While this view is far from purely externalist, it does not suggest an overly-intellectualized conception of epistemic responsibility. Such conceptions stem from the attempt to meet Agrippan (regress) skepticism head on, which we should not do. Agrippan skepticism depends on misrepresenting the entitlement structure of the space of reasons: the relation between managing one's beliefs in an epistemically responsible$_2$ (duly diligent) fashion and making proper use of reasons and evidence. The skeptical argument presupposes a severe claimant-questioner asymmetry, according to which epistemic authority is always to be earned, whereas a mere claim to such authority (even an implicit claim) creates a right to question. But if personal justification is a defeasible concept, the skeptic's asymmetry is a myth. Everyday practices of knowledge attribution mandate a *reasonable distribution* of epistemic burdens among claimants and questioners. Sometimes, epistemic authority must be earned, explained or defended; but the same goes for epistemic questions and challenges.

"Reasonable distribution" does not mean "equal distribution." The defeasibility structure I envisage replaces the skeptic's severe anti-claimant bias with a *moderate* claimant-challenger/questioner asymmetry, but tilted in the opposite direction. This pro-claimant bias is reasonable because challenges and epistemic questions interrupt inquiry, conversation or practical projects, thereby imposing opportunity costs. Pragmatism counsels us to take seriously our interests (practical and theoretical) and finite resources. When a belief is one of our own, we are (rationally) not ordinarily interested in investigating its credentials, unless we find reason to do so.

Conclusion

I have argued that we can usefully apply Hart's ideas about ascriptive sentences and defeasible concepts to epistemic vocabulary. This is because epistemic vocabulary is itself best understood in deontological terms, as a matter of rights and responsibilities. But there are two problems to solve. First, to rescue Hart's ideas, we need to adopt of generalized use-theoretic approach to the constitution of meaning. When we do, we can separate the idea that the ascriptive role played by certain sentences plays a decisive role in determining their conceptual content from Hart's unfortunate dualism of ascriptive *versus* descriptive sentences. Second, it is necessary to head off the charge that a deontological approach to epistemic concepts leads to an overly-intellectualized, thus humanly unrealistic, view of the role of reasons and evidence in creating and sustaining epistemic authority. But over-intellectualization is not the result merely of taking a deontological approach to epistemic vocabulary. Rather, it results from attempting to deal with the skeptical problem of the regress of justification while acceding to the skeptic's radically unequal distribution of epistemic rights and responsibilities between claimants and questioners. But while knowledge requires both reliability and responsibility, personal justification (grounded in epistemically responsible belief-management) is a defeasible concept, in Hart's sense. The conditions of epistemic accountability ensure that epistemic authority is often possessed by default, while open to defeat by an appropriate challenge or unanswered question. In such a defeasibility structure, claims may require defence or explanation, but so may challenges or questions. Neither claimant nor challenger starts with all the rights or all the responsibilities. Hart didn't get everything right, but he opened lines of inquiry that continue to repay exploration.

References

Alston, William 1993:"Epistemic Desiderata". *Philosophy and Phenomenological Research* 53, 527–51.

Austin, John L. 1961: "Other Minds". In: *Philosophical Papers*. Oxford: Oxford University Press, 44–84.

Brandom, Robert 1994: *Making It Explicit*. Cambridge, MA: Harvard University Press.

Craig, Edward 1990: *Knowledge and the State of Nature*. Oxford: Oxford University Press.

Fogelin, Robert 1994: *Pyrrhonian Reflections on Knowledge and Justification*. Oxford: Oxford University Press.

Geach, Peter T. 1960: "Ascriptivism". *The Philosophical Review* 69, 221-25.

Goldman, Alvin 1976: "What Is Justified Belief?". In: George S. Pappas (ed.), *Justification and Knowledge*. Dordrecht: D. Reidel, 1–23. Reprinted in: Ernest Sosa, Jaegwon Kim, Jeremy Fantl, & Matthew McGrath (eds.) 2008, *Epistemology: An Anthology*, 2nd edition. Oxford: Blackwell, 333–47.

— 1999: "Internalism Exposed." *Journal of Philosophy* 6, 271–93. Reprinted in Sosa et al. 2008, 379–93.

Hart, H. L. A. 1948-49: "The Ascription of Responsibilities and Rights". *Proceedings of the Aristotelian Society*, New Series 49, 171–94.

Horwich, Paul 1998: *Truth*, 2nd edition. Oxford: Oxford University Press.

— 2001: "A Defence of Minimalism". *Synthese* 126, 149–65.

Kappel, Klemens 2010: "On Saying that Someone Knows: Themes from Craig". In: Adrian Haddock & Alan Millar (eds.), *Social Epistemology*. Oxford: Oxford University Press, 69–88.

Macarthur, David & Price, Huw 2007: "Pragmatism, Quasi-Realism and the Global Challenge". In: Cheryl Misak (ed.), *The New Pragmatists*. Oxford: Oxford University Press. Reprinted in: Huw Price, 2011: *Naturalism Without Mirrors*. Oxford: Oxford University Press, 91–120. Quotation from this reprinting, p. 211.

Pollock, John 1967: "Criteria and Our Knowledge of the Material World". *Philosophical Review* 76, 28–60.

Sellars, Wilfrid 1997: *Empiricism and the Philosophy of Mind*. Edited with Study Notes by Robert Brandom. Cambridge, MA: Harvard University Press.

Sosa, Ernest 1999: "How to Defeat Opposition to Moore." *Philosophical Perspectives* 13, Epistemology, 141–53.

de Vries, Willem A. & Triplett, Timm 2000: *Knowledge, Mind and the Given*. Indianapolis: Hackett.

Williams, Michael 2013: "How Pragmatists Can Be Local Expressivists". In: Huw Price (ed.), *Pragmatism, Expressivism and Representationalism.* Cambridge: Cambridge University Press, 128–144.
Williams, Michael forthcoming: "Internalism, Reliabilism and Deontology". In: Hilary Kornblith (ed.), *Goldman and His Critics.* Oxford: Blackwell.

Grazer Philosophische Studien
87 (2013), 37–57.

KNOWLEDGE, DEFEASIBILITY, AND THE GETTIER PROBLEM[1]

Klemens KAPPEL
University of Copenhagen

Summary

It is natural to assume that since knowledge requires doxastic justification (whatever the exact nature of this), then if doxastic justification is defeasible, as many would assume, then so is knowledge. In the paper I argue that knowledge is defeasible in a way that does *not* depend on the purported defeasibility of doxastic justification, but rather in a way that relates directly to the famous Gettier Problem. And, though less important in this context, even if doxastic justification is defeasible, this does strictly speaking not make knowledge defeasible.

1. *Introduction*

Knowledge is defeasible in a way that relates directly to the famous Gettier Problem, or so I argue in this paper. To many readers it might not seem terribly surprising that knowledge is defeasible, but perhaps this is because they have the defeasibility of doxastic justification in mind. Since knowledge requires doxastic justification (whatever the exact nature of this), then if doxastic justification is defeasible, as many would assume, then so is knowledge. What I suggest in this paper, however, is that knowledge is defeasible in a way that does not depend on the purported defeasibility of doxastic justification. Even if doxastic justification were not defeasible, then knowledge would nonetheless be defeasible for the reasons that I will lay out below. And perhaps more surprising, but less important in the present context, even if doxastic justification is defeasible, this does

1. A precursor of this paper was presented at the conference Defeasibility in Epistemology, Ethics, Law and Logic, Goethe-Universität, Frankfurt am Main, September 24–26, 2010. I would like to thank participants at that event for comments and inspiring discussion, especially (in alphabetical order): Claudia Blöser, Mikael Janvid, Hannes Ole Matthiessen, Hans Rott, R. Jay Wallace, Michael Williams, Marcus Willaschek.

strictly speaking not make knowledge defeasible, as I shall explain below. I hope that all of this is at least mildly surprising. Moreover, I will argue that there is an intimate connection between the sort of defeasibility that I have in mind and the Gettier Problem that has troubled modern epistemology since its inception by Edmund Gettier in 1963.[2] The basic idea I want to propose and defend is quite simple: some event that would constitute a Gettier-style obstacle to a true and justified belief being an instance of knowledge is a defeater to that item of knowledge. And since such events are always possible, knowledge is defeasible. In this paper, I develop this view in some detail.[3]

2. *Defeater-structure*

Consider first what it is for something to be a defeater of something else. Here and in the ensuing discussion I will assume the following:

> *Defeater-structure*. Some object O and properties P and Q have a defeater-structure just in case (i) O has property P *in virtue* of having property Q, (ii) unless there is a defeater. A *defeater* is any property R, such that Q and R are co-possible, and yet (Q & R) entails that O does not have P.

There are many well-rehearsed examples of phenomena that seem to have a defeater-structure (the object O can be many different types of entities, as the examples below illustrate). Legal duties may be a case in point. Suppose that some part of the legislation specifies that I have a legal duty to do so and so, or a legal right to this and that. Normally it is understood that circumstances may be such that my legal duties or rights don't apply, all things considered. My duties or rights might be outweighed by other concerns, or circumstances might be such that the legal duties or rights simply cease to apply, though this is often not specified in the legal documents. So, in many cases, specific legal rights and duties seem to display a defeater-structure. Legal rights and duties apply to individuals in virtue of the proper legislation being enacted, and yet there are circumstances that void the rights and duties, despite the legislation still being in place.

2. In his (Gettier 1963).

3. The main discussion of the Gettier Problem draws some material from my longer and more detailed discussion 'Knowledge, Truth by Luck, and What Solves the Gettier Problem' (in preparation).

Similarly, moral reasons may have a defeater structure. Your pain is a reason for me not to harm you. But there might be special and perhaps unusual circumstances in which your pain ceases to be any reason at all for me to act in certain ways.[4] This is a well-known if also somewhat controversial view in moral theory.

Other and perhaps less controversial instances of defeater structures link these structures essentially to a specific dialectic, a practice of challenge and rebuttal. For example, on the view developed by Marcus Willaschek (Willaschek 2007), a subject S may by default be doxastically justified in her belief that p given the right sort of conditions C. But if that belief is appropriately challenged by someone else (or, presumably, by S herself), then it may be that S then is no longer justified, though she is still in condition C. S may then rebut the challenge, and perhaps S thereby regains her status as being justified in her belief. Again, this exemplifies a defeater-structure of the kind I have in mind.[5]

It is worth pausing for a moment to consider an obvious objection to the applicability of the notion of a defeater-structure. The objection is that in the cases that are supposed to instantiate a defeater-structure, it is just not true that the object O has property P *in virtue* of Q. The reason is the trivial one that when some object O indeed has property P, this is not *merely* in virtue of Q, but in virtue of Q *in conjunction* with the absence of any candidate property R. More generally, the suspicion would be that the very definition of a defeater-structure refers to the empty class because when (ii) applies, then (i) is false. When some property P depend on the absence of a defeater R, then it is not true that O has property P *in virtue* of some base property Q. So, defeater-structures are never instantiated.[6]

Formally speaking, this seems right. There is a more inclusive but still reasonable way of reading 'in virtue of' such that in the candidate cases, O has property P not merely in virtue of Q, but in virtue of Q in conjunction with the absence of any candidate property R applying. So, on this more inclusive reading of 'in virtue of' the suspicion just voiced is correct: there are no objects displaying defeater-structures. But the implication of this is not that the proposed notion of a defeater-structure is devoid of interest. What we should realise, however, is that the suggested notion of

4. A view of this sort is defended in (Dancy 2004).

5. Cf. also the introduction to this volume.

6. This objection to the notion of a defeater-structure grew out of a comment made in discussion by Hans Rott.

a defeater-structure depends on a less than fully inclusive reading of 'in virtue of'. Some object O can possess property P in virtue of possessing some other property Q, and yet P in some broader sense also depends upon any property R not applying. I do not think that this deprives the notion of defeasibility of general interest in philosophy, and this is so for a couple of reasons which are, I believe, well known.

First, as is often suggested, it might be that for certain defeater-structures there is no non-trivial way of delimiting the set of possible defeaters. When this is so, we may be barred from illuminating the nature of a defeater-dependent property P by citing Q and listing a disjunction of defeaters. We simply cannot point to a set of disjunctive properties upon which a defeasible property P depends in an indefeasible way. When this is so, it is at least sometimes more enlightening and helpful to provide a partial explanation of property P by saying that P defeasibly depends on Q. I shall argue that this is exactly what we get in the case of knowledge. Something similar holds when we can in principle produce a list of possible defeaters, but when this list turns out to be too long an unwieldy. In such cases it might be much easier to comprehend the nature of P by learning that P defeasibly depends on Q than to grasp an entire and very large disjunction of possible defeaters.

Second, in many cases of purported defeater-structures, it seems natural to think that the relation between P and Q has a certain priority. There may, for example, be a salient causal or constitutive relationship between P and Q that one does not find between P and any disjunctive condition that would constitute a defeating circumstance. Again in these cases, it might be illuminating to learn that P has a defeater-structure.

Finally, but not unrelated to the two previous points, it may be heuristically helpful for us to think of properties as related by a defeater-structure. Suppose I know that P defeasibly depends on Q. If I wonder whether P applies to some object O, I may start by looking for Q. If Q applies, it may be heuristically wise to assume that P applies as well, until I eventually come across defeating circumstances. This way of proceeding relieves me of the cognitive task of scanning all possible defeating circumstances in advance. Maybe I am not even able to form a conception of each possible defeater, though if a defeater were to arise, then I would be able to determine that. So, understanding that some phenomenon has a defeater-structure may play into a cognitive heuristic that might be useful to us. Whether this would be a good heuristic, would of course depend on the probability distribution of defeating circumstances. If defeating circumstances are comparatively rare, the described heuristic might be quite reliable and efficient, at least compared to the alternative of searching through the entire set of possible defeating circumstances before forming an opinion about whether P applies to O. Surely, these remarks might not conclusively settle the uneasiness that some may feel about the coherency of the notion of a defeater-structure, but I will set aside remaining worries and from now on take the notion of a defeater-structure for granted.

3. *Does knowledge have a defeater-structure?*

The question I want to address now is this. Are instances of knowledge instances of a defeater-structure? It is important to note that the question is not whether warrant, epistemic reasons, evidence or epistemic entitlement is defeasible in some sense. To be sure, it seems sensible to hold that some of these properties have a defeater-structure. Add to this, that on most views, knowledge requires some factor such as evidence, epistemic reasons, warrant or reliable belief formation. I shall simply use the label doxastic justification for this constituent of knowledge, but apart from that leave the nature of doxastic justification open. Combining these two lines of thought one may suggest that knowledge is defeasible simply in virtue of having doxastic justification as a constituent part, where doxastic justification is itself defeasible. The idea would simply be that if some belief is known and some factor then undermines the doxastic justification of that belief, then the belief is no longer known but defeated.

Surprisingly perhaps, this line of argument fails to show that knowledge is defeasible, given the specification of a defeater-structure that I offered above. Why is this? Assume that doxastic justification displays a defeater structure. So, a subject can be doxastically justified in a belief in virtue of, say, the evidence or epistemic reasons for the belief possessed by the subject. Yet, there could be defeating circumstances that would void the doxastic justification, though the evidence or reasons would in a sense be left intact. But since knowledge requires doxastic justification, there wouldn't be knowledge in such cases. Now, we can see that the fact that knowledge has *this* dependency on defeasible doxastic justification does not entail that knowledge has a defeater-structure. Surely, when a belief is known, it is in part in virtue of being doxastically justified. However, when the doxastic justification of a known belief is defeated, then what we have is an unjustified but true belief. We do not have a doxastically justified true belief that due to defeating circumstances fails to qualify as knowledge. So, we do not have an instance of a belief being known *in virtue* of a property Q, yet the presence of a defeater R which is *co-possible* with Q, makes it the case that the belief is not known. So even if doxastic justification both necessary for knowledge and defeasible, knowledge is not thereby defeasible, given the way I have defined defeasibility.

What I want to suggest, however, is that knowledge is defeasible, independently of doxastic justification being defeasible. So, even abstracting from the possibility that doxastic justification is both defeasible and required for knowledge, knowledge is still defeasible. How can this be? What I propose is that the defeasible nature of knowledge is exactly the lesson to learn from the difficulties of solving the Gettier Problem. What I will argue is that there are strong reasons to think that solutions to the Gettier Problem have the following form: Knowledge is true doxastically justified belief, unless a Gettier Incident has occurred. Below, I shall say more about what I mean by a Gettier Incident, but for now just take it to be the kind of odd occurrence that features in the well known cases invented by Edmund Gettier, and which served to show that knowledge is not equivalent to true, doxastically justified belief. I will argue that when a belief is known because true and doxastically justified, there is, so to speak, nothing that secures against such Gettier Incidents. A genuine case of knowledge could be just as it is with respect to the truth and doxastic justification of the belief in question, and yet circumstances could have conspired to make up a Gettier Incident. But then we get that possible Gettier Incidents make up a set of defeating circumstances to knowledge. So, knowledge is defeasible in ways that have nothing to do with doxastic justification being defeasible.

Of course, the idea just floated raises many questions of which I can only briefly address a few, and I will do so in the next section.

4. *The Gettier Problem—why the solution is to see that there is no solution (of a certain kind)*

So, the general proposal is that in response to the Gettier Problem we should basically say that knowledge is doxastically justified true belief, unless some Gettier Incident has happened. This is why knowledge is defeasible. Now, is this really what we should say in response to the Gettier Problem? Unfortunately, space does not permit a full discussion, but I will outline an argument that I defend in more detail elsewhere.[7]

Consider the JTB account of knowledge according to which knowledge just is doxastically justified true belief. As is familiar, the Gettier Problem arises because there are possible (and indeed actual) cases in which the JTB conditions are fulfilled, and yet something has gone wrong. Here is a version of a Gettier Case, i.e. the style of cases invented by Edmund Gettier:

> At 10 AM Jones sees the old clock in the hall, which shows 10 AM. Accordingly Jones forms the belief that it is 10 AM. Unbeknownst to Jones, however, the clock stopped yesterday exactly when showing 10 AM.

Here Jones seems to be doxastically justified in believing that the time is 10 AM, his belief is true, and yet Jones fails to know. So, there is a counter-example to the JTB account of knowledge. As is already clear, I refer to the kind of incidents that make for these types of counter examples to the JTB-account of knowledge as Gettier Incidents (the class is slightly broader).

Now, when the Gettier Problem became known, epistemologists started looking for a solution to the problem. Roughly, the ambition was to find a definition of doxastic justification that would rule out the kind of cases just illustrated. Alternatively, one would try to achieve the same by finding some fourth condition that could be appended to the condition on doxastic justification. I will assume that the underlying assumption behind this approach was a particular view about what would constitute a satisfactory solution to the Gettier Problem. I will state this assumption as follows:

> *The Strong Criterion of Adequacy (SCA)*. A solution to the Gettier Problem is successful if and only if it identifies a property W, such that WTB entails the impossibility of a Gettier Incident.

Here the property W arises as a suitable interpretation of the J-condition, or the J-condition in conjunction with a suitable anti-Gettier clause. So, on this approach, knowledge is assumed to be definable as WTB, and the

7. In forthcoming work on the Gettier Problem.

task is then finding property W while also meeting the Strong Criterion of Adequacy.

It is not surprising that many epistemologists have been tempted to The Strong Criterion of Adequacy. Indeed, there is a very compelling rationale for it. Suppose one denies SCA. Then one's theory would permit that the WTB properties could apply, and yet there would be the possibility of a Gettier Incident. But this would be tantamount to conceding that there are possible cases in which the WTB properties apply, and yet the believer is subject to a Gettier Incident. But then a definition of knowledge in terms of WTB would be subject to counterexamples of exactly the same structure as the ones bringing down the JTB account of knowledge. These are cases in which the JTB properties apply, and yet due to a Gettier Incident, the subject in question does not know. So, the conclusion must be that only a property W that together with the truth and belief conditions rules out *even the possibility* of a Gettier Incident suffices for a solution to the Gettier Problem.[8] As we all know, it has proved hard to find a plausible candidate for W.

As we shall see, one reason why this is so emerges when we consider now another assumption it is tempting to make about the nature of W:

> *Fallibilism.* It is possible that S believes that p, and has the property W, and yet S's belief that p is false.

It is clear why Fallibilism looks attractive. It is natural to assume that W is a property of the way in which a believer acquires her belief. So W is a property that depends on S's evidence, her method of inquiry, her background beliefs and patterns of reasoning, as well as certain features of S's environment. But this surely looks fallible. Whatever the exact features that make W apply, they seem to permit cases in which W apply, and yet the target belief is false.

A very interesting implication of this is that the Gettier Problem now not only looks hard, but unsolvable. Taking Fallibilism and the Strong Criterion of Adequacy as premises, it seems provable that there is no solution to the Gettier Problem. This is what I call the Argument from Fallibility, and it goes as follows:

8. In forthcoming work, I explain why the rationale for (SCA) in a certain sense begs the question, and therefore is not as strong as it appears on first sight.

(F1) A solution to the Gettier Problem is successful if and only if it identifies a property W, such that WTB entails the impossibility of a Gettier Incident (SCA).
(F2) There are possible cases C* in which a subject S believes that p, and possess property W, and yet S's belief that p is false.
(F3) But if there are such cases then there will also be cases C** just like C*, except that some freak accident has made that same belief p true after all. These are Gettier Incidents.
(F4) This entails that there are possible cases in which the WTB conditions are fulfilled, and yet a Gettier Incident occurs.
(F5) However, this means that the Gettier Problem has not been successfully solved (from (F1) and (F4)).

So, the intended conclusion of the Argument from Fallibility is, as I said, that the Gettier Problem has no solution. No wonder that the problem has seemed so hard!

As readers familiar with the recent literature on the Gettier Problem will recognise, this is not all entirely new. Trenton Merricks and Linda Zagzebski have presented similar arguments to the effect that warrant must be infallible. Essentially, they both think that no form of fallibilism can avoid the Gettier Problem for reasons captured in (F3) and (F4).[9] This led Merricks to the conclusion that warrant in Plantinga's sense must be infallible, and presumably this would count in favour of an infallibilist solution to the Gettier Problem. Zagzebski also proposed a form of infallibilism in response to the Gettier Problem, or more specifically, to an argument similar to the Argument from Fallibility. So, Merricks and Zagzebski may be interpreted as proposing that a solution to the Gettier Problem must go via a rejection of (F2). However, as far as I can see, neither Merricks nor Zagzebski seem to have noted that their arguments depend on the Strong Criterion of Adequacy. Consequently, they do not consider the option of rejecting that assumption rather than fallibilism as a general strategy of responding to the Gettier Problem.

The upshot of the Argument from Fallibility is, I suggest, that we are faced with a choice between three options. First, we might abandon Fallibilism in favour of some form of infallibilism. I will discuss and reject two such approaches in a moment. Second, we might admit that the Gettier Problem admits of no solution. As anyone familiar with the lit-

9. See (Zagzebski 1994; Merricks 1995b; Merricks 1995a; Merricks 1997; Zagzebski 1999).

erature on the Gettier Problem can tell, this is a rather popular option. I will not discuss it in detail here, in part because I am not confident what this option really involves. Instead I will suggest that we pursue the third option, which is to abandon the Strong Criterion of Adequacy, that is reject (F1) in the argument from fallibility. Rather than finding a property that rules out even the possibility of a Gettier Incident, we should settle for less. What should we settle for? The answer I will propose and develop in more detail below will be this: we should identify a property W, such that when a belief is true and has property W, then it is known, unless a Gettier Incident has occurred.

One major reason why we should reject (F1) rather than (F2) is that abandoning fallibilism on its own will not solve the Gettier Problem, or this is what I will argue now. Why couldn't we respond to the Gettier Problem and the argument from fallibility by turning to infallibilism? To see why, consider first what one might call:

> *Substantial infallibilism.* There is a property R of believers or their cognitive systems and parts of their cognitive environment such that having R with respect to p ensures that S gets it right regarding p.

The idea behind substantial infallibilism is that some of our cognitive systems are so powerful and well functioning that they never get it wrong. When we exercise these powers the underlying features ensures that we are not let down. So, in substantial infallibilism the order of dependence is that *because* S has R with respect to p, S is always right about p.

Suppose that such a property R existed. We could then try to define knowledge in terms of it. That is, we could capture our target property W in terms of whatever features of believers and their environment that renders them infallible. The result would be that for subjects possessing property W, Gettier Incidents would be ruled out. Their possibility would be prevented by knowledge requiring not only ordinary doxastic justification but substantially infallible cognitive powers. This would block the template for generating Gettier Incidents provided in premises (F2) and (F3).

The rather significant problem with substantial infallibilism is that such a property R is hardly or never instantiated, given our actual cognitive systems. Perhaps some of our cognitive systems are infallible in the substantial sense at stake, or they are close to being so. But surely the majority of them are not. So, if knowledge requires substantial infallibility, then the implication would be that we do not know much. So, this avenue leads to a very rampant and all embracing scepticism. On this ground I think we can disregard it as a solution to the Gettier Problem.

In a widely read paper, Zagzebski offers a diagnosis of the Gettier Problem in which the fallibility of our cognitive powers plays a crucial role similar to what I said above.[10] Zagzebski then goes on to offer a solution to the Gettier Problem that takes issue with just the assumption of infallibility. As she says, the lesson to be learned is this: 'Success in reaching the truth must be an intrinsic part of the sense in which each instance of knowledge is good'.[11] The general definition of knowledge she proposes is this: 'Knowledge is belief arising out of acts of intellectual virtue'.[12] It is important here to understand exactly what is meant by 'act of intellectual virtue'. Zagzebski defines this as follows: 'An act of intellectual virtue *A* is one that arises from the motivational component of an intellectual virtue, it is an act that person with virtue *A* characteristically do in those circumstances, and is successful in reaching the truth because of these other features of the act'.[13]

Note a couple of important things. If we exercise our intellectual capacities, that is, try to determine the truth of some proposition, but fail to be successful in doing so, this does not count as exercising an intellectual virtue. This is because the term 'intellectual virtue' is defined as a success-term. It applies only in the good cases. We might exercise our intellectual capacities in just the same way, and yet due to unfortunate circumstances, we do not arrive at a true belief, and in such cases our endeavours do not count as intellectually virtuous. As a consequence of this, knowledge can then be defined as 'belief arising out of acts of intellectual virtue'.[14] This addresses the Gettier Problem in the following way. Since the term 'intellectual virtue' applies only to the exercise of our cognitive capacities when they are in fact successful, there can be no cases in which one is intellectually virtuous, and yet adopts a false belief. Consequently, there are no cases just like these, except that some fluke has rendered the belief true nonetheless. So, there are no Gettier Incidents. If a belief is acquired by intellectual virtue, then it is not only true but also Gettier-proof.

---

10. In (Zagzebski 1999). In the negative part of her discussion, Zagzebski seems to accept what I have called the Strong Condition of Adequacy, though she does not discuss it.

11. (Zagzebslki 1999, 105)

12. (Zagzebski 1999, 109)

13. (Zagzebski 1999, 108)

14. (Zagzebski 1999, 109)

So, Zagzebski offers a form of infallibilism as a solution to the Gettier Problem. As should be clear, however, what she has in mind is not the substantial infallibilism that we discussed above. Zagzebski's claim is not that we are in possession of cognitive powers that invariably deliver true beliefs whenever we exercise them. Rather, what she says is that the exercise of these powers count as intellectual virtues only in the good cases. A virtue that has failed is no virtue, and this is the sense in which acts of intellectual virtues are infallible.

I will label this type of view *nominal infallibilism*. Let me now try to characterise the general format of nominal infallibilism in more detail, in order to get a clear grasp of the way in which this sort of view may provide a solution to the Gettier Problem. According to nominal infallibilism, there is some property R of believers that tends to make them get it right with respect to certain beliefs. If we follow Zagzebski, property R would consist in the exercise of our cognitive powers or faculties, but one could imagine other ways of filling out the details. The important point is that, whatever their nature, when we exercise theses powers, we do not always get it right. But often enough we do. So, there are possible cases in which R is instantiated (and we exercise the relevant capacities), and yet the resulting belief is false. These are the bad cases. But there are also the good cases. These are the cases in which property R is conjoined with cognitive success. These are the cases in which S gets her belief right in virtue of (or because of) property R (and the exercise of the relevant capacities).

With this in mind, we can now define our target property W roughly as follows: some subject S instantiates property W just when she instantiates property R and gets her target belief right in virtue of that. So, instantiating property W is just instantiating property R in the good cases. Knowledge, in turn, is defined in terms of W, as WTB (and one should now bear with the truth condition being redundant).

Formally speaking, W is infallible, just as we would expect. There are no possible instances in which W applies, and yet the subject in question gets it wrong. We can then see why the template for generating Gettier Incidents given in (F3) and (F4) would seem to be blocked. When a subject possesses property W as now defined, no Gettier Incident is possible. This is why nominal infallibilism solves the Gettier Problem.

It should be obvious why nominal infallibilism is to be distinguished from substantial infallibilism. Substantial infallibilism turns on the highly implausible claim that we possess cognitive powers that, at least in certain domains, never let us down. Nominal infallibilism, however, does not commit us to this claim. Rather, nominal infallibilism holds that when such errors occur, we do not instantiate the property that together with that truth and belief conditions would be necessary for knowledge.

There is a lot to be said about nominal infallibilism, but here one rather brief remark will have to suffice. Effectively nominal infallibilism solves the Gettier Problem by silently rejecting (SCA), the Strong Condition of Adequacy. Nominally, of course, the strategy identifies a property W such that when this property is instantiated, then no Gettier Problem is possible. A believer cannot instantiate property W and yet fall victim to a Gettier Incident. But this is merely a consequence of the way in which property W is defined. By definition, if a subject uses her otherwise reliable cognitive powers, but is subject to a strange incident of the sort that Gettier made legendary, then property W does not apply. But then defining knowledge in terms of W amounts to proposing a property W such that knowledge is WTB, except when a Gettier Incident has occurred. So, nominal infallibilism effectively abandons (SCA), the strong condition of adequacy.

Or so is the suspicion at least. Before proceeding I want to note a complication here. Zagzebski argues that in the good cases, the cases in which acts of intellectual virtue results in us arriving at the truth, a subject must arrive at it 'because of' certain features of the act, that is because the underlying intellectual capacities the exercise of which is involved in the act.[15] Or so she says. But she offers no analysis or characteristic of the crucial '*because of* relation'[16]. One might think that if such an analysis were forthcoming, nominal infallibilism would solve the Gettier Problem without abandoning (SCA). However, though I cannot show this here, I believe that this hope is in vain. Unless one wants to turn nominal infallibilism into substantial infallibilism, there is no way to solve the Gettier Problem that does not involve discarding (SCA).[17]

This is why I think that infallibilism does not provide a solution to the Gettier Problem. Let's now consider what is involved in discarding (SCA), the strong condition of adequacy. As already said, the alternative that I want to consider is the following:

15. See (Zagzebski 1999), especially at pages 108, 111, 112.

16. (Zagzebski 1999, 108)

17. In forthcoming work, I argue in detail why a form of nominal infallibilism that assumes (SCA) cannot succeed, on pain of collapsing into substantial infallibilism.

The Weak Condition of Adequacy (WCA). A solution to the Gettier Problem is successful if it identifies a property W, such that WTB is a known belief, unless some Gettier Incident has occurred.

We have seen that (WCA) suggests answers to the Gettier Problem of the following form. Knowledge is internally justified true belief (where no Gettier incident has happened). Or, if one prefers a virtue account, the general line would be that knowledge is a belief acquired by intellectual virtue, except when some Gettier Incident has been involved in the process. A generic reliabilist account would have that knowledge is true belief acquired by a reliable method, provided that no Gettier Incident has happened. As implied, I take (WCA) to delineate a wider class of solutions to the Gettier Problem, rather than one specific solution. So, whether we should opt for a reliabilist account or some other would then depend on other matters; the basic way these theories respond to the Gettier Problem will be the same.

Clearly, this family of responses to the Gettier Problem raises some important challenges and questions. First of all, there is a question whether the notion of a Gettier Incident, which plays a pivotal role here, can be independently defined. If we could capture this notion only as incidents whatever else their nature such that when they occur they prevent a true and otherwise doxastically justified belief from being known, then the whole approach might face a problem about being un-illuminating, or circular in a vicious sense.

I cannot address these important concerns in details, but I will try to illustrate both how the strategy plays out, and suggest how one can address the worries just mentioned. I will do so by applying the basic idea ventured to process reliabilism. Assume that process reliabilism asserts that necessary conditions on knowledge are that beliefs are true and acquired by reliable processes.[18] What other conditions are required is a question we will return to. Consider again our now familiar case:

At 10 AM Jones sees the old clock in the hall, which shows 10 AM. Accordingly, Jones forms the belief that it is 10 AM. Unbeknownst to Jones, however, the clock stopped yesterday exactly when showing 10 AM.

---

18. A form of process reliabilism about doxastic justification was proposed in the seminal (Goldman 1979). A more extensive discussion is found in (Goldman 1986) and in (Goldman 2011). See also the discussion in (Goldberg 2010).

Let us assume that Jones's belief is formed by a process that consists of visual inspection of certain features of the clock combined with a distinct pattern of processing of this visual input, and let us refer to this process as M_{clock}. We do not need to make any particular assumptions about the nature of M_{clock}, but we should assume that M_{clock} is reliable under normal circumstances. There is an important and difficult issue about how to identify what for a given process counts as normal circumstances. But clearly, for talk about a process' levels of reliability to make sense, we need to relativize the used processes to some set of circumstances. However, for the sake of the current discussion, let us abstract from this problem, and merely grant the process reliabilist a notion of normal circumstances and a way of pairing individual processes with normal circumstances.

So, returning to Jones's case, let us assume that relative to M_{clock}, there is a set of circumstances that we can regard as normal circumstances of M_{clock}, however the pairing of process and normal circumstances comes about. Moreover, let us assume, again for the sake of argument, that Jones's circumstances are in fact normal in the relevant sense. So, when Jones relies on his visual perception of the old clock in the hall to form a belief about what time it is, he is relying on a process that is reliable under normal circumstances, and Jones's circumstances are normal.

Assume now that though M_{clock} is reliable under normal circumstances, this process is nonetheless fallible even when circumstances are in fact normal. Indeed, Jones's case requires just this assumption of fallibility under normal circumstances; if M_{clock} were not fallible under normal circumstances, then it would not be fallible under the circumstances in which Jones uses it. But then the kind of error that paved the way for a Gettier Incident to occur could not have happened. So, fallibility is needed for a Gettier Incident to arise. Of course, this feature of the case is just an instance of the general lesson we saw exploited in the Argument from Fallibility. Fallibility is a necessary condition for Gettier Incidents to be possible. And, as the Argument from Fallibility brings out, Fallibility with other trivial conditions is also sufficient for Gettier Incidents to be possible. The reason is familiar by now. If a belief forming process is reliable and yet fallible in normal circumstances, then there are cases in which this reliable process issues a false belief in normal circumstances. But then there are also cases just like these, in which the same process issues a belief that would have been false, except for a freak incident intervening and making the resulting belief true nonetheless. Such cases are, of course, Gettier Incidents.

So, given the above stipulations, process reliabilism is susceptible to the Gettier Problem, as is all too familiar. Now, what I suggest is that the process reliabilist should simply respond as follows: knowledge is true belief acquired or sustained by a reliable process under normal circumstances, unless a Gettier Incident has occurred. Again, a reliable process is here a process that tends to generate true beliefs under normal circumstances. As mentioned, the process reliabilist needs to assume that for each type of process there is a set of circumstances—however individuated—that counts as normal circumstances, and relative to which the reliability of the process is defined. Of course, most belief forming processes can be used under a variety of circumstances, not all of which are normal. But assume that for a reliable process to generate knowledge, it must not only be reliable in normal circumstance, but also actually operate under normal circumstances. As we have just seen a belief may be true, formed by a process which is reliable under normal circumstances, and which is operating under normal circumstances, and yet, due to a Gettier Incident, it fails to be known. This is what Jones's case above shows. So, what needs to be added to the process reliabilist definition of knowledge is that no such incident has occurred.

Let me immediately consider two objections. First, why not simply say that circumstances are not normal in Jones case, and that this is why Jones fails to know? This would permit the process reliabilist to respond to the Gettier Problem, while retaining (SCA), the Strong Condition of Adequacy. While this might seem a natural objection to make, there is a decisive problem with it. For consider how we need to think of normal circumstances for this strategy to succeed. We would have to conceive of normal circumstances as being such that when a reliable process operates under normal circumstances no error can occur. Only this form of infallibility would ensure that no Gettier Incident can occur when circumstances are normal. But if our cognitive processes are anything like what defenders of process reliabilism would normally take them to be, then they are fallible when they operate under normal circumstances. To avoid such fallibility, normal circumstances would need to be specified in such a way as to ensure the infallibility of the entire packet. But this seems hopeless.

Second, why not simply say that in Jones's case, though circumstances are normal, contrary to what we initially assumed about the case, the process used by Jones's is not reliable after all (under what we now assume to be normal circumstances). This is why Jones fails to know; though circumstances are normal, he does not form his belief by a reliable process. Again, this strategy is vulnerable to a decisive objection. Because consider what it would require of Jones' process to count as reliable in the actual circumstances of the case. It would, for example, require no less than the capacity to discover that the clock has stopped several days ago merely by looking at it. Indeed this extraordinary process would require not just the capacity to discover this event, but also the capacity to detect many other events which would make ordinary visual processes fail to be accurate. Again, this is hopeless, and it is hopeless because it slides into substantial infallibilism. For a process to count as reliable in normal circumstances, it would effectively need to be infallible in those circumstances, but there are hardly any such processes.

What we see here, of course, is that if a process reliabilist intends to respond to the Gettier Problem while retaining (SCA), she is led towards infallibilism. Either normal circumstances need to be individuated in such a way that a reliable process operating under normal circumstances is infallible. Or reliability needs to be understood in such a way that a reliable process is infallible under normal circumstances. In both cases, of course, process reliabilism turns into a version of substantial infallibilism. But again, on the assumption that our psychology and the world we inhabit have not bestowed us with such remarkable powers, this is a hopeless strategy.

With these responses to our two objections in mind, return to the approach I suggest. In response to the Gettier Problem, the process reliabilist should say, roughly, that a known belief is a true belief acquired by a reliable process under normal circumstances, provided that no Gettier Incident has occurred. I will now spell out this a bit more, among other reasons in order to alleviate concerns that the approach is not illuminating or somehow viciously circular.

What Jones's case suggests is that apart from Jones's belief forming process being reliable and the actual circumstances being normal, a range of other conditions need to be met for a true belief formed under those circumstances to qualify as known. For example, the clock that Jones is looking at should not have stopped exactly 24 hours before Jones is looking at it. And the clock should in other respects work as we expect clocks to do. Consider for example the possibility that the clock works in the unusual way that it started ticking at exactly double speed at precisely 10 pm yesterday, and Jones happens to look at the clock at 10 am today. This unlikely event would prevent Jones from knowing. But this is far from enough. We can readily see that there are many, many further such conditions that need to be in place. For example, there should be no holographic presentation of a fake clock that misleads Jones to think that he is watching the genuine clock. And atmospheric conditions should be such that there is no local aberration of light-rays that unbeknownst to Jones makes visual perception often yield false beliefs under those very specific conditions. And so on.

Let's use the label 'background conditions' to refer to the relevant set of conditions. So, relative to a reliable belief forming process, and its set of normal circumstances, there is a set of background conditions. They have to be met for the reliable process to generate knowledge in normal circumstances. What's in the set of background conditions? Reflection on examples like the above ones suggests the obvious way of defining the set of background conditions. When background conditions are not met, a reliable process operating in normal circumstances fails to generate a high ratio of true beliefs. So, a background condition, relative to a belief forming process M is any condition that, if it not met, means that the process is not reliably producing true beliefs, even when operated under normal circumstances.

Clearly, if a process is reliable, and operates under normal circumstances, and yet some background condition fails to be met, then the resulting beliefs will often be false. But they need not be false; chance may have it that they come out true. This permits us to define what a Gettier Incident is. A Gettier Incident is what you have when a reliable process is operating under normal circumstances, and one or more of the background conditions fail to be satisfied, and yet the process produces a true belief. Exactly this constitutes the class of Gettier Incidents. Note here that the notion of a Gettier Incident is now not defined negatively, say, in terms of some event that prevents an otherwise true and justified belief from being known. This is quite crucial, of course, as it shows that there is a non-circular and illuminating characteristic of the notion of a Gettier Incident to be offered.

Having now defined the notion of a Gettier Incident, we can offer a process reliabilist definition of knowledge that does not use the notion of a Gettier Incident: A known belief is a true belief acquired by a reliable process, in normal circumstances, when all background conditions are met. Given the way the notion of a Gettier Incident has been defined, the last clause is equivalent to the clause that no Gettier Incident should have occurred. So the view arrived at is just what we had earlier: a known belief is a belief which is reliably produced or sustained in normal circumstances, provided that no Gettier Incident has occurred. But what has been shown now is that the last clause can be independently specified. This confirms that, when unpacked, the approach can be relieved of the charge of being circular or not illuminating.

Again one might object that if one or more of the background conditions are not met, then surely the conditions are not normal. So, why not simply say that in Jones's case, the conditions are not normal? Why talk both about normal conditions, and background conditions? Why not lump them together into one set of conditions. But we have already seen where this leads. This strategy takes us to the claim that circumstances are normal only when they ensure that a reliable process is infallible. As before, though it is tempting, we need to reject this strategy. We do not trade in infallible cognitive processes.

Let me expand on some remarks made earlier. Consider the condition relevant in Jones's case, namely that that the clock didn't run at double speed for exactly 24 hours. The intuitive thought is that for Jones to know, this must not have happened. So Jones's knowledge is in this sense lucky—it depends on a kind of external luck. When we know stuff, this depends on the absence of Gettier Incidents, but nothing that makes a belief known prevents such incidents from occurring. Given the way we have applied this strategy to process reliabilism we can now make this modal claim a bit more precise. The modal claim is simply that a cognitive subject may operate a reliable belief forming process in normal circumstances, and yet all this does not fix the status of the background conditions.

By a similar measure, we can illuminate a kind of open-endedness to background conditions, and thereby to the set of possible Gettier Incidents. The detailed specification of the appropriate set of background conditions is, in a sense, open-ended: there seems to be endless ways in which they may fail to obtain. This is hard to argue in detail, but let me suggest some examples of why this seems to be so. Consider the specific condition that the clock that Jones is looking at should not have been running at double speed since 10 am yesterday. If we count this as one separate background condition, we can easily see that there are innumerable other similar conditions (any positive integer will do). Just change the number of days with any number you want. Or change the factor that the speed of the clock is multiplied with (any positive integer will do). Or multiply speed with negative integers, and make the clock run backwards. And so on. The lesson is that Jones' knowing that it's 10 am requires not only that conditions are normal, but that an additional endless set of possible scenarios are not actual. We cannot enlist the members of this set for the simple reason that for any item we identify, there are countless variations of this item. And for the reasons already implied there is no obvious other way in which we can specify the members of the set of background condition. One might suggest, for example, that background conditions should be captured in terms of nomological possibility. But quick reflection will reveal that this is a non-starter. None of the cases so far discussed can be ruled out as nomologically impossible.

As we have seen, there is fortunately another way of deciding whether a candidate condition is indeed a member of the set of background conditions. It is this: some condition C is a background condition relative to a reliable method M and its normal circumstances N just when N and not-C are co-possible, and M fails to generate a high ratio of true belief when used in N, and C is the case. Though this does not permit us to generate the full set of background conditions relative to a given method, we can nonetheless use this criterion to decide whether any proposed condition is a member of the set of background conditions.

If the above is right, knowledge is defeasible in a certain way. Roughly, we might say that knowledge is justified true belief, except when a Gettier Incident has occurred. If a given belief is known, it is known in virtue of being true and justified. However, for any known belief, there is a class of possible events that constitute defeaters to that belief's being known. Were any of these events to occur, the belief would be true and justified, but not known. This makes knowledge fit the template of what I called a defeater-structure. So, in this sense knowledge is defeasible. In the light of parts of the tradition in epistemology, this might seem an odd view about the nature of knowledge, rendering knowledge more fragile and susceptible to chance than might have been assumed in epistemology. What I have argued is that reflection on the Gettier Problem gives us very robust reasons to think that knowledge is fragile in just this way.

References

Dancy, Jonathan 2004: *Ethics Without Principles*. Oxford: Oxford University Press.

Gettier, Edmund 1963: "Is Justified True Belief Knowledge?". *Analysis* 23, 121–133.

Goldberg, Sanford 2010: *Relying on Others: an Essay in Epistemology.* Oxford: Oxford University Press.

Goldman, Alvin 1979: "What Is Justified Belief?". In: George S. Pappas (ed.), *Justification and Knowledge.* Dordrecht: Reidel, 1–23.

— 1986: *Epistemology and Cognition.* Cambridge: Harvard University Press.

— 2011: "Reliabilism". Edward N. Zalta (ed.), *The Stanford Encyclopedia of Philosophy (Spring 2011 Edition).* URL http://plato.stanford.edu/archives/spr2011/entries/reliabilism/.

Merricks, Trenton 1995a: "A Dilemma for any Theory of Knowledge". *American Philosophical Quarterly* 32, 279–284.

— 1995b: "Warrant Entails Truth". *Philosophy and Phenomenological Research* 55, 841–855.

— 1997: "More On Warrant's Entailing Truth". *Philosophy and Phenomenological Research* 57, 627–631.

Willaschek, Marcus 2007: "Contextualism about Knowledge and Justification by Default". *Grazer Philosophische Studien* 74, 251–272.

Zagzebski, Linda 1994: "The Inescapability of Gettier Problems". *The Philosophical Quarterly* 44, 65–73.

— 1999: "What is Knowledge". In: John Greco & Ernesto Sosa (eds.), *The Blackwell Guide to Epistemology.* Oxford: Blackwell, 92–116.

Grazer Philosophische Studien
87 (2013), 59–73.

THE CHALLENGES OF TRAVELING WITHOUT ITINERARY: THE OVERRIDING CASE

Mikael JANVID
Stockholm University

Summary

As an important step towards a comprehensive model of challenges and defeaters, it is here argued that securing a previously held epistemic status for a belief in the face of an overriding challenge does not require us to reach a higher epistemic standard than the one the belief originally reached. In the course of the investigation, criteria for when the epistemic status of beliefs are challenged and defeated are suggested. At the end of the paper, these results are then more briefly applied to shed some light on the problem of misleading evidence.

I.

Consider the following scenarios:

1. A traveling couple wants to know whether their flight to New York will have a layover in Chicago. They overhear a fellow traveler saying that she knows that the aircraft will land in Chicago since she has checked the flight itinerary. The couple challenges the reliability of the itinerary on the grounds that it might contain a misprint or be outdated. The couple concludes that the fellow traveler does not know that the flight has a layover in Chicago.
2. A couple about to fly to New York wants to know whether their flight will have a layover in Chicago. They decide to go to the information desk at the airport to find out. While waiting in the queue at the desk, they overhear a fellow passenger saying that she knows that the aircraft will land in Chicago since she has checked the flight itinerary. At that moment the couple arrives at the desk and are told that the flight has no stops at all. The couple is thus told both that the flight has a layover in Chicago and that it has

not by reliable sources and has no reason to question either source except for the fact that they contradict each other.

How should these scenarios be analyzed epistemologically? Both scenarios have in common that a challenge is directed against a knowledge-claim. They differ in that the first scenario contains an undermining challenge (in fact two) while the second contains an overriding challenge. An overriding challenge to an epistemic claim p provides warrant for non-p, while an undermining challenge to p challenges the warrant provided for p. In the latter case, no warrant has thereby been provided for non-p.[1] More precisely, if warrant is a relation r with at least two *relata*, the ground or evidence e and the proposition p, then an undermining challenge can either challenge e or challenge that e stands in r to p.[2]

Note that the truth of an overriding challenge to p may be compatible with the truth of the evidence e for p as well as with the truth of p itself. If p is "There is a computer on the desk" and e is "It appears to me that there is a computer on the desk", then "I see no computer", as uttered by the challenger, without being incompatible with e or p itself, constitutes, nevertheless, an overriding challenge to p.

The scenarios also differ in that, unlike scenario 2, scenario 1 has received a lot of attention in the recent epistemological debate. For instance, contextualists like Stewart Cohen and Keith DeRose claim that challenging a knowledge-claim p in such a scenario raises the epistemic standard originally in place.[3] In order to gain knowledge that p in the new context created by raising the challenge, the subject or someone else, must reach a higher epistemic standard than in the original context.[4]

1. The distinction is usually drawn in terms of defeaters, see (Pollock and Cruz 1999, 196) and (Casullo (2003, 44-45). (Pollock employs the terms rebutting for overriding and undercutting for undermining defeaters.) For this author, a challenge differs from a defeater primarily by constituting a *prima facie* characterization. See below.

2. Sometimes defeating e may override p, as in the case of an inductive inference concerning the color of swans: The observation of a non-white swan overrides the generalization that all swans are white. In those cases we have thus instead come across an overriding defeater. A relevant example of defeating e, and thereby undermining the warrant for p, would instead be where an alleged sighting of a white swan indeed was of a white bird but not of a swan.

3. See (Cohen 1999 and 2000), (DeRose 1995) and (Janvid 2008) for further details. In brief, their version of contextualism (sometimes distinguished from other versions by adding "semantic" or "attributor") holds that the truth value of knowledge ascriptions of the form "S knows that p" vary with the context of the attributor. See also notes 4 and 5 below.

4. According to contextualism, the challenge thus creates a new context and it is in order to know p in this context that a higher epistemic standard must be reached. The subject continues

According to contextualism, it is the introduction of previously ignored error possibilities that raises the epistemic standard. The error possibilities in scenario 1 constitute undermining challenges that undermine the warrant provided for p: the itinerary may contain a misprint or be outdated. In (Janvid 2008), this author criticizes the view that undermining challenges raise the epistemic standard. Briefly, by raising an undermining challenge, one does not demand a higher level of warrant. If one suspects that the flight itinerary is outdated, then one suspects that the *original* warrant is defective. Raising such a challenge does not amount to a rise in standard of warrant since an outdated itinerary does not provide sufficient warrant in the original context (nor in any context!) to begin with. This analysis can thus account for the fact that subjects tend to withdraw their epistemic claims when faced by an undermining challenge without bringing in a rise in standard of warrant.

However, in that paper, this author also conceded that overriding challenges do seem to conform to an analysis in which the epistemic standard is raised. The initial dialectical stalemate between p and non-p in scenario 2 plausibly starts a competition where the one that succeeds in assembling the strongest warrant in favor of one of the claims wins and the assembled stronger warrant sets the standard for the positive epistemic status in question, which thus has been raised to a higher standard than in the original context. In this paper we shall investigate whether the intuitive pull towards such an analysis withstands closer scrutiny.

Notwithstanding the intuitive attraction of the standards-shifting picture, just noted, it is not clear whether those epistemologists who claim that the epistemic standard rises when undermining challenges are introduced also think that the same phenomenon occurs in the case of overriding challenges in scenario 2. As noted above, overriding challenges have not

---

to know according to the standard of the old context. Contextualism formulates this claim in a meta-language where these different contexts and corresponding standards thus employ different senses, or different contents, of "know". See (Janvid 2008) for further details and criticism. The conversation can swing back to the old context with its lower standard, but accounting for such a "semantic descent" is a problem for contextualism. See (Pritchard 2001) for this convincing objection.

Note, however, that although contextualism entails the aforementioned rise of standard, the converse entailment does not hold. One could hold that the epistemic standard rises in the face of challenges without committing oneself to the semantic hypothesis that the sense of "know" changes from the old to the new context or that conversational mechanisms have any epistemic relevance in scenarios 1 and 2. Although the presumption of a raise in epistemic standard does not entail contextualism, this author suspects this presumption makes the contextualist solution intuitively attractive.

received the same amount of attention. The following analysis is thus not intended as an objection to contextualism or any other currently held epistemological position, but is primarily motivated by the *desideratum* of arriving at a comprehensive model of challenges and defeaters.

The analysis of scenario 2 provided in this paper is thus independently motivated. As a consequence, this author shall take the opportunity of changing the focus of the analysis somewhat (thereby further diminishing the possibility of the upcoming analysis targeting any of the aforementioned positions): whereas epistemologists that discuss scenario 1 focus on the ascription of knowledge,[5] the upcoming analysis will be conducted in terms of *warrant.* One upshot of this paper is that the tendency, sometimes deliberately, sometimes less so, to jump directly to the knowledge ascription thereby overlooks the complicated but important epistemic dialectic of warrant, challenge and defeat – a dialectic that should condition such ascriptions and may sometimes make for the incorrectness of such ascriptions.

Moreover, both philosophers and non-philosophers tend to have fewer, or less determinate, intuitions about these scenarios, when they are posed as questions about warrant rather than knowledge. This author regards this as a virtue of this warrant-centered approach rather than as a vice since it encourages a more theory driven approach compared to an intuitive, piecemeal, case by case, approach. If our intuitions all pointed in the same direction, then the latter approach should perhaps be recommended, or yield the same result as the former approach. However, since our intuitions conflict, certain intuitions must be discarded in favor of others, and these decisions must be theory driven.[6]

---

5. The puzzle arising in scenario 1 is that the couple, on the one hand, grants knowledge to the fellow passenger, but, on the other hand, seems epistemically or rationally obliged to inquiry further into whether the flight really stops in Chicago, which smells of paradox. Contextualists argue that the solution is contextualization: the ascription of knowledge is given in a context where the epistemic standard is low while the need for further investigation occurs in another context where the epistemic standard is high (and where thus the fellow passenger lacks knowledge).

6. As we noted above and following the model developed in (Lewis 1979 and 1996), the rise in required epistemic standard consists in an expansion of the range of relevant alternatives, or error possibilities, the subject must be in a position to eliminate in order to count as having gained that epistemic status. However, in ordering the error possibilities as close or distant, thereby measuring epistemic strength, contextualists rely on intuitions rather than any systematic method. Even though contextualism is developed systematically in other aspects, the crucial reliance on intuitions here thus makes the capacity to eliminate error possibilities a poor measure of epistemic strength since the suspicion lingers that its verdicts articulate the intuitions

Having made these preliminary points and rehearsed the analysis of scenario 1, we shall in the next section turn to scenario 2 where this author argues that reaching a higher epistemic standard constitutes neither a necessary, nor a sufficient, condition for defeating an overriding challenge.

II.

Firstly, reaching a higher epistemic standard is not a necessary condition for a subject being warranted in believing that p, when she is faced by an overriding challenge, since the subject may instead defeat the overriding challenge to p by an undermining defeater that undermines the warrant provided for non-p. For instance, the subject in scenario 2 notices that the agent at the service desk is too stressed to provide any reliable information. If the overriding challenge is undermined, then p is not challenged anymore and since no challenge has been directed against the warrant provided for p, i.e. no reason to doubt the sufficiently high epistemic strength of the warrant for p, the original epistemic status of p for the subject is thereby preserved without the subject having acquired new warrant with a higher epistemic strength.

Secondly, reaching a higher epistemic standard is not a sufficient condition since providing stronger warrant for p than the subject originally possessed is not enough given certain assumptions. Showing non-sufficiency is a bit more complicated and we therefore need to spell out the scenario further in order to more fully display the often overlooked epistemic dialectic of challenge and defeat. Truth conduciveness constitutes a criterion of the relation of warrant r, of which the evidential *relatum* e constitutes one of the *relata*, in the view of this author. Although not free from problems of its own,[7] truth conduciveness offers a way of measuring epistemic

---

rather than providing independent support for them See (Janvid 2008). For similar criticism, see (Baumann 2005, 232–8) and, in admirable detail, (Wilburn 2010).

That the standard is determined in common sense contexts, prior to any epistemological inquiry, is a further problematical idealization that is subjected to criticism in (Janvid 2008) where it is argued that what rises as a result of philosophical reflection is not the epistemic standard, but rather the *standards of precision* regarding the epistemic terms in question.

Concerning the role that "folk intuitions" should play in epistemology, the favorite example of this author is that most colleagues and students assent to the claim that strawberries are berries while denying that bananas are even though the converse, in fact, is true. Why, then, should folk botanic carry less weight than folk epistemology?

7. See, for instance notes no. 8 and 9 below.

strength, more precisely strength of warrant, precisely in degree of truth conduciveness. The strength of a challenge and defeater is measured in the corresponding way: the strength of an overriding challenge by the truth conduciveness of the warrant for non-p while the strength of an undermining challenge is measured by the truth conduciveness of the warrant against e or r.

This suggestion thereby holds the promise of offering a unified way of determining and assessing warrant and defeat. It is hard to see why given such a view on warrant, defeaters should not be treated in the same way.

If the strength of a challenge to p outweighs the strength of p, then p is defeated and the challenge thus turns into a defeater to p. Alternatively, in the case of an undermining challenge, if the challenge outweighs the strength of the warrant for p, then the warrant is defeated and the undermining challenge turns into an undermining defeater. Whereas a challenge is a *prima facie* characterization that is determined by *accessible* warrant, the notion of a defeater is determined by the strength of the warrant the challenge in fact possesses in comparison to the warrant for p, irrespective of whether anyone has access to the former warrant in that context. In scenario 1 and 2 various sources of information regarding the flight are more or less reliable and it is their reliability that determine to what extent the subjects are warranted or defeated in their beliefs. Although the upcoming analysis does not depend on this particular view on defeaters, *defeater* is thus an externalist concept for this author, while *challenge* is an internalist one.

Returning now to the question of sufficiency, let us postulate that checking the itinerary yields an epistemic strength, that is truth conduciveness, for p over 0.5, say 0.6 and that receiving information at the information desk yields a strength of warrant for non-p of 0.7.[8] Faced with this overriding challenge to p, the couple goes to the hall of departures and gazes at the electronic billboard and there reads that the flight has a layover in Chicago. Let us further assume that the strength of warrant in receiving information in this way is 0.8. Has the passenger now secured the relevant epistemic status albeit at a higher epistemic standard than in the original

8. Estimating epistemic strength, i.e. truth conduciveness, in quantitative terms simplifies the analysis, but the same upcoming result could be obtained solely by using the terms slightly higher and lower epistemic strength. Probability is of course a difficult and controversial philosophical concept. This author has regrettably at present nothing to add over above Alston's attempt to give an account of objective probability within epistemology in (Alston 2005).

context? Not necessarily, since in virtue of the slight difference in strength of warrant, the overriding challenge has not thereby been sufficiently met. Just as the original overriding challenge to p leaves us in a state of ignorance regarding p rather than securing a positive epistemic status for non-p, merely providing new slightly stronger, but non-conclusive, warrant for p does not allow us to secure the epistemic status for p. What is missing is an undermining defeater to the overriding challenge (that may also explain the strong warrant for non-p). Then, and only then, has the passenger secured the epistemic status for p—something that the she might thus have done without acquiring stronger warrant for p as long as she comes across the undermining defeater to the overriding challenge to p.

Slight differences in epistemic strength are not sufficient to secure the epistemic status of p against challenges since as prima facie their epistemic strength are approximations based on the available evidence that therefore may fluctuate in any direction in the course of the dialectic as new evidence is brought in. A sufficient margin of epistemic strength is therefore required. Cases of slight differences in epistemic strength should thus be treated as cases where the epistemic strength of the warrant in favor of p and non-p are equal. When the subject cannot rely on a sufficient margin of epistemic strength in favor of her belief that p, then she has no other option than to attempt to come up with an undermining defeater against the warrant provided for non-p, to secure her epistemic status concerning p.

The result of this analysis of scenario 2 regarding sufficiency thus illustrates the common constraint on warrant that in order for a subject to be warranted in her belief that p, the belief must not only be based on sufficiently strong, i.e. truth conducive, warrant for p, there must also not exist any challenges to p.[9]

Here undermining challenges differ from overriding challenges. Faced with an undermining challenge, it is sufficient to secure the epistemic status for p by providing new warrant for p from another source

9. See, for instance, (Alston 1989, 238f.) although Alston there retains an internalist constraint on warrant as well in that defeaters may only arise from "what is in the subject's perspective on the world" whereas in this paper that would count as yet another stage of prima facie assessment towards the goal of determining warrant where no internalist constraints hold. This author is hopeful that such a "no defeater" clause can argued for externalistically, but such an argument deserves a paper of its own.

The basing relation is a crucial feature of any substantial externalist position. For an attempt to give an account of this notoriously difficult relation, see (Alston 2005, Ch. 5 and 6).

that is at least equally strong as the warrant provided from the original source.

While scenarios subject to the condition of slight differences in strength of warrant are common enough, it should be conceded that in scenarios where a great difference in strength of warrant exists, or when conclusive warrant is provided, reaching a higher epistemic standard does secure a previously held epistemic status. However, this author is happy to make this concession. Note that the first proviso is never fulfilled when the strength of the overriding challenge is very high, since then a sufficient difference in strength of warrant will not be obtained. The warrant will then not secure a sufficient margin of strength over the overriding challenge.

Nevertheless, with these provisos in place, we can tentatively conclude that reaching a higher epistemic standard constitutes neither a necessary nor a sufficient condition for defeating an overriding challenge.

However, the case may not be closed since non-epistemic factors, which, so far, we have not taken into account, may be of relevance. More specifically, some philosophers think that practical factors like what is at stake for the participants raise the epistemic standard in the case of undermining challenges.[10] May such factors be of epistemic relevance in the case of overriding challenges? Insofar as they would, high stakes would make overriding challenges with a low degree of warrant salient for beliefs whose warrant possesses higher epistemic strength, which under lower stakes would not challenge the targeted belief. This would in turn raise the epistemic standard.

The response is twofold. First the harsh answer, insofar as one holds that the epistemic status of a belief is determined by the epistemic strength of the warrant that the belief is based on, as this author does, then the answer is no. Since practical factors do not make any difference in truth conduciveness, challenges consisting of making practical factors salient lack epistemic strength on their own. Practical factors therefore lack epistemic relevance.[11]

10. See (Henderson 2009), (Grimm forthcoming) and (Stanley 2005) for three different versions of that view and (Reed 2010) for an opposing view. In scenario 1 the practical factor consists in the couple having an important business contact in Chicago.

11. As this author has argued in (Janvid 2008) where undermining challenges are considered. There it is also tentatively suggested that the irrelevance goes in the other direction as well, i.e. that epistemic states like knowledge are irrelevant for practical reasoning. Since the publication of that paper, Douven has given more substantial arguments for that conclusion in (Douven 2008).

One way to claim that practical factors are epistemically relevant in cases like scenario 2, where the warrant for p is strong to begin with, would be to argue that high stakes scenarios

Second, the more nuanced answer, for those who hold that the epistemic status of a belief is not exclusively determined by the epistemic strength of the warrant, which the belief is based on. Certain practical factors could, for instance, determine *how* strong the warrant is required to be in order to secure a certain epistemic status, like knowledge. This view, nevertheless, looks less promising in the case of overriding challenges where two propositions compete than in the more discussed case of undermining challenges. A great difference in epistemic strength simply is a deciding factor in assessing epistemic status between competing propositions. Moreover, if practical factors like high stakes are relevant in determining epistemic status in the way indicated above, by raising the standard for when a belief is sufficiently warranted as to constitute knowledge, then it seems that it is *the presence of these high stakes themselves* that raise the epistemic standard rather than the presence of an overriding challenge. The latter thus constitutes a superfluous element in the rise of epistemic standard.

It can easily be conceded that in high stakes scenarios, the subject may loose faith in her warrant for p and therefore ceases to believe that p and thus for *that* reason ceases to know that p,[12] but this psychological phenomenon is a result that takes place without, and thus not due to, any change in epistemic strength.

This concession may be complemented with the hypothesis that a challenge that consists of making the high stakes involved salient may be rephrased along the following lines: "I understand that your evidence for the flight having a layover in Chicago is strong, but I, nevertheless, want to be sure since I have an important business meeting there". Put in this way, it seems like an understandable psychological "quest for certainty", but

---

entail indefeasibility or infallibilism, i.e. that only indefeasible and infallible warrant suffices for the epistemic status in question in high stake scenarios, but this constitutes an unwarranted leap that requires further, and other kinds of, arguments. Fallibilism is often defined as the view that a subject can know that p even though the existence (or truth) of the warrant that the belief that p is based on is compatible with the falsity of p. For further discussion of such high epistemic standards, see (Janvid 2008) and sec. III below.

12. Steven Luper suggested this reply in conversation as a comment on (Janvid 2008). This may also be a case where ascription of knowledge differs from ascription of warrant in that the former ascription, due to the doxastic condition, is more sensitive to practical factors than the ascription of the latter property is, which this author regards as a further advantage of the present approach.

If the above considerations concerning the epistemic irrelevance of practical factors are correct, then, since a challenge consisting in making high stakes salient thus lacks epistemic relevance, such a challenge should be classified as an *empty* challenge. See below.

as fallibilists, we have, nonetheless, good epistemological reasons to deny that knowledge requires certainty.[13] The introduction of practical factors does thus not force a rise in epistemic standard in the case of overriding challenges. The tentative conclusion that we reached above, is therefore still standing.

As a general reflection, this author suspects that one reason many epistemologists fail to take the intricate epistemic dialectic of warrant, challenge and defeat into full account is the tacit assumption that challenges come cheap so that the burden of proof, accordingly, always is upon the subject (claimant). This is an assumption that one critic of this traditional view, Michael Williams, has expressed as follows:

> *Claimant-challenger asymmetry*. Whenever knowledge is claimed, the burden of justification lies with the claimant. If I represent myself as knowing that p, I invite you to ask me how I know. There is nothing you have to do, or no way that things have to be, in order for you to have the right to enter a challenge. (Williams 2007, 99)[14]

Epistemologists who reject this assumption instead often propose an asymmetry in the other direction: subjects are in certain contexts *default* warranted in certain of their beliefs. Frequently the notion of *entitlement* is used to depict that form of warrant. Even though the epistemic claim being challenged in scenarios 1 and 2 is a very unlikely candidate for enjoying a default status, one may still wonder what relation the approach advocated here stands to a "default and challenge" model of warrant and knowledge.

There are indeed similarities. Both approaches reject empty or naked challenges; that is challenges simply consisting in asking "why?" or "Are you sure?". Since such challenges are not based on any warrant they do not *per se* carry with them any epistemic strength. Possessing such strength is a requirement not only for a belief being warranted, but also for challenges to qualify as genuine challenges. Two guiding principles of the approach adopted in this paper here come to the fore: firstly, the conditions for raising challenges and defeaters deserve as much attention as conditions

---

13. On this point see (Reed 2010) who argues that we should instead regard the subject as still knowing that p, but that certain contexts of practical deliberation, where the stakes are high, demand certainty. From the externalist perspective of this author, this author would instead be inclined to omit any epistemic requirement on the state, which an agent must be in to be rationally permitted to act. See note no. 11.

14. See also (Williams 2001) especially Ch. 13 and 14.

for warrant have traditionally received within epistemology and, secondly, that results gained concerning warrant are highly relevant for challenges and defeaters as well as vice versa.

However, the approach proposed here does not entail the existence of default entitled beliefs that would enable subjects to enjoy positive epistemic status to beliefs in the absence of any warrant. The approach suggested here may thus instead advocate *symmetry* of warrant between epistemic claim and challenge where both the claimant and challenger must possess warrant in order for their respective epistemic claims to be warranted or, respectively, constitute a genuine challenge.[15]

On the basis of the framework adopted here and the results reached so far, in the next and final section some tentative remarks concerning the problem of misleading evidence will be given.

III.

A subject is in the epistemic state of knowing that p, but is faced with an overriding challenge c. Can the counterevidence that the overriding challenge rests upon, thereby, without further consideration, be dismissed as misleading? Such a dismissal seems dogmatic and, yet, the subject actually knows that p![16]

Even though this author has already taken the liberty of specifying the misleading evidence in question as an overriding challenge, the case is still under-described. The problem of misleading evidence will here be spelled out further with the help of the terminology and results from sections I and II in order to see whether we thereby can at least reduce its mystery. The ambition is thus to employ the results from the former sections to shed some light on the issue, not to address this complex problem in its entirety. This author is aware of how intuitive the puzzle is and, undoubtedly, will remain.

First of all, the knowledge ascription depends on the warrant on which the subject's knowledge that p is based. An epistemological investigation of these cases should not be based on independent access to the truth of p, but, as was stated in section I, precisely proceed via the warrant that the belief that p is based on. Furthermore, the warrant that the belief that

15. These paragraphs are indebted to discussions with Marcus Willaschek. For more on empty challenges, see (Janvid 2008).

16. See (Sharon & Spectre 2010) for a more extensive analysis of the problem.

p is based on is sufficiently strong and, given that truth conduciveness constitutes the criterion of warrant, the warrant thus enjoys a sufficiently high degree of truth conduciveness. Now, from these considerations alone we are certainly not in a position to categorize the overriding challenge as misleading in the sense of c being false and/or that the warrant for c is lacking truth conduciveness for non-p. The next question is then how strong the warrant for non-p is. There are three possible answers. (I) If the strength of the counterevidence is considerably lower than the strength of the evidence for p, then knowledge is preserved. (II) If the strength of the counterevidence is sufficiently close to the strength of the evidence for p, then knowledge is defeated and the subject becomes ignorant of p. (III) If the evidence for non-p is considerably stronger than the evidence for p, then the subject is even warranted in believing that non-p.[17]

From a fallibilist point of view, the first case is compatible with the truth of the overriding challenge c.[18] In that case, the challenge is only misleading in the sense that it might lead us to reject p even though the strength of the warrant for non-p is lower than the strength of the warrant for the belief that p is based on.

In the second case, we need to draw on the results reached in section II in order to determine how the subject can secure knowledge that p. Recall that we are considering an overriding challenge. No undermining challenge has been raised against the original warrant for p, so this warrant thus stands unchallenged. Nevertheless, we saw that in close cases, the subject needs additional undermining evidence against the overriding challenge, in order to count as knowing or being warranted in her belief that p. (If possessing such an undermining defeater counts as knowing not only that p, but also *how* the evidence is misleading, is a terminological question.) However, from the perspective argued for here, it may be the case that warrant for p, which is sufficiently strong to base knowledge that p, might still in the face of an overriding challenge need additional undermining evidence against the overriding challenge in order to preserve knowledge that p.[19] For this author, this does not outright smell of paradox and shows

17. Depending on how strong warrant is required to be in order to ground knowledge and how large a difference must be in order to be considerable, the third alternative might be impossible. It will, in any case, not be further analyzed here.

18. As the example with not seeing the computer on the desk illustrates in sec. I.

19. It might be the case that the subject within her total evidence already possesses the relevant undermining evidence ahead of the overriding challenge. What the subject then needs

how the unified externalist approach proposed here can to some extent dispel that smell by carefully investigating the intricate epistemic dialectic of warrant, challenge and defeat.

What if the supposedly misleading evidence instead has the form of an undermining challenge? Since knowledge is at hand, the warrant for p must be sufficiently strong. From a fallibilist point of view, such strength of warrant is, nevertheless, compatible with the existence of evidence against e or r. In the aforementioned computer scenario, an example of challenging e would be that the challenger points out that the subject has a low technical expertise, which is true but the subject still recognizes that particular kind of computer when she sees one. An example of challenging r (for a specific computer model) would be that the challenger points out that the presence of visual characteristic x, which the subject provides as warrant is not a reliable indicator of newer models. This is indeed the case, but since another visual characteristic y is also present which together with x constitute a reliable indicator of an older model, the challenge is defeated. In the case of undermining challengers we thus actually seem to be in the position to dismiss the counter-evidence as misleading in the way the examples illustrate—albeit not in any dogmatic way. However, since the subject herself may not know that she knows, she may not herself be able to reason in this way—recall the externalist conditions on defeaters from section II. At least part of the mystery of misleading evidence resides in the clash between the factive state of knowledge and natural internalist intuitions regarding evidence and defeaters. That the unified externalist approach suggested here does not cause quite the same clash is therefore not surprising.

Moreover and perhaps somewhat counter-intuitively, when the problem of misleading evidence is spelled out in this way, the warrant for the belief that p in a case of knowledge is thus robust against defeaters in a way which the belief that p itself is not! In any case, just as in the case of overriding challenges, once we pay sufficient attention to the admittedly complex epistemic dialectic, the mystery of misleading evidence does not disappear, but is at least somewhat diminished.[20]

---

to do to defeat the overriding challenge is to put the pieces together.

20. Thanks to Albert Casullo, David Henderson, Steven Luper, Levi Spectre and an anonymous referee for helpful comments. An earlier version of this paper was presented at the conference "Defeasibility in Epistemology, Ethics, Law and Logic" in Frankfurt in September 2010. This author is grateful to the participants, including the "DDD-group": Claudia Blöser, Claudia Cuadra, Hannes Ole Matthiessen and Marcus Willaschek, for useful comments and stimulating

References

Alston, William 1989: "An Internalist Externalism". In his *Epistemic Justification.* Ithaca: Cornell University Press, 227–245.

— 2005: *Beyond "Justification". Dimensions of Epistemic Evaluation.* Ithaca: Cornell University Press.

Baumann, Peter 2005: "Varieties of Contextualism: Standards and Descriptions". *Grazer Philosophische Studien* 69, 229–245.

Casullo, Albert 2003: *A Priori Justification.* Oxford: Oxford University Press.

Cohen, Stewart 1999: "Contextualism, Skepticism and the Structure of Reasons". In: *Philosophical Perspectives 13. Epistemology.* Oxford: Blackwell, 57–89.

— 2000: "Contextualism and Skepticism". In Ernest Sosa & Enrique Villanueva (eds.), *Skepticism. Philosophical Issues 10.* Oxford: Blackwell, 94–107.

DeRose, Keith 1995: "Solving the Skeptical Problem". *The Philosophical Review* 104, 1–52.

Douven, Igor 2008: "Knowledge and Practical Reasoning". *dialectica* 62, 101–118.

Grimm, Stephen (forthcoming): "Knowledge, Practical Interests and Rising Tides". In: John Greco & David Henderson (eds.), *Epistemic Evaluation: Point and Purpose in Epistemology.* Oxford: Oxford University Press.

Henderson, David 2009: "Motivated Contextualism". *Philosophical Studies* 142, 119–131.

Janvid, Mikael 2008: "Defeaters and Rising Standards of Justification". *Acta Analytica* 23, 45–54.

Lewis, David 1979: "Scorekeeping in a Language Game". *Journal of Philosophical Logic* 8, 339–359.

— 1996: "Elusive Knowledge". *Australasian Journal of Philosophy* 74, 549–567.

Pollock, John & Cruz, Joseph 1999: *Contemporary Theories of Knowledge.* (2nd ed.). Oxford: Rowman & Littlefield.

Pritchard, Duncan 2001: "Contextualism, Scepticism and the Problem of Epistemic Descent". *dialectica* 55, 327–349.

Reed, Baron 2010: "A Defense of Stable Invariantism". *Noûs* 44, 224–244.

Sharon, Assaf & Spectre, Levi 2010: "Dogmatism Repuzzled". *Philosophical Studies* 148, 307–321.

Stanley, Jason 2005: *Knowledge and Practical Interests.* Oxford: Oxford University Press.

Wilburn, Ron 2010: "Possible Worlds of Doubt". *Acta Analytica* 25, 259–277.

---

discussions. Work on this paper was funded by the Deutsche Forschungsgemeinschaft project "Defeasibility and Discourse Dependence".

Williams, Michael 2001: *Problems of Knowledge: A Critical Introduction to Epistemology.* Oxford: Oxford University Press.
— 2007: "Why (Wittgensteinian) Contextualism is not Relativism". *Episteme* 4, 93–114.

Grazer Philosophische Studien
87 (2013), 75–97.

ENTITLEMENT AND PUBLIC ACCESSIBILITY OF EPISTEMIC STATUS[1]

Hannes Ole MATTHIESSEN
Université de Fribourg

Summary

In recent epistemological literature, epistemic entitlement is understood as a personal epistemic status that does not require elaborate justificatory activity on behalf of the entitled individual. It is nevertheless internalist in a weaker sense, since it is said to be grounded in perceptual experiences.

It seems, however, that the conditions under which an epistemic right holds should, like in cases of most other rights, be publicly observable, because they have implications for the ways others are required to treat the entitled individual. Therefore I suggest an alternative to the weakly internalist conception of epistemic entitlement as based on mental episodes. I show how we can construe epistemic rights as being based on external conditions that are publicly observable. This social externalist approach is then defended against internalist and externalist challenges.

Two broad classes of epistemic status concepts have dominated the epistemological debate until recently. On the one hand we have somewhat deontological notions such as *justification* and *reason* that stem from an internalist tradition. These are intimately connected to agentive rationality. On the other hand we have more abstract notions such as *warrant* and *safety* that have been introduced by externalist minded epistemo-

1. Precursors of this paper have been presented at the Conference "Defeasibility in Epistemology, Ethics, Law and Logic" in Frankfurt, at the research Colloquium in Fribourg (Switzerland) and at the 22nd Congress of the DGPhil in Munich. I would like to thank the audiences for many helpful remarks, particularly Klemens Kappel, Gianfranco Soldati, Cain Todd and Michael Williams. I am also grateful to Fred Dretske and an anonymous referee for Grazer Philosophische Studien for voicing important criticism. My special thank goes to my collaborators in the DFG-funded research project "Defeasibility and Discourse Dependence" Claudia Blöser, Claudia Cuadra, Mikael Janvid and Marcus Willaschek, whose influence on the development of my thoughts was invaluable.

logists. They immediately concern the relation between a belief and its truth.

In the last two decades, the concept of *epistemic entitlement* has gained some attention in the epistemological literature, notably in attempts to explain *perceptual* knowledge. The idea that the central epistemic notion is one of an *epistemic right* seems initially attractive if one looks for a position in between the two camps, because it can accommodate externalist and internalist intuitions: We may sometimes be entitled to a certain belief independently of our ability to offer a justification, whereas special circumstances may require us to give reasons in order to be entitled. Authors such as Fred Dretske, Tyler Burge, Peter Graham, Christopher Peacocke, Crispin Wright and Martin Davies have offered original accounts of entitlement as a kind of epistemic status that comes with weaker internalist requirements than justification.[2] Although these accounts differ in important respects, it is nevertheless possible to extract something like a common core, a "standard account" of epistemic entitlement.

Having summarized the standard account in section 1, I will argue (in section 2) that epistemic entitlements—just as other kinds of rights—should meet an accessibility requirement: since someone's having a right to do something has consequences for how others are required to treat that person, entitlements have to be publicly accessible. After showing (in section 3) that entitlements as understood in the standard account have problems meeting this requirement, I present a social externalist alternative in section 4, according to which entitlements are grounded in a set of accepted default conditions. In sections 5 and 6 I discuss ways in which this account can deal with various objections driven by internalist intuitions.

1. *The standard account of epistemic entitlement*

Here is what I take to be the *four central elements* of the standard account of epistemic entitlement.[3]

2. Cf. (Altschul 2011), (Burge 1993, 2003), (Casullo 2007), (Davies 2004), (Dretske 2000), (Janvid 2009), (Graham 2012), (Peacocke 2004), (Williams 2000), (Wright 2004).

3. In extracting the standard account I am putting weight on commonalities between the authors. Not all four theses I am putting forward are shared by all authors. Wright and Davies, e.g., are not talking about entitlements for specific perceptual beliefs, but are rather interested in a conception of entitlement that helps to set sceptical worries at rest. Peter Graham does not commit himself to the weakly internalist aspect of entitlement (namely, to the idea that entitlement somehow grounds in perceptual experience), and so on. But since these deviations are the

First, entitlement is an epistemic status or a kind of warrant that is not strongly internalist. It does not require the demanding kind of subjective access that features in traditional accounts of justification. If one is entitled to a belief, one does not have to justify it. Here are some representative quotes: "Entitlement is *epistemically externalist* inasmuch it is warrant that need not be fully conceptually accessible, even on reflection, to the warranted individual" (Burge 2003, 504); "entitlements, like all rights, confer an advantage. In the case of epistemic rights it is relief from the burden of justification" (Dretske 2000, 593), where justification is understood "as the reasons, the *propositions one already accepts as true,* which one can appeal in support of P" (ibid., 592). Graham uses the term "'entitlement' for warrants that are not reasons" where reasons are understood as "warranted beliefs and other cognitive propositional attitudes." (Graham 2012, 452); "[Entitlement is] a type of rational warrant which one does not have to *do any specific evidential work* to earn" (Wright 2004, 174).

These quotes do not by themselves imply that entitlement is a purely externalist epistemic status. A requirement to offer propositional justification is certainly an internalist requirement, but not the only one one might think of. To get things a bit clearer here, it is useful to introduce some distinctions. Speaking very broadly, internalism comes down to the thesis that positive epistemic status requires an epistemic subject to have some kind of reflective access to what warrants her belief. Let us call the source of warrant the *ground* of the belief. Then, following William Alston (Alston 1989, 237-242; cf. also Casullo 2007), we can distinguish between at least three internalist requirements of different strength:

IR1: *The ground of S's belief that p has to be accessible.*
IR2: *IR1 + The adequacy of the ground of S's belief that p has to be accessible.*
IR3: *IR2 + The epistemic norm governing the ground of S's belief that p has to be accessible.*

According to IR1, positive epistemic status requires that what warrants a belief has to be accessible to the believer. If for example a belief is warranted by a perceptual experience, then the epistemic subject must be able to access this ground by consciously "having" the experience.[4] The

exception, I think it is nevertheless worthwhile to try to get an overall picture of what the term epistemic entitlement stands for in the recent debate.

4. An internalist account along IR1 would thus allow for positive epistemic status for subjects

stronger condition IR2 additionally requires that the epistemic subject be aware of the ground of her belief *as a ground*, and assess its adequacy as an entitling ground. She has to be able to entertain thoughts of the form "It now appears to me that there is a red cube in front of me, and that is a reason to believe that there is a red cube in front of me". The strongest condition IR3 requires, in addition, that the entitled individual has access to the general rules that govern the epistemic impact of grounds for belief. She must be able to entertain thoughts like "It now appears to me that there is a red cube in front of me, and that is a reason to believe that there is a red cube in front of me, because appearances with the content *that p* entitle epistemic subjects to beliefs with the content *that p*".

The quotes given above show that entitlement is neither internalist according to IR2, nor according to IR3 (as we shall soon see, it is internalist in the sense of IR1). After all, being in a position to evaluate one's ground as warranting a belief requires *conceptual access* to the ground (which Burge denies for entitlement), and comes down to "giving reasons" (which is denied by Dretske and Graham) or "providing evidence" (which Wright takes not to be required for entitlement). Also, the authors under discussion often remark that entitlement is a form of basic warrant that is not only possessed by mature humans, but already by children and—perhaps—higher animals, as well. Now, whereas the capacity to access the grounds of a belief (that may simply consist in being aware of a perceptual experience) is a capacity that not only mature humans possess, thinking of these grounds *as grounds* for a certain belief, and thinking of these grounds as instances of a certain kind of ground is something we cannot expect from small children and animals.

We can say, therefore, that epistemic entitlement is a kind of epistemic warrant that requires neither access to the adequacy of the grounds of a belief, nor access to the norms governing the grounds of beliefs.[5] If entitlement is an internalist epistemic status, then at best in a weak sense.

Second, the proponents of entitlement agree on the further point that entitlement is not a thoroughly externalist kind of warrant. It is not sufficient for an entitlement to a belief that the belief in question, as a matter of fact, meets some externalist anti-luck condition (i.e. that it is safe, or tracks the truth, or that the process leading to the belief was in fact reliable).

---

who perceive things in an ordinary fashion, but, contrary to some externalist accounts, not for unenlightened chicken-sexers or blind-seeing subjects.

5. Casullo (2007) lucidly demonstrates this point for Burge's account.

The main reason for this is that being entitled, though it does not require any elaborate cognitive *activity*, nevertheless takes the subject's epistemic perspective into account. We find two different internalist requirements for entitlements in the literature:

On the one hand, most authors affirm (or at least imply) that perceptual entitlements are *grounded in* perceptual states. Here, again, are some representative quotes: "Entitlement to perceptual beliefs [...] is grounded in perceptual states with content fashioned through reliable interaction between the environment and sense-perceptual systems." (Burge 2003, 548); "A perceptual experience which represents a content as correct, and which is instance individuated with respect to that content [that is to say that the judgement only contains observational concepts, H.O.M.], is also one which entitles a thinker to judge that content, in the absence of reasons for doubting that he is perceiving properly" (Peacocke 2004, 447); "How do perceptual experiences entitle us to form beliefs about the objective world? It is this question, perennial and fundamental, that I will be addressing" (Peacocke 2004, 441). Peter Graham forms a notable exception. His notion of entitlement is more externalist in spirit than the notions defended by other authors: "For all I say here, subjective perceptual phenomenology may be a kind, source, or aspect of entitlement. [...] I leave the issue open, tabling the role of subjective conscious perceptual phenomenology in perceptual entitlement for another occasion" (Graham 2012, 453). But apart from Graham the authors share the thesis that entitlement is grounded in perceptual experiences. In this sense, then, entitlement is an internalist notion according to the criterion IR1, because it requires access to the grounds of the belief, which, in this case, consist in perceptual episodes. I will call this the *experience condition* of the standard account.

On the other hand, our authors see a connection between entitlement and rational or at least epistemically blameless behaviour—there is a *blamelessness requirement* for entitlement. Dretske formulates this requirement in terms of supervenience on the subjective resources of the subject, where these are construed broadly enough to include the abilities to test and revise beliefs.[6] Other authors state that you can only be entitled to a belief as long as you are not aware of counter-evidence. You are not entitled to take your perceptual experience at face value if you recognize (or at least

6. "Entitlements supervene on the subjective resources of the believer—facts the believer either is, or can be made, aware of." (Dretske 2000, 597)

reasonably believe) that you are in a situation where your senses are not to be trusted.

Experience condition and blamelessness requirement are then related in the following way: Entitlements are *based* on perceptual experiences representing the world in a certain way. But these experiences entitle you only if you are not aware of defeating conditions that would require you to call the deliverances of your senses into question. The blamelessness requirement, then, is a purely negative condition. It does not require subjects to do something, i.e. to engage in some sort of cognitive activity, in order to be entitled to a belief. It only excludes that you are entitled if you are aware of defeating conditions. Therefore, it is compatible with the idea that entitlements are only weakly internalistic.

Third, entitlements are introduced as epistemic rights, that is, as rights to believe. Dretske is most explicit on this point. He compares epistemic entitlements to legal rights such as the right to park a car in a certain place, or the right to vote.

It seems that *some* epistemic rights have to be earned—if, e.g., I claim to know that a highly controversial mathematical proposition is true, one will only grant me the right to that belief—in the sense that I will not be regarded as a hasty or negligent mathematician—if I can present a proof, or something that comes reasonably near to that. In *other* cases, our right to believe does not depend on our "proving" or "providing evidence for" the believed proposition. What kind of positive steps could be reasonably required to be taken by a man who, truly and in ordinary circumstances, claims that he has got two hands, or that there are three bottles on the table? Entitlements, according to Dretske, are epistemic rights of the latter kind. If you have a right to believe, then you are not criticizable for doing so, and you are not required to engage in some kind of cognitive behaviour to earn that right.

The argument of the following sections builds on this Dretskean idea that entitlements are fundamentally epistemic rights. Maybe the textual basis for regarding this as a feature of the standard account is rather thin, since only Dretske explicitly compares epistemic entitlements to legal rights. But I think we can at least say the following:

On the one hand, the other proponents of entitlement might easily follow Dretske is this respect and agree that entitlements, as the legal terminology already suggests, are basically epistemic rights. Even if some of the authors use the quasi-legal term "entitlement" interchangeably with more neutral words like "warrant" and "positive epistemic status", they explicitly commit themselves to the idea that epistemic entitlement—contrary to more elaborate epistemic statuses—confers an *advantage* to the entitled individual, the advantage of being allowed to hold a belief without being required to justify it. In this minimal sense, then, entitlement is always a kind of right: a status that *allows* me to do something without taking steps towards earning this status.

On the other hand, it might well be the case that some of the authors would tend to deny that epistemic entitlements are rights in this way. In this case, my reconstruction of the standard account may be more of a idealization. It is not clear to me, however, why these philosophers who opted for the legal terminology should resist the idea that entitlements are rights.

Finally, all proponents of entitlement agree that entitlements are *defeasible.* That means, minimally, that an existing entitlement to a belief can be challenged in the light of evidence speaking in favour of the belief's being false (or only accidentally true). The defeasible character of entitlements follows from the claim that entitlements are compatible with perceptual errors, together with the weak rational requirement that entitlement is not compatible with the subject's awareness of a defeating condition: In case a subject is entitled to a false belief it is generally possible that she should become aware of that fact (which would constitute a challenge) and hence no longer be entitled to the belief in question.[7]

To sum up, then, the standard account comprises the following four claims about epistemic entitlement:

1. Entitlement is not an internalist epistemic status in a strong sense, since it requires no access to the adequacy of the ground of one's belief, and no access to the rules governing grounds of beliefs.

7. Perhaps Dretske's account diverges in this respect; Dretske understands entitlement as more robust than most other authors. In order to be entitled to a belief P there has to be "nothing a responsible agent could have done to avoid believing P" (Dretske 2000, 601). This seems to exclude situations in which it would have been possible to find a challenge after some investigation. However, in other places Dretske is more liberal and requires only that the belief is "unavoidable *for an epistemically responsible agent,* for someone who has done all he or she should have done to reach the truth" (ibid., 603). This would allow for defeasible entitlements, since we are usually not required to *do* literally everything we *could do* to avoid false beliefs.

2. Entitlement is not a thoroughly externalist epistemic status because it takes the subject's epistemic perspective into account. Entitlements have their grounds in perceptual experiences (experience condition), and are incompatible with epistemically irrational behaviour (blamelessness requirement).
3. Entitlement is a kind of epistemic right, i.e. a right to hold a belief.
4. Entitlements are defeasible.

Having thus summarized what I take to be the central ideas that make up the core of the concept of entitlement, I shall continue by concentrating on the second and third features of entitlement. My aim is to show that a serious difficulty lies in the combination of understanding an epistemic status as a right and claiming that the status is grounded in something which is, fundamentally, inside the believer's mind.

2. *Entitlements and accessibility*

Let me continue with some simple observations about entitlements in general. We can, of course, be entitled to all sorts of things. One can be entitled to vote in France. One can be entitled to pitch one's tent in a certain place. One can be entitled to park one's car in a certain parking space.

Such entitlements can be ordered along two distinctions: There are *earned* and *unearned* entitlements, on the one hand; and entitlements *for some people* and entitlements that hold *for virtually anybody*, on the other. The entitlement to vote in France holds only for French citizens. Moreover, it can be an earned or unearned entitlement: Some people have to apply for French citizenship in order to be entitled to vote in France, while others do not have to do so because they were born in France. In Scandinavian countries, anyone is entitled to set up a tent and camp out for a few nights (unless one is camping on or very close to someone's private property), so this is an unearned entitlement holding for everybody. In most other European countries you are entitled to set up your tent only on camp sites, and you have to pay for this privilege. So outside Scandinavia, the entitlement to camp is an earned entitlement that holds only for those who earned it. Some parking spaces are for everyone (unearned, for everyone), some are reserved for people with a physical handicap (unearned, for some), or for those who have bought a parking ticket (earned, for some, but everybody can earn the entitlement). Sometimes the entitlement to park a car in a certain space has to be earned, but can only be earned by some people, e.g. residents (earned, for some, only some can earn the entitlement).

A feature shared by all these types of entitlements is that they have an impact on how others are required to treat those who possess them. If I am entitled to vote, I cannot be denied the right to vote and sent away from the polling station (if there is a valid election going on). If I am entitled to set up my tent somewhere, then nobody has the right to send me away, or to carry my tent to another place. If I am entitled to park my car in a certain parking space, then I cannot be charged with parking illegally there, and there is no legal basis for towing my car. This general feature of entitlements can be expressed by the following conditional: *If S is entitled to do A, then others are not allowed to act in a way that prevents or hinders S from doing A.* Being entitled to A, however, means not only that others are not allowed to do things that make it *actually impossible* for me to do A, such as carrying my tent away or towing my car. The fact that someone is entitled to do A also makes some weaker forms of criticism inappropriate: If someone does A, and is entitled to do so, it is usually not adequate to ask her to justify her behaviour, or to require her to take additional steps to earn the entitlement.

It is important to note that the immunity to criticism provided by an entitlement is limited in some respects. Someone who was legally entitled to set up her tent here may still be criticized for various reasons: she may have chosen a very uneven place, an ugly place, a place far away from water, a place in the shade on a chilly day, and so on. We can say, roughly, the following: An entitlement of a certain kind (legal, moral, prudential, aesthetic ...) can usually not be criticized by reasons from the same sphere, although it may be open to criticism from other spheres.

Now, the fact that *my* entitlement imposes duties (not to act in ways that violate my entitlement) on *others* has a remarkable consequence: *entitlements must be publicly accessible.* There can be no duties to treat entitled individuals in certain ways if it is impossible to tell when someone is entitled to something. I will call this the *accessibility requirement* for entitlements.

Stated thus boldly, the accessibility requirement may seem to be of little help, since it is far from clear what degree of public accessibility is needed in order for S to be entitled to A. Does it have to be immediately obvious to everybody that S is so entitled? Or is it enough that everybody *could* easily establish that S is entitled? Is it sufficient that an entitlement can easily be detected by certain persons? And how easy must that be?

The answer to these questions is: it depends. As a look at a couple of practical entitlements reveals, there are differences concerning the accessibility of entitlements. Sometimes, only specialists are able to establish entitlements, sometimes entitlements are in principle accessible by everyone while only people with a certain role care to establish them, and some entitlements are obvious and accessible to all members of the relevant practice on a quick glance.

Here is the first example: As a matter of fact, you can purchase tickets for the German Bundesbahn via the internet. You have to carry a printed page with you on the train. Now, the only thing that distinguishes a "real" ticket from an—easily producible and visually indistinguishable—piece of forgery is a unique barcode on it. The guard, carrying a fancy electronic device, is in a position to establish that the ticket is one that entitles the passenger to the passage. What we have here is a case of an entitlement that can be established by only one person on the whole train.

Next, consider cases of entitlements that can in principle be established by everyone, but—due to the circumstances—there are typically only few persons who are interested in the entitlement. Examples would be the right to purchase alcohol and cigarettes, the right to vote or the right to park one's car in a resident's parking area. While in principle everybody is in a position to find out whether or not someone has a parking permit displayed under the front window of her car, there are some restrictions for the other two entitlements. Although there is no special complication in determining whether or not someone is over eighteen, or living in the region where elections are taking place, by taking a quick glance at the passport, these entitlements are typically only established by shopkeepers and electoral assistants, by persons who have a special responsibility to make sure that only those who are entitled will be allowed to do a certain thing. Usually, you have to be in such a special position in order to ask someone to show you her passport.

To get nearer to the case of our epistemic practice, we should look for examples of entitlements that are not only assessed by people who have a special authority or responsibility, but more or less by everyone. Such examples can be found in everyday practice. Consider the entitlement to regain one's position in a queue which one has left for a short while. Before leaving, one tells the person standing behind oneself that one is going to return soon, and asks her to keep the position reserved. When returning on time, one can take one's former position.[8] The entitlement to take a position in the middle of the queue is then based on one's having been in that position before. And others determine that one has this entitlement by recognizing one as that very person. But who is the one who establishes the entitlement? It would be too quick to respond that it is the person (who was and is going to be) standing behind you in the queue. Depending on the situation, it may often be the case that several people in later positions of the queue will observe who is trying to get a place before them, and there may be protest if no-one except the person behind you remembers you. It seems to be the case that a considerable part of the queue is establishing the entitlement collectively.

Another case: Generally, when someone who is old and frail, physically disabled, or pregnant enters a fully occupied bus or train, then someone will leave that person his or her seat. Failing to offer one's seat to such a person is impolite or may even be regarded as rude. So, in a sense, these people, contrary to other passengers, have an entitlement to a seat even in a fully occupied vehicle. This is an entitlement which is assessed by all other passengers, and it is accessible to them because the property that grounds the entitlement is directly visible.

These examples show two things: First, we can draw a distinction between those entitlements which are normally established by persons who have a special kind of responsibility and those entitlements that are typically established by several participants of the relevant practice. And second, it seems to be the case that entitlements that are accessible by bigger groups of people are—generally—easily accessible, often at first glance.

Nothing I have said so far establishes that there is a conceptual necessity for rights to be publicly accessible in any of the described ways. It may sometimes even be desirable to be able to speak of a person being entitled to do something even if nobody is (even in principle) able to establish that she is so entitled. But what seems to be quite obvious is that entitlements that play a role in a human practice and are such that they do not hold for every individual (such that it can become important to distinguish between those who are entitled and those who are not) must meet the accessibility requirement. How else could we explain that they are attributed with ease and correctly most of the time?

8. There seem to be significant cultural differences in queuing techniques. I got acquainted with the described practice in Russia, but I also encountered it in Germany. To draw the distinctions I am after it wouldn't matter if the practice was merely hypothetical.

My suggestion is that perceptual epistemic entitlements can plausibly be regarded as entitlements of just this sort: The distinction between epistemically entitled believers and believers who are in charge to provide a justification is one that is applied by all of us on a regular basis. And it appears obvious that there are no experts, or people with special authority, to check epistemic entitlements. Moreover, since in attributing these entitlements we do not inquire a lot, epistemic entitlements are entitlements of the easily accessible sort.

Having said that, two questions need an answer: First, what is it, exactly, that an *epistemic* entitlement entitles you to do? And second, what kind of behaviour towards an epistemically entitled subject is inappropriate? The answer to the first question is straightforward: epistemic entitlements are entitlements to form or hold a belief. That is a thesis shared by the proponents of the standard account.[9] The clue to answering the second question lies, I think, in the first feature of epistemic entitlement we discussed above: entitlement is an epistemic status that does not depend on justification where justification is understood as requiring an evaluation of one's reasons. If being entitled implies that one is not required to justify one's belief in order to be allowed to hold it, then it is not appropriate for others to require a justification for it. If the entitlement to park my car here depends on my buying a ticket, then I am required to buy the ticket if I want to leave my car there, and therefore it is appropriate to remind me of this duty, or to request me to purchase a ticket, or to criticize me if I don't. If I am *already* entitled to park my car there, then such reminders and requests are inappropriate. We can say the same about epistemic entitlements: some kinds of positive epistemic status may depend on justification, and it *is* appropriate to request the epistemic subject to give such a justification. But if someone is entitled to a belief—i.e. is allowed to hold the belief without a justification—then it is not adequate to insist on a justification, and to criticize the believer if she does not provide one.

I hope these considerations help to make the idea that epistemic status can fruitfully be understood as a kind of right plausible. There may be good reasons for epistemologists to work with epistemic notions that are based on rational behaviour or truth-conduciveness. But once we take a look at our epistemic practice, it makes much more sense to talk about rights. There is a sense in which people who bear an epistemic status

9. Only (Wright 2004) discusses the possibility that entitlements might only be entitlements to weaker doxastic states such as *acceptance* or *trust*.

have a kind of advantage, or privilege: Contrary to others, they are not normally required to justify their beliefs towards others. In everyday situations of knowledge-ascriptions, this privilege becomes apparent in the fact that we see no point in asking, pointedly, how a person knows as long as she is entitled. Someone who is looking into the fridge will not normally be asked why she believes that there is still milk in it. And her unwillingness to provide us with a reason does not seem to undermine her epistemic status. The fact that we find it inappropriate to insist on a justification in such a case, then, speaks in favour of the idea that epistemic rights have an influence on the kinds of epistemic behaviour towards the entitled individual.

As I said, in our epistemic practice we *distinguish* between those who deserve criticism for holding a belief as long as they do not justify it from those who are not required to justify their beliefs because they are (already) entitled. In order to do so *properly*, facts about entitlement have to be publicly accessible. If my entitlement implies that others are obliged to treat me in a certain way (they shall not insist that I justify my belief), then the fact that I am entitled has to be publicly accessible. Moreover, our shared practice of mutual epistemic evaluation suggests that epistemic entitlements—at least in such everyday matters as perceptual beliefs—are attributed *instantly*. They are easily accessible.

Even if one agrees with my observation that parts of our epistemic practice can be described in terms of rights and duties, one may of course regard this observation as philosophically unimportant. One may think that such a description is possible, but does not give us any insight into the natures of epistemic statuses, because these need to be explained by something else. At this point all I would like to do is to invite you to take these kinds of epistemic practice phenomena seriously and see in how far a plausible epistemological theory can be construed out of them.

3. *Public accessibility in the standard account*

If we understand entitlement as an epistemic right—that is, as a normative status with implications for how one deserves to be treated, epistemically, by others—we have to construe it as *publicly accessible.* Moreover, they seem to be *easily* accessible because we usually determine whether or not somebody is entitled to a perceptual belief in an instant—without any inquiry or inference involved.

But, as soon as we take a look at the standard account, there seems to be a tension between this accessibility requirement and the second key feature of entitlement that states that entitlements require access to the grounds of a belief qua being based on perceptual experiences. The problem is, of course, that it is not obviously a public fact whether or not someone has access to the grounds of her beliefs *qua* her perceptual experience. Experiences (no matter how exactly one chooses to interpret the term) are paradigmatically private episodes. And this generates a tension to the accessibility requirement. This is not to say that we properly never know how it is, perceptually, with others. But whenever we have knowledge about perceptual experiences other than our own, this knowledge is *derived* from facts we know about the perceiver and her environment. I will therefore suggest that the *proper* starting point for an account of perceptual entitlements is a subject's perceptual situation, and not her conscious experience.

While accepting the accessibility requirement for entitlements, a proponent of the standard account may of course explain how we acquire knowledge about other's perceptual experiences in the following way: Once we know the perceptual situation a subject is in, we also know how the world presents itself to her perceptually, that is, we know what her experiences are like. If someone is sitting opposite to me I have no difficulty determining the makeup of her visual field, for example. I can tell which sides of objects she is able to see, and how they look to her, and which objects are blocked from her sight by other objects, etc. The same applies to other sense modalities. I know what people feel when they jump into the cold water of the lake, and I know someone sitting next to me will experience roughly the same smells and sounds as I experience, and so on. So one could claim that subjects are entitled to perceptual beliefs in virtue of being in the right kind of conscious perceptual experience, and that we establish whether or not someone else has such an experience by reference to her perceptual situation, that is, her situation in respect to perceivable things.[10]

I do not want to say that this picture is completely implausible. But I think we can say that it is at least a bit awkward. If everything that matters

10. Another way to establish how the world appears to others is to simply ask them. Note, though, that this is something we hardly ever do. Physicians, optometrists and psychologists sometimes make use of this method, but their aim is not the evaluation of epistemic status. It is rather a means to study or test the patient's perceptual apparatus and thus presupposes, in a way, knowledge about what the patients should be able to perceive in their perceptual situation.

for the establishment of a perceptual entitlement is the perceiving subject's perceptual situation, why then should we introduce the intermediary condition that the subject must undergo an appropriate perceptual experience? It seems to me that construing entitlement as dependent on conscious experiences needlessly complicates matters. Moreover, taking into account that entitlement is meant to be a normative status implying that one does not have to justify a belief, it is unclear why—although entitlement is attributed on the basis of perceptual situations—there should also be an at best indirectly accessible condition that *really* grounds entitlement.

To be clear, nothing said so far excludes the possibility that epistemic entitlements are grounded in experiences, and that we attribute entitlements on the basis of observed perceptual situations because they indicate that the subject has the right kind of experience. But as long as there is no good reason to assume that the right to hold a belief without being required to offer a justification is grounded in a mental state, it seems to be good policy to prefer the simpler model to the more complicated one.[11]

Note that at this point it matters that we chose some kind of a reconstructive approach. One certainly can defend epistemic status concepts that do not contain such a practical element. Of course a belief can be formed reliably, or be fully internally justified without these facts being easily publicly accessible. It is only by taking the quasi-legal character of epistemic status—that seems a plausible element in a reconstruction of the way we actually treat each other epistemically—seriously that one has to worry about the accessibility requirement. Let us see in how far this starting point can be further developed.

4. *An alternative suggestion*

My suggestion is that we should construe entitlement as grounded in a subject's perceptual situation, rather than in the subject's experiences.

11. Probably the reason why most of our authors accept that entitlements must be grounded in perceptual states is something like this: an experience as of p is reliably connected to it being the case that p. You have the right to take experiences at face value because they are likely to represent the world adequately. But this explanation does not give the standard account an advantage over the suggested account according to which entitlement grounds in a perceptual situation. After all, people who judge that p while being in a perceptual situation in which one can normally tell that p are also very likely to be right.

Entitlement to a perceptual belief depends on one's being properly situated in a perceptual environment.[12] Such an account can deal with the accessibility requirement much better than the standard account can.

As mentioned before, we can determine quite well how it is with someone's perceptual experience once we take into account her perceptual perspective. But since the introduction of this inner element adds nothing to the way we in fact determine somebody else's entitlement, it seems that what really interests us when we seek to establish somebody's entitlement is the *perceptual situation itself*, and not the perceptual experience we may expect the subject to have in such a situation.

I understand the term *perceptual situation* quite literally. Just being in the right place with your eyes open and good light entitles you to judge about the objects in your surroundings. Holding something in your hand entitles you to judge its weight and temperature, and so on. There are different entitling conditions for beliefs about different kinds of objects and qualities (taste, loudness, colour, texture, etc.). But they do have something in common: Those perceptual situations that entitle a subject to a belief that p are situations that are commonly acknowledged as situations in which people generally can tell whether or not it is the case that p. This implies that once someone is in an entitling perceptual situation, anyone with access to the fact that the subject is in this situation could reasonably assume that the subject is reliable in her belief-formation.

This picture also offers a plausible *explanation* for why being in a perceptual situation in which we could reasonably regard a subject as reliable *entitles* the subject to a belief: Just remember that being entitled to a belief is a normative status with the implication that insistence on a justification, or criticism if the entitled subject does not justify her belief, is inappropriate. It is indeed very plausible that we do not require justifications from those who are in favourable perceptual circumstances, i.e. situations in which people usually get things right. We are not *making a point* by asking a person why she believes that there is a bird in the tree, if she has it clear in view. The account of entitlement suggested here may be called social externalist—*externalist* because entitlement is grounded in facts that are observable from a third person perspective, and *social* because the perceptual situations that ground entitlements are essentially of such a sort that they enable others to determine whether or not someone has a right to believe.

---

12. Similar ideas are developed by (Brandom 1994, 226) and (Willaschek 2007, 2012)

5. *Objections to the social externalist account*

My proposal, as it stands, seems to have an implausible implication. Although subjects who find themselves in appropriate entitling perceptual situations make correct judgements most of the time, there are also plenty of cases where they are mistaken. Someone who is colour-blind may be in a situation in which we expect people to judge correctly whether an object, say, a cup, is red or green. According to my account such a subject would be entitled to her belief if she judged the cup to be green, although all she can do is guess. But, certainly, it would be odd to say that this subject is entitled to believe that the cup is green, since that would imply that it would be inappropriate to insist on a justification. In fact, however, we would very much like to know why she believes the cup to be green (or, perhaps, why we should rely on her testimony), since unlike most other people she cannot tell just by looking whether the cup is green or red. In cases like this, justification is needed, and this shows that there is no entitlement. The social externalist account seems to imply that one can be entitled to a belief even if one lacks the appropriate perceptual experience, and this is implausible.

But this does in fact not follow. It is, after all, possible to distinguish between a *ground* or a *basis* of something on the one hand, and a *necessary condition* on the other. An entitlement to attend a play at the theatre is grounded in the purchase of a ticket. If I interrupt the performance by shouting or threatening other members of the audience, I may lose my entitlement to remain at the performance. So it is *necessary* for my right to attend the whole performance that I do not behave outrageously. But it seems odd to say that my entitlement to attend a theatre performance in the first place *depended* on or was *grounded* in an adequate behaviour, or that I had the right to be in the audience *because* I was quiet. What we would rather say is that buying a ticket entitles me to attend the specified performance, *unless* I behave outrageously. My inappropriate behaviour may be the basis of a challenge to my entitlement. So a necessary condition for an entitlement need not be a ground of the entitlement. I suggest that whereas perceptual entitlements are grounded in perceptual situations, and not in perceptual experiences, the appropriate perceptual experience is nevertheless necessary, since its absence is incompatible with being entitled, as we could see from the example of a colour-blind subject.

We have to stress, that is, that epistemic entitlements are—just as they are in the other current accounts—defeasible. The attributions of entitlement based on a subject's being in entitling conditions may have to be retracted when *additional circumstances* make it unreasonable to regard the subject as reliable in her belief-formation. I will refer to these circumstances as *challenge conditions.* We should also allow for the possibility that a challenged entitlement may be re-established if the subject is able to justify her belief, that is, is able to explain why she is nevertheless to be regarded a reliable. Let us call these entitlements *earned entitlements*. To avoid confusion, I will call those entitlements that hold just in virtue of entitling conditions *unearned* or *default entitlements*. I will also use the term *default conditions* to refer to those perceptual situations in which subjects are by default entitled to a perceptual belief. A colour-blind subject who happens to believe that a cup is green may be default entitled to the belief, but as soon as the fact that she is colour-blind becomes salient, the entitlement is subject to a challenge.[13]

So we must distinguish between factors that *constitute* or *ground* an entitlement, and factors that are only *necessary* for an entitlement, in the sense that the absence of these factors constitutes a challenge against the entitlement. In this sense, having it appear to one that p is necessary for an entitlement to the belief that p, although the entitlement is grounded in something else, namely in one's being in appropriate default conditions. Thus the account captures the intuition that perceptual experiences are necessary for an entitlement (the experience condition) while avoiding the implication that what constitutes an entitlement is not accessible from an external perspective. In a similar way, the social externalist default and challenge model of entitlement is able to meet the blamelessness requirement, which, remember, is part of the standard account. Being entitled to a belief is not compatible with the subject's possession of counter-evidence: once we learn that a subject is aware of a challenge condition, we retreat from our ascription of entitlement.

It is interesting to observe, that the distinction between *grounds* of an entitlement and *"mere" necessary conditions* is already contained in the accounts I discussed in the beginning. The classic proponents of entitlement hold that although entitlement is grounded in perceptual experiences, it is nevertheless necessary for an entitlement that the subject not be aware of counter-evidence. One can thus say that whereas these authors conceptualize the blamelessness requirement only negatively (in that an

13. The colour-blind usually do not perceptually judge things to be green, and if so, they can be expected to be aware of the holding challenge condition instantly.

entitlement holds only in the absence of counter-evidence) I go a step further and suggest that anything internal to the agent's mind, including her perceptual experiences, is relevant for entitlement only in the sense that its absence makes a challenge legitimate.

To sum up, then, these are the essential features of the social externalist conception of perceptual epistemic entitlement so far:

1. Just as in traditional conceptions of entitlement, entitlement is understood as an epistemic right. Therefore, having an entitlement has an impact on what you are allowed to do (namely, to hold a certain belief), and on how others are required to treat you (namely, they must not insist on a justification for your belief). I tried to show that an *accessibility requirement* follows from this: Implications for the appropriate behaviour of others only make sense if it is relatively easy for other participants of the epistemic practice to establish that someone is entitled to a belief.
2. Contrary to other proponents of entitlement, I deny that entitlements are grounded in anything internal to an agent's mind. Rather, I suggest that entitlements are based on a subject's fulfilment of default conditions that consist in her being in a kind of perceptual situation in which she may be expected to be reliable in her judgement.
3. Nevertheless, the experience condition and the rationality requirement are met by my proposal; not because these internal factors are constitutive of entitlement, but because they are necessary in the minimal sense that their absence counts as a challenge condition against the entitlement.

6. *Two types of entitlement*

One important intuition has not been mentioned, yet: Isn't there a sense in which *some* people who are not entitled according to the social externalist account (because they are not in conditions in which they could reasonably be regarded as reliable) are nevertheless entitled in some sense, because they—reasonably—evaluate their epistemic situation as being much more favourable than it in fact is? Cases of this sort exist in real life, such as cases where people are cleverly deceived. However, the infamous brain in a vat forms perhaps the clearest example. What shall we say here? If we claim that entitlements are based on the satisfaction of social externalist default conditions, then, surely, a BIV lacks epistemic entitlement altogether. However, many people are convinced that such a result is untenable. Dretske for example takes his intuition concerning the case as the major motivation for his account of entitlement: "I can imagine some benighted soul—a brain in a vat will do—whose beliefs are false but whose total evidence—both the evidence he has and the evidence he can, by assiduous effort, obtain—is the same as mine. If his beliefs are false and mine true, it nonetheless strikes me that he has the right to believe whatever I have the right to believe. If I see that the lights are on and he, having the same experiences as me, merely thinks he can see they are on, then he has as much right to believe they are on as I do." (Dretske 2000, 595) If Dretske's internalist intuition is to be taken seriously, then the social externalist account of entitlement seems to fail in one important respect.

But remember that there is, in the approach suggested here, more to entitlement than being in conditions that make it reasonable to regard one as reliable. An internal element is also necessary—not in the sense that it is a precondition for entitlement, but in the sense that lacking an appropriate experience or being epistemically blameworthy is incompatible with entitlement. What this shows is that entitlement can be seen as containing two elements: an element of non-accidentality and an element of non-blameworthiness. Both elements are defeasibly ascribed to subjects in default conditions. Someone in an entitling perceptual situation is *usually* reliable, and someone who holds an appropriate belief in such circumstances is *usually* epistemically blameless. The entitlement can be challenged if either exceptional circumstances make it unreasonable to regard the subject as reliable or in case the epistemic subject is epistemically to blame for her belief—for example because she is aware of counter-evidence.

If both elements are necessary for entitlement, one may still hold that each element of entitlement is individually sufficient for some kind of weaker epistemic status. One may imagine cases of epistemically blameworthy behaviour in which the subject is still reliable. Someone who has been convinced that her senses deceive her may be irrational when she takes their deliverances at face value, but we can still regard her as reliable. So whereas she is not *properly* entitled to her belief, she is at least a reliable perceiver.

In the case of the BIV, now, the subject is far from being reliable, but after all she is not to blame for her beliefs. So what one may say here is that the BIV is not *properly* entitled to her beliefs, but at least not to blame for them. One might say that the BIV is not entitled to her *beliefs*, but is entitled to *take herself* to be so entitled. Her case is similar to that of someone who bought an invalid theatre ticket on the street from a completely honourable looking person. Such a person is not entitled to attend the performance, but it seems that she is entitled to take herself to be so entitled. As a consequence, although she has no right to attend the performance, she nevertheless deserves better treatment than someone who tried to get into the theatre although she knew her ticket to be forged. Note that *blamelessly* taking oneself to be entitled to do something may count as an excuse in court if one does something that is in fact forbidden. If a mistake of law was unavoidable, this can sometimes lead to suspension of the principle *ignorantia juris non excusat* (ignorance of the law is no excuse). I think we should explain the intuition that a BIV is somehow entitled to many of her beliefs by this common trait of legal systems: If one unavoidably but mistakenly takes oneself to be entitled, this does not give one an entitlement, but we may to some degree excuse persons in such circumstances. To come back to Dretske's internalistic intuition: My suggestion is not that we should say that the unfortunate brain in a vat has the same epistemic entitlement as her real-world twin. To the contrary, her entitlements—unlike those of her mental twin in normal circumstances—are subject to the standing challenge that she lacks any normal access to facts in her environment. Nevertheless, as long as she is unaware of her situation, we will not criticize her for her false beliefs in ways we do criticize epistemic subjects who hold on to their beliefs while knowing a challenge condition to obtain.

7. *Conclusion*

To sum up, in the social externalist account, just as in the standard account, entitlement is understood as a defeasible epistemic status that need not be earned by the entitled individual through justification and which is internalist in the sense that an appropriate perceptual experience and an element of epistemic blamelessness are *necessary* conditions, although these internalist elements do not ground the entitlement. It especially highlights the quasi-legal character of entitlements. Entitlements are rights to hold beliefs without being required to justify them. This has certain implications for the kinds of behaviour that are appropriate towards the entitled subject.

I have tried to show that, since we generally ascribe epistemic entitlements instantly, such a status must be construed as easily publicly accessible. Therefore I suggested—contrary to the standard account—that entitlements are grounded in nothing that is internal to the believer's mind, but are rather grounded in the believer's perceptual situation. You are defeasibly entitled to the belief that p (that is, you do not have to be able to offer a justification for the belief that p) in virtue of being in a perceptual situation in which people normally can tell whether or not it is the case that p (default condition). Nevertheless, the lack of an appropriate experience, or various sorts of epistemically blameworthy behaviour, can suffice for a challenge to the entitlement. Thus the weakly internalist requirements of the standard account are captured by the social externalist account.

References

Alston, William P. 1989: *Epistemic Justification.* Ithaca: Cornell University Press.

Altschul, Jon 2011: "Epistemic Entitlement". *The Internet Encyclopedia of Philosophy (version May 2011)*, URL: (http://www.iep.utm.edu/ep-en/).

Brandom, Robert 1994: *Making it Explicit.* Cambridge, MA: Harvard University Press.

Burge, Tyler 1993: "Content Preservation". *The Philosophical Review* 102, 457–488.

— 2003: "Perceptual Entitlement". *Philosophy and Phenomenological Research* 67, 503–548.

Casullo, Albert 2003: *A Priori Justification.* Oxford: Oxford University Press.

— 2007: "What Is Entitlement?". *Acta Analytica* 22, 267–279.

Davies, Martin 2004: "Epistemic Entitlement, Warrant Transmission and Easy Knowledge". *Proceedings of the Aristotelian Society* 78, 213–245.

Dretske, Fred 2000: "Entitlement: Epistemic Rights Without Epistemic Duties?". *Philosophy and Phenomenological Research* 60, 591–605.

Graham, Peter J. 2012: "Epistemic Entitlement". *Nous* 46, 449–482.

Janvid, Mikael 2009: "The Value of Lesser Goods: The Epistemic Value of Entitlement". *Acta Analytica* 24, 263–274.

Peacocke, Christopher 2004: "Explaining Perceptual Entitlement". In: Richard Schantz (ed.), *The Externalist Challenge.* Berlin: de Gruyter, 441–480.

Plantinga, Alvin 1993a: *Warrant: The Current Debate.* Oxford: Oxford University Press.

— 1993b: *Warrant and Proper Function.* Oxford: Oxford University Press.

Willaschek, Marcus 2007: "Contextualism about Knowledge and Justification by Default". *Grazer Philosophische Studien* 74, 251–272.
— 2012: "Non-Relativist Contextualism about Knowledge". In: Christoph Jäger & Winfried Löffler (eds.), *Epistemology: Contexts, Values, Disagreement.* Frankfurt: Ontos, 53–62.
Williams, Michael 2000: "Dretske on Epistemic Entitlement". *Philosophy and Phenomenological Research* 60, 607–612.
— 2001: *Problems of Knowledge.* Oxford: Oxford University Press.
Wittgenstein, Ludwig 1953: *Philosophical Investigations.* Oxford: Blackwell.
Wright, Crispin 2004: "Warrant for Nothing (and Foundations for Free)?". *Proceedings of the Aristotelian Society* 78, 167–212.

Grazer Philosophische Studien
87 (2013), 99–128.

STRAWSONIAN EPISTEMOLOGY. WHAT EPISTEMOLOGISTS CAN LEARN FROM "FREEDOM AND RESENTMENT"

Marcus WILLASCHEK
Goethe-Universität Frankfurt am Main

Summary

This paper investigates the possibility of applying P. F. Strawson's method in his seminal paper "Freedom and Resentment" (1962) to issues in epistemology. In that paper, Strawson sheds light on our concepts of responsibility and free will by looking at practices in which we employ these concepts not directly—by judging that someone is free or responsible—but rather indirectly by adopting "reactive attitudes" such as resentment and gratitude that presuppose that their targets are free and responsible in relevant respects. In a similar way, we may be able to shed light on the concept of knowledge by looking at aspects of our communicative practice such as assertions and their acceptance. In accepting as true what others assert, the paper argues, we typically attribute knowledge to the asserter. This connection between acceptance and knowledge-attribution can then be used to argue that the concept of knowledge implicitly employed in our communicative practice is externalist in spirit, but also includes internalist elements.

0. *Introduction*

With his seminal article "Freedom and Resentment" (Strawson 1974 [1962], henceforth *FR*), P. F. Strawson added a completely new dimension to the traditional debate about free will. One central move in that paper consists in addressing the free will issue *indirectly*, through a description and analysis of a practice in which freedom and responsibility are attributed implicitly, namely the practice of responding to other people's actions with "reactive attitudes" such as resentment and gratitude. The aim of the present paper will be to investigate whether a parallel move can be helpful in epistemology. After a recapitulation of Strawson's paper, in which I will offer a novel reading of Strawson's overall argumentative strategy and highlight some often neglected aspects of his argument (section 1), I will look at an epistemic practice that might serve as a basis for a "Strawsonian" approach to epistemology, namely simple forms of everyday communication in which we *accept* as true what others assert (section 2). Next, I will argue that in typical cases of accepting as true what others say, we implicitly attribute knowledge to the asserter (section 3). Finally, I will outline what a Strawsonian approach might look like with respect to the debate between internalism and externalism in epistemology by offering a "Strawsonian" argument for (a generic version of) externalism (section 4). Obviously, my aim will not be to give a comprehensive defense of externalism, but only to indicate how an approach modeled on Strawson's strategy in "Freedom and Resentment" might be fruitfully applied in epistemology.

1. *"Freedom and Resentment"*

Strawson's starting point in "Freedom and Resentment" is the traditional debate between compatibilists (Strawson: "optimists") and incompatibilists ("pessimists") about freedom and determinism (cf. *FR*, 1). While compatibilists claim that our actions and decisions can be free and we can be responsible for them even if determinism is true, incompatibilists deny this. According to Strawson, this debate (as it had been conducted in the 20th century until the time of Strawson's essay) suffers from the fact that the traditional versions of compatibilism are committed to implausible consequentialist accounts of punishment and reward (cf. *FR*, 2ff.): If determinism were true, it may seem that the only rationale for punishment and reward could lie in influencing people's *future* behavior. But this would ignore the essentially backward-looking dimension of punishment and reward which is associated with the idea that punishing or rewarding someone is unfair unless they *deserve* this on the basis of what they have *done.* As incompatibilists have rightly pointed out, traditional compatibilism cannot account for this central aspect of our moral practice. But according to Strawson, incompatibilists in turn have overreacted by positing contra-causal freedom as the basis of moral desert and responsibility. Strawson's aim is to offer a modified version of compatibilism that takes non-consequentialist notions of moral desert and responsibility on board but that remains neutral with respect to the truth of determinism (cf. *FR*, 4). He tries to achieve this aim, however, not directly by analyzing, or constructing, appropriate concepts of desert and responsibility, but rather indirectly, by giving a structural description of our practice of *attributing* responsibility. And the most fundamental, and most common, way in which we attribute responsibility is not verbally by *saying* of someone that they are responsible for some act or event, but rather by taking certain *attitudes* towards people, which Strawson calls "reactive attitudes" and of which resentment and gratitude are the paradigmatic cases (cf. *FR*, 5). In taking such an attitude towards some agent we *hold* them responsible for what they have done and thus *implicitly* attribute responsibility to them.

Now Strawson has often been understood as trying to provide an argument *for* compatibilism and thus *against* incompatibilism (e.g. Wallace 1994, 96ff.). I will return to this point below. But given Strawson's official goal of *mediating* between compatibilists and incompatibilists,[1] I take it that his primary aim is not to refute incompatibilism, but rather to offer the compatibilist a non-consequentialist account of responsibility that is acceptable to incompatibilists. Thus, Strawson's official strategy, as I understand it, must be to show two things: First, our practice of attributing responsibility is *not consequentialist in character*, since it is organized around values such as interpersonal goodwill and mutual esteem and reacts to the moral quality of *past* actions. And second, both the legitimacy of responsibility-attributions within this practice and the legitimacy of the practice as a whole are independent from the truth or falsity of determinism.

Accordingly, Strawson must first provide us with a plausible picture of the practice of attributing responsibility. Strawson achieves this by giving what might be called a "structural description" of one particular aspect of that practice, that is, a description that identifies some of its fundamental moves, viz. the reactive attitudes, and states the conditions under which we do and the conditions under which we don't take these attitudes towards ourselves and others. The description will be successful if we, as competent participants of the practice, can recognize it as adequately depicting some of the fundamental moves and guiding principles of our communal practice.

Strawson intends the resulting description to represent what he thinks of as a part of human nature.[2] For this reason, his account of the reactive

1. Cf. Strawson's remark that his argument "is intended as a move towards reconciliation" (FR, 1).

2. "[A]ll these types of attitude alike have common roots in our human nature and our membership of human communities" (*FR*, 16).

attitudes has often been taken to be purely descriptive. However, the conditions for adopting reactive attitudes reconstructed by Strawson are not just conditions under which we typically *do* adopt such attitudes, but also conditions under which it would be *appropriate* to do so, as Strawson himself emphasizes.[3] Therefore, Strawson can fruitfully be read as offering a reconstruction of (some of) the *norms* that govern our practice of attributing responsibility by describing the conditions under which it is appropriate to adopt the reactive attitudes.

Strawson first traces our practice of reacting to harmful and beneficial actions with feelings of resentment, gratitude and other reactive attitudes (cf. *FR*, 5f.). We expect a certain minimal amount of goodwill and consideration from others. If their actions are harmful and thus seem to disclose a lack of goodwill, we feel resentment; if they show more goodwill than what may be expected, we feel gratitude. Restricting our discussion to harmful actions, these natural reactions will be, and ought to be, inhibited in two kinds of cases (cf. *FR*, 6–10): (i) the action, although harmful, was not done from a lack of goodwill, but accidentally, inadvertently, from ignorance etc. (so-called "excuses" in the post-FR-literature)[4]; (ii) the agent was "incapacitated" in such a way that he or she was unable to fully engage in normal interpersonal relations either temporarily (e.g. the agent is a child or she was out of her mind) or permanently, e.g. in cases of certain mental disorders (so-called "exemptions"). If someone is permanently incapacitated and therefore not an apt target of the reactive attitudes, we often take what Strawson calls an *objective attitude* to that person, which means that we see her as an object of treatment, manipulation and social policy (cf. *FR*, 9).

Notice that Strawson, in effect, describes a default-and-challenge pattern. *Normally*, we react to other people's harmful or beneficial actions with reactive attitudes, *unless* it is a case of an excuse or an exemption. No inquiry into people's motivation and their capacities is required unless there is reason to assume that there is an excuse or exemption.[5]

3. "It is one thing to ask about the general causes of these reactive attitudes I have alluded to; it is another to ask about the variations to which they are subject, *the particular conditions in which they do or do not seem natural or reasonable or appropriate*; and it is a third thing to ask what it would be like, what it is like, not to suffer them. I am not much concerned with the first question; but I am with the second; and perhaps even more with the third" (*FR*, 6; emphasis added).

4. Cf. Watson 1987, Wallace 1994; also cf. Claudia Blöser's contribution to the present volume.

5. This is an aspect of Strawson's account that it shares with related work by H. L. A. Hart (Hart 1948) and J. L. Austin (Austin 1956).

Corresponding to the reactive attitudes (by which we react to goodwill, or lack thereof, against ourselves and those we love) there are impersonal, generalized, or vicarious analogues, such as moral indignation or moral admiration, by which we react to the moral quality of actions done to others (including those done to people completely unknown to us). Again, these vicarious attitudes are natural reactions and will be inhibited only in exceptional circumstances that are basically the same as the excuses and exemptions that also inhibit the personal reactive attitudes.

In sum, the first part of Strawson's overall argument consists in providing us with a structural description of the conditions under which we typically adopt, or refrain from adopting, the reactive attitudes, thereby articulating the norms that govern the *appropriate* adoption of these attitudes (and thus the appropriate attribution of responsibility). Given this description, we can see that our practice is not consequentialist in spirit, since it consists in reactions to *past* actions and to the agent's *motivation* (goodwill or lack thereof) quite independently of considerations of present or future utility. Moreover, we distinguish between situations in which it is fair, or appropriate, and those in which it is unfair, or inappropriate, to adopt reactive attitudes. So the second part of Strawson's argument must consist in showing that this practice, and hence the concept of responsibility it implicitly employs, is compatible with the truth of determinism. If it were not, this would mean that the truth of determinism would require us to give up the reactive attitudes and to adopt an objective attitude towards everyone (let's call this a "universal objective attitude").[6]

Strawson's argument for the claim that our practice of adopting reactive attitudes is compatible with the truth of determinism comes in three steps: First, Strawson observes that for *logical* reasons the truth of determinism cannot require us to suspend all reactive attitudes. Determinism is a completely general thesis, whereas, given Strawson's description of our practice, refraining from adopting reactive attitudes requires either an excuse or an exemption, each of which hold only under very specific conditions. It does not follow from determinism that each individual act was done accidentally, or inadvertently etc., nor does it follow that each human being is incapacitated (cf. *FR*, 11ff.). Therefore, it cannot be a consequence of determinism that we have to adopt an objective

6. Cf. *FR*, 11. Strawson himself does not distinguish terminologically between the objective attitude toward individuals and what I have called the universal objective attitude. As we will see in what follows, however, this distinction will help to clarify the structure of Strawson's overall argumentative strategy.

attitude in each individual case. The objective attitude is required only in cases of "psychological abnormality" and "it cannot be a consequence of any thesis which is not itself self-contradictory that abnormality is the universal condition" (*FR*, 11). This has been called Strawson's "argument from excuses".[7]

Second, Strawson argues that even if we wanted to, it would not be possible for us to give up the practice of adopting reactive attitudes altogether by adopting what I have called here a universal objective attitude, since the reactive attitudes are part of human nature. It is simply not up to us whether or not to engage in them; engaging in them is part of what we are as human beings. Conversely, human beings, as the natural beings they are, are not able to adopt a universal objective attitude for more than a limited time. This has been called the "naturalist argument" (cf. Wallace 1994, 96).

Third, even if we could adopt a universal objective attitude, belief in the truth of determinism *should not* (rationally) lead us to do so, since whether we should adopt a universal objective attitude depends not on the truth of an abstract thesis such as determinism, but on "the gains and losses to human life", that is, on the practical, social, and political issue of how we want to live our lives and organize our societies (cf. *FR*, 13). Abandoning the reactive attitudes would mean a severe impoverishment of human life, since it would be incompatible with serious interpersonal relationships such as love or friendship as we know them. Even if we were willing to accept these costs, the truth of determinism in itself would not be a sufficient reason to do so. This has been called the "pragmatic argument" (cf. Wallace 1994, 99).

One may wonder whether the naturalist and pragmatic arguments are really necessary for Strawson to achieve his official goal, which he may seem to have reached already with the argument from excuses. After all, this argument, if successful, shows that, given our actual practice of attributing responsibility, the truth of determinism would not count as a reason to give up the reactive attitudes; hence, the concept of responsibility we implicitly employ in that practice is compatible with the truth of determinism. Moreover, this practice is not consequentialist in that it makes the appropriateness of the reactive attitudes depend on the goodwill, or lack thereof, displayed in an action and on whether the agent is a proper

7. Cf. McKenna 2005, 167; Wallace refers to this as Strawson's "internal arguments" (Wallace 1994, 96).

target of reactive attitudes (and hence on fairness-conditions). With this, Strawson has shown what he had announced, namely that compatibilism is not committed to an impoverished consequentialist conception of punishment and moral praise and blame (as mere means of social policy) since it can incorporate the reactive attitudes with their thick conception of moral desert and responsibility. So there seems to be no need for the further steps in Strawson's argument.[8]

Many readers have therefore taken Strawson to argue for a stronger claim that might require the naturalist and pragmatic arguments, namely the falsity of incompatibilism. This argument would consist of two steps: (i) incompatibilism is at odds with our actual practice of attributing responsibility; (ii) it is neither possible (naturalist argument) nor rationally desirable (pragmatic argument) for us to give up this practice. So if either our practice or incompatibilism has to go, it must be the latter.—But even if there may be a basis in Strawson's text for such a reading, I think that it does not represent the philosophically most convincing reading of Strawson's overall argument.

The naturalist and pragmatic arguments should not be seen as self-standing arguments against incompatibilism, but rather as part of a complex dialectic into which they are entered only in order to fend off an objection against Strawson's general strategy. According to this objection, the argument from excuses only shows that the truth of determinism, because it would be a general truth pertaining to all actions and all agents in the same way, could not be a reason not to adopt reactive attitudes in *each individual case*, since this would require case-specific excuses or exemptions for each case. This, however, seems to leave open the possibility that, if determinism were believed to be true, we would, and should, adopt what I have called above a *universal* objective attitude—an objective attitude towards anyone, *independently* of whether any of the recognized excuses or exemptions applies to them. It is only in order to rule out this possibility, and thus to block an incompatibilist objection based on this possibility, that Strawson invokes the naturalist and the pragmatic arguments. Hence, they form an integral part of Strawson's overall strategy, even if they are not intended as independent arguments against incompatibilism.

It may be questioned, however, whether they succeed even in this limited task. The naturalist argument rests on the assumption that the reactive attitudes are an immutable part of human nature—a claim which can

8. Thanks to Andreas Maier for suggesting this point.

be, and has been, rejected: First, Strawson's naturalism about the reactive attitudes is an empirical assumption for which he does not argue. Second, there is empirical evidence against it based on the differences in the reactive attitudes between people from different times and cultures. And third, we may well be able to develop our moral sensibilities in such a way as to overcome at least "negative" reactive attitudes such as resentment and guilt (cf. Pereboom 2008). Even without going into the details of these objections here, I think it must be granted that they make it exceedingly difficult to defend Strawson's naturalist argument.[9]

But there still remains the pragmatic argument. Against it, it has been claimed that the truth of determinism is relevant after all for the question of how to live, since, if determinism were true, it would be *unfair* to engage in the reactive attitudes and the related practices of praise and blame, punishment and reward. This objection, however, obviously presupposes the truth of incompatibilism. And if the pragmatic argument is not meant as an independent argument against incompatibilism, but is put forward only in order to reject an objection to Strawson's central claim that our practice of adopting reactive attitudes is compatible with the truth of determinism, then it is the incompatibilist who must not presuppose the truth of his own position in countering the pragmatic argument. Conversely, since Strawson's aim is only to supply the resources for an improved compatibilism, his argument may presuppose the truth of that view. Moreover, that presupposition is not unargued for, but motivated by the previously given description of our practice of adopting the reactive attitudes. It therefore seems to me that the pragmatic argument is successful at least in the limited sense of countering the objection that the truth of determinism would make it rationally imperative to adopt a universal objective attitude.

In conclusion, Strawson has achieved what he had set out to do, namely to provide the compatibilist with a non-consequentialist account of praise and blame. Given that compatibilism's dependence on consequentialism about praise and blame had been one of the central targets of the incompatibilist critique, this amounts to an important indirect argument for compatibilism.

If we now turn to the question of what epistemologists might be able to learn from "Freedom and Resentment", I take the central point to be

9. For a thorough analysis and critique of Strawson's naturalist argument cf. Russell 1992. For a defence of Strawson's naturalism cf. Magill 1997.

this: Instead of trying to analyze a contested concept directly, it may be more promising to look at the practices in which the concept is being used, including those in which it is used only implicitly. This helps to avoid a mistake Strawson attributes to traditional compatibilists and to incompatibilists alike, namely the mistake of "over-intellectualizing" our practices (cf. *FR*, 23). I think that this is an idea that can be fruitfully employed in epistemology as well. Instead of trying to analyze concepts such as knowledge and justification directly, let us look at the practices in which these concepts are being used, including those in which they are used only implicitly. In the next section, I will turn to the task of giving a structural description of a practice that may be able to do for epistemological issues what the practice of attributing reactive attitudes does for the debate about freedom and responsibility. It will be important that this practice is "primitive" in the sense of being independent from, and more basic than, the explicitly epistemological vocabulary in which philosophical theories are couched. As we will see, there are many structural similarities between the practice described by Strawson and the one we are going to consider now.

2. *Communication, acceptance, and knowledge*

Many human practices employ epistemic notions either explicitly or implicitly. On the more explicit end of the spectrum, there are practices such as science (or specific scientific disciplines), the law, and, of course, epistemology. On the other end of the spectrum, there are certain simple forms of everyday communication: Speaker A tells hearer B that it is raining outside, and B comes to believe this (that it is raining outside) *because* A said so. Let us say that in such a case, B *accepts* that p *from* A. If A does not accept that p, we can say that B *rejects* that p.[10]

Note that the notion of acceptance we are interested in here differs from the one sometimes contrasted with belief (where belief is typically thought of as involuntary and acceptance as voluntary)[11] in that it is a three-place-relation: A accepts that p from B. Consider the following definition:

10. Note that this means that "rejecting that p" does not imply believing that not-p, but is compatible with suspension of belief about p.

11. Cf. e.g. Lehrer 1990; Engel 1998, Tuomela 2000. I will ignore the belief/acceptance distinction here and define "acceptance of" in terms of belief.

(A1) B accepts that p from A $=_{Def}$ (i) A asserts that p and (ii) B comes to believe that p because A has asserted that p.

This doesn't give us what we need, though, because it would allow for cases in which B uses A merely as a "reliable indicator", for instance if A asserts that it's raining by using the French words "Il pleut" and B, not understanding French, comes to believe that it's raining because he has noticed that every time A says these words it happens to be raining. Although cases like that are clearly possible, they seem to be relevantly different from typical cases of communication. In order to exclude cases like this, we might try the following definition:

(A2) B accepts that p from A $=_{Def}$ (i) A asserts that p and (ii) B comes to believe that p because B takes A to have asserted that p.

But still there are counter-examples: B may take A to be lying about p but also to be systematically mistaken about whether or not p, so that A asserts that p just in case A believes that non-p and A believes that non-p just in case that p. B can then learn that p from A's assertion that p without "accepting", in any intuitive sense, that p from A. I therefore suggest working with the following definition of acceptance:

(A3) B accepts that p from A $=_{Def}$ (i) A asserts that p and (ii) B comes to believe that p by taking A's word for it.

Here the colloquial expression "taking someone's word for it" serves as a technical term meant to exclude the kinds of indirect means of gathering information compatible with A1 and A2. If B comes to believe something by taking A's word for it, this means that without second-guessing and theorizing about A's intentions, B simply comes to believe that p because this is what A *asserts*. In order to avoid misunderstandings, let me stress that acceptance, by definition, only concerns propositions B doesn't already believe independently of A's assertion.

Although the practice I suggest for consideration is one of communication, and although asserting that p is a way of testifying to others that p, I am not particularly interested here in the epistemology of testimony. The point I will focus on is not whether and how B can acquire *knowledge* by relying on A's assertions; rather, my focus will be on the attitude B must have towards A in order to acquire *beliefs* on the basis of what A asserts, independently of whether B's beliefs amount to knowledge or not. In particular, I will be interested in the epistemic status B must ascribe to A with respect to p in order for it to be correct for B to accept that p from A. While the epistemology of testimony is interested primarily in the *transmission* of information and knowledge in communication,[12] I will be interested in the concepts and standards of *epistemic appraisal* that lie in the background of any successful act of communication. Following Strawson's lead, I will offer a structural description of (some aspects of) our communicative practice by describing some of the fundamental moves that are possible in it (so far, I have mentioned assertion, acceptance, and rejection) and the conditions under which they are appropriate, thereby outlining the normative structure of that practice.

The first thing to note about the role of acceptance in our communicative practices is that, at least in fundamental cases, *acceptance is the default.* By "fundamental cases" I mean cases in which no prior experience has lead B to take A to be, for instance, dishonest or incompetent. Lacking a history of misinformation or deception linking speaker and hearer, people typically accept what they are told unless they take there to be some special reason against acceptance. Moreover, this is just what the norms that govern human communication require. If someone in my office tells me that the copy-machine is not working and I don't accept this, I need a reason for non-acceptance in order for my response to be appropriate. This is not just a demand of politeness, since, absent some reason for rejection, it would seem to be inappropriate not to accept what the person says even if I keep my reserve to myself. By contrast, I do not need a reason for *acceptance*—over and above the fact that this is what the person said to me. So just as adopting reactive attitudes is the default in our practice of attributing responsibility, acceptance is the default in our communicative practices. Note that this does not exclude the possibility of acceptance that is *not* appropriate by default. However, in this case B needs some special reason for acceptance. For instance, if B takes A to be a notorious liar, it will not be appropriate by default for B to accept that p from A. But if the given situation is such that A would not profit from a lie and B knows this, for instance, it might still be appropriate for B to accept that p from A.[13]

12. For a critique of the widespread assumption that the transmission of belief/knowledge lies at the heart of testimonial knowledge, cf. Lackey 2008, Ch. 2.

13. If B accepts that p from A even though B takes A to be a notorious liar, then the fact that in this case A would not profit from a lie does not serve as the basis for some inference

Notice that this does not commit us to any view about testimony as a source of knowledge; my claim here is not that one is by default epistemically justified in believing what one is told, but only that acceptance is the default according to the standards that govern everyday acts of communication. According to these standards, rejecting what someone tells me without a particular reason for this rejection would be inappropriate. This alone does not imply that acceptance without further reason is *epistemically* permissible or even required, since it might in principle be possible that our communicative standards are less demanding than our epistemic ones. (Although I will argue in what follows that in typical cases of acceptance we attribute knowledge to the asserter, and that the conditions under which it is appropriate to accept that p from A include A's knowing that p, it is important here that the standards for appropriate acceptance can be reconstructed independently of any prior epistemological commitments.)

Next, let us turn to reasons for rejection, that is, a reason that defeats the default. These defeaters can be grouped in three broad categories, depending on whether they concern, (i) the proposition asserted, (ii) the person who makes the assertion, or (iii) the epistemic relation between that person and the proposition asserted.

First, there are reasons that have to do with how plausible p is given the rest of B's beliefs. For instance, if B holds beliefs that are incompatible with p, or beliefs that make it seem highly unlikely that p, then this will typically count as a reason against accepting that p.

The second category comprises those reasons for non-acceptance that have to do with the person making the assertion. If there is reason to believe that A might be lying, for instance because A has been dishonest before or because A would profit from my falsely believing that p, I thereby have a reason not to accept what A says. In the same category belong cases in which A, either temporarily or permanently, is not the kind of person whose utterances can have the force of full-blown assertions or, if they do have that force, do not have the kind of authority that warrants acceptance. Young children, for instance, or people who are drunk, belong in this class.

The third category has to do with the relation between A and what A asserts; in particular, whether or not A *is in an epistemic position to assert*

to the conclusion that p, but rather makes it appropriate for B, in this special case, to take A's word for it after all.

that p. Let me first try to explain the notion of "being in a position to assert" by way of examples: If I am looking outside the window at a tree in plain daylight and nothing obstructs my view, I am in a position to assert that there is a tree in front of the window. By contrast, if the shutters are closed or if it is too dark to see, I am not in a position to assert this, unless I have some other access to the fact that there is a tree in front of my window, for instance by remembering it or by inferring it from other things I know. Typically, A will be in a position to make assertions about what happened to him yesterday. By contrast, if A makes an assertion about something that happened to *me* yesterday in A's absence, it is at least not obvious how A can be in a position to assert this.

We can try to specify somewhat more generally what it means for someone to be in an epistemic position to assert that p by appealing to the so-called "Knowledge Rule for Assertion" (KR). According to KR, one is in an epistemic position that makes it appropriate to assert that p only if one knows that p. Its most prominent proponent is Timothy Williamson, who has claimed that the following principle is constitutive of assertion: "One must: assert *p* only if one knows *p*."[14] That knowledge that p is a condition for appropriately asserting that p, and that therefore assertion is an implicit knowledge-claim, has been maintained by many other philosophers, too (cf. e.g. Brandom 1994, Williams 2001, DeRose 2002, Hawthorne 2004, Stanley 2005).

But KR has also been contested. Some of its critics have denied that KR is valid as a rule for assertion by citing counter-examples to KR (e.g. Lackey 2007, Weiner 2005). Some critics have held that other rules can explain all relevant data in a more convincing or theoretically elegant way (e.g. Douven 2006, Lackey 2007, Weiner 2005). I cannot enter into a discussion of KR and its alternatives here. What must suffice for our purposes is the observation that even most of these critics admit in one way or another that KR does hold for *most* cases of assertion and that *typically*, by asserting that p one conveys that one knows that p (cf. e.g. Brown 2008, 91, Douven 2006, 469).

14. Williamson 2000, 243. Williamson adduces three kinds of considerations in favor of KR. First, unlike some other candidates for rules governing assertion, KR can account for the fact that it is somehow improper to assert "Your lottery ticket will lose", even if the chances of its winning are minimal and if later, after the drawing, it turns out that the ticket *has* lost (ibid., 249ff.). Second, "How do you know that?" can be a proper response to an assertion, which it couldn't be if assertion wasn't an implicit claim to knowledge (ibid., 251-3). Third, there is something paradoxical and inappropriate about Moorian assertions of the form "p, but I don't know that p", a fact that can be easily explained by appeal to KR. (ibid., 253ff.).

And indeed, it seems hard to deny that if I assert without any sign of reservation, say, that Naples, Florida, is south of Naples, Italy, and it later turns out that I didn't know this and merely guessed, my assertion was not in accordance with the norms that govern our communicative practice. This does not mean that there cannot be counter-examples to KR. Lackey for instance constructs three such examples based on the idea that it can sometimes be appropriate to assert that p if one takes all the available evidence to tell in favor of p but, for personal reasons, one cannot bring oneself to believe that p (and hence doesn't know it) (cf. Lackey 2007). But cases like that are clearly exceptional. They do not tell against the claim that typically, in the vast majority of cases, it is inappropriate to assert something (without indicating any reservation) unless one knows it to be true. So I think that we can learn from the discussion of the Knowledge Rule that at least the following negative default rule seems to hold:

(DKR) If A does not know that p, A will *typically* not be in an epistemic position to assert that p *unless* there is some exceptional reason why it is appropriate for A to assert that p even though A doesn't know that p.

Since A's not being in an epistemic position to assert that p is a defeater for the default of acceptance, this means that A's not knowing that p will *typically* be a defeater to the default of acceptance, too. If A doesn't know that p, it will be appropriate for B to accept that p from A only if there are special reasons that either make it appropriate for A to *assert* that p in the absence of knowledge that p or make it appropriate for B to *accept* that p from A even though A doesn't know that p.[15]

We can sum up our brief overview of possible defeaters by saying that *typically* it will be appropriate for B to accept that p from A unless (i) p is implausible, (ii) A is dishonest or incapacitated, or (iii) A doesn't know that p (where "typically" indicates that it can be appropriate to accept that p even in the presence of a defeater given special reasons for acceptance).

This brief presentation of possible defeaters is doubly ambiguous between (a) a normative and a factual reading and (b) an 'objective' and a 'subjective' account of defeaters. Both ambiguities are closely connected. According to a factual reading, while competent participants in our com-

15. For examples of the first type of reasons, see Lackey 2007; for an example of the second type, see section 3 below.

municative practice typically *accept* what others assert, they regularly do not do so in the presence of a defeater. According to the normative reading, by contrast, it is *appropriate* to accept what others assert unless there is a defeater. On a *subjective* account of defeaters, defeaters are reasons against acceptance only if, and insofar as, the hearer is, or at least ought to be, *aware* of them, while on an *objective* account, the factual presence of a defeater is sufficient to make acceptance inappropriate. Another way of bringing out the contrast between subjective and objective accounts of the relation between default and defeat is by saying that, on an objective account of default-appropriateness, B's acceptance is appropriate *unless* there *is* a defeater, while on a subjective account, B's acceptance is appropriate *until* B becomes *aware* of a defeater.

Given these distinctions, I want to suggest that all four possible combinations (factual/subjective, factual/objective, normative/subjective, normative/objective) are relevant for the purposes of a description of our communicative practice. (1) People generally accept (factual reading) what others assert unless they take there to be (some indication of) a defeater (subjective account). But since most people are correct most of the time in their beliefs about the presence or absence of defeaters, this also means (2) that people generally accept (factual reading) what others assert unless there really is a defeater (objective account). Further, (3) it is (objectively) appropriate for a participant in our communicative practice (normative reading) to accept what others assert unless there really is a defeater (objective account). But (4) it is (subjectively) appropriate for a participant in our communicative practice (normative reading) to accept what others assert, even in the factual presence of a defeater, until he or she becomes, or ought to become, aware of the defeater. In what follows, I will primarily be interested in the normative side of our practice. Where it will be necessary to distinguish terminologically between the subjective and the objective accounts, I will speak of *correctness* instead of objective appropriateness and *entitlement* instead of subjective appropriateness. The term "appropriate" will be used as neutral between these two readings. Note that even though (objective) correctness and (subjective) entitlement mostly go hand in hand, they can diverge: If B accepts what A asserts in the presence of a defeater of which B was not, and need not have been aware, B is (subjectively) entitled to accept that p from A even though the acceptance is (objectively) incorrect.

So these are the outlines of a structural description of some basic aspects of our communicative practices: There are three fundamental moves that can be made within this practice (assertion, acceptance, rejection) and two types of secondary moves (challenges and responses to challenges). The default response to A's asserting that p is B's acceptance of p, and there are three types of reasons that defeat this default, namely (i) that p is implausible, (ii) that A is dishonest in asserting that p or is in some sense "incapacitated" (a child, drunk, confused), and (iii) that A, in the given situation, is not in a position to assert that p. Given any of these defeaters, it will be inappropriate for B to accept that p from A unless there is a special reason to do so.

3. *Acceptance as implicit knowledge-attribution*

Obviously, the above is only a very general description of some aspects of our communicative practice to which much fine structure could be added if needed. I hope, however, that it has become apparent already that this practice is of great potential interest for epistemologists. Since the conditions for appropriate acceptance include the epistemic standing of the asserter, this practice must include standards of epistemic appraisal that, in themselves, are a novel and largely unexplored field for epistemological inquiry. Here, however, I will try to show that our communicative practices are also relevant for more traditional epistemological concerns. In order to do so, it will be important to link the structural description of our practice given so far to the central concept of traditional epistemology, the concept of knowledge. I will do this by arguing for (some qualified version of) the following claim:

(AIKA) Acceptance is an implicit knowledge-attribution.

By this I mean that in accepting that p from A, we commit ourselves to attributing knowledge that p to A. Put negatively, the claim is that it would be inappropriate to accept that p from A and at the same time, if confronted with the question of whether or not A knows that p, not to assent to the claim that A knows that p. If something like this claim is correct, this would constitute a strong and important analogy between acceptance and the reactive attitudes, which can play the theoretical role they play for Strawson precisely because they are implicit attributions of responsibility and free will.

Now AIKA clearly has some initial plausibility. This can be illustrated by cases such as Steward Cohen's airport scenario: A and B are at the airport waiting to board a plane to New York. They wonder whether their flight will have a stop-over in Chicago, where they have an urgent business appointment at the airport. They overhear C saying to D: "I know that the flight stops in Chicago, I've checked the itinerary". A says to B "The itinerary might contain a misprint or they might have changed the schedule at last minute. So C doesn't *know* that the flight stops in Chicago. Let's check with the airline".[16] Cohen has used this scenario in order to argue that knowledge-attributions are context-sensitive and that one aspect of the context is determined by how much is at stake for the attributor. While A may be correct to claim knowledge relative to a low stakes-situation, B is correct in denying knowledge to A given that there is a lot at stake for B and C. Whether or not this kind of contextualist interpretation is plausible, note that there is a minimal interpretation of the scenario according to which B doesn't accept from A that their flight stops in Chicago *because* B doesn't take A to *know* that their flight stops in Chicago. No matter what else one might want to say about the scenario, this minimal interpretation seems hard to deny. And this strongly suggests that acceptance is an implicit knowledge-attribution. Note that otherwise, it would have been an option for B to deny that A knows that the flight stops in Chicago, but still to accept that the flight stops in Chicago from A. But this does not seem to be an admissible move in our communicative practice. We can explain this if we assume that acceptance that p requires that one takes the asserter to know that p.

Against this, it might be objected that knowledge may be an unnecessarily strong condition for acceptance; rather, *warranted* belief might seem to be sufficient.[17] In the airport-case, for instance, B takes A's belief that the plane stops in Chicago to be insufficiently warranted, which is enough to explain why B doesn't accept from A that the plane stops in Chicago. But note, first, that in a negative case like this, lack of warrant implies lack of knowledge. So the point of the objection can only be that in the positive case, warranted belief can be sufficient for appropriate acceptance even in the absence of knowledge. But this is an illusion. Let's assume that B attributes warranted belief to A and that B accepts that p from A. From the fact that B accepts that p from A it follows (i) that B takes A to believe

16. Adapted from Cohen 1999.

17. I use the term "warrant" here to cover both internalist and externalist conceptions of the kind of epistemic standing a belief must have in order to count as knowledge (at least in a non-Gettier situation). It is important for me here to stay neutral with respect to internalist and externalist accounts of knowledge for reasons that will become apparent in section 4.

that p (ii) that B takes p to be true. But then, whenever B accepts that p from A on the basis of attributing the warranted belief that p to A, B will also attribute to A the warranted *true* belief that p. Even if, depending on the account of warrant one favors, warranted true belief may not always be sufficient for knowledge because of Gettier cases, it follows that at least for non-Gettier situations requiring warranted belief for appropriate acceptance comes to the same thing as requiring knowledge.

Nevertheless, there are counter-examples to AIKA: Imagine you know a person you consider to be *wise* (in the sense that their knowledge is wider and their judgment is better than most people's, including your own). Now this person tells you that in the 21st century there will be wars about water. You may think that it is impossible to *know* such a thing (because it concerns the contingent future), but still accept what the person says because you trust their judgment.

However, while this kind of example shows that AIKA cannot be correct as it stands, it is compatible with the weaker claim that A's lack of knowledge is a defeater for *acceptance by default*: If you don't take A to know that p, you may still accept that p from A, but in this case you need some reason to accept that p even though A does not know that p – in the example, the reason consists in the fact that the asserter is particularly wise. So the example seems to confirm, rather than disconfirm, that in order to be entitled by *default* to accept what others assert (i.e. for accepting that p from A to be correct in the absence of special reasons over and above A's asserting that p), one implicitly commits oneself to attributing knowledge to them.

Let's call this weaker principle DAIKA (with "D" for default):

(DAIKA) If B is default-entitled to accept that p from A, and B accepts that p from A merely on the basis of A's asserting that p, B implicitly attributes knowledge that p to A.

That B is default-entitled to accept that p from A means that it is "subjectively" (i.e. from B's perspective) appropriate to accept that p from A merely on the basis of A's asserting that p, that is, independently of any positive assumptions about A's person (his being generally honest, or particularly wise) and without investigating A's reasons for believing, and asserting, that p.[18] Now here's an argument for DAIKA:

18. For a possible worry that the definition of acceptance might seem to rule out the possibility of non-default acceptance, cf. fn. 13 above.

(1) It is correct (objectively appropriate) for B to accept that p from A only if *either* A knows that p *or* there is some special reason to accept that p from A (such as A being wise, or particularly competent, etc.) (premise)

This premise follows from the above description of our communicative practice, in particular from our discussion of the Knowledge Rule: If A doesn't know that p, then this defeats the default of acceptance, so that B needs some special reason for acceptance in case A doesn't know that p.

(2) B does not have a special reason to accept that p from A (such as A's being wise or particularly competent, etc.) (assumption)
(3) B's accepting that p from A is correct only if A knows that p (from 1,2).
(4) B accepts that p from A (assumption)
(5) B takes her accepting that p from A to be correct (assumption)

Note that "taking her acceptance to be correct" here is understood in the weak sense that B, if asked, would assent to the claim that her acceptance was correct (or deny that it was incorrect). Therefore, (5) will typically hold, since it is rationally impossible to come to believe that p while denying that the way by which one came to believe that p was correct; any reason to deny this would be a reason not to come to believe that p in this way (or, if it's too late for that, to give up the belief that p).

(6) B is a competent participant in our communicative practice (assumption)
(7) If (a) it is correct for B to do F only if C is the case, and (b) B does F, and (c) B takes her doing F to be correct (according to the standards of some practice P of which doing F is a part), and (d) B is a competent participant in P, then B is committed to the claim that C is the case.

That (7) is highly plausible can be seen if we apply it to a simple example: If it is correct for B to cross the street only when the lights are green, and B crosses the street, and B is a competent participant in the practice of road traffic, and B takes her crossing the street to be correct (according to the traffic rules), then B is committed to the claim that the lights are green. Of course, if B knowingly crosses the street when the lights are red, B is not committed to the claim that the lights are green. But in this case she either is not a competent participant of the practice of road traffic (since she doesn't know one of its basic rules) or B cannot consistently take her crossing the street to be correct. Applied to the case at hand, since (3) corresponds to (7a), (4) to (7b), (5) to (7c) and (6) to (7d), it follows that:

(8) B is committed to the claim that A knows that p.

So in cases where B (i) accepts that p from A (ii) in the absence of any special reason that would make it correct to do so even if A did not know that p and where B (iii) is competent and (iv) takes her acceptance of p from A to be correct, B is committed to attributing knowledge that p to A. Since typical cases of default-entitled acceptance satisfy conditions (i) - (iv), we can say (with a grain of salt) that default-acceptance is an implicit knowledge-attribution.

4. *A Strawsonian argument in epistemology*

Finally, let us look very briefly and in general outline at an epistemological debate that may benefit from being considered from a Strawsonian perspective—*the debate between epistemological internalists and externalists* that has divided epistemologists since some of the early reactions to Gettier brought the option of externalism to general attention. Just like the compatibilist account of punishment, the externalist account of knowledge can seem to leave out something important, namely the fact that human beings are capable of reflective attitudes, and that knowledge, in many cases, seems to require not just de facto reliability, but that the subject has reflective access to the factors that turn a true belief into knowledge. So perhaps we can improve the externalist case by showing that our communicative practice (a) is fundamentally externalist in spirit but (b) also contains elements the recognition of which allows us to honor the fact that we are reflective beings.

In what follows, it will not be possible to discuss the pros and cons on both sides of the debate in any detail and to distinguish between the many different versions of internalism and externalism, including various intermediary positions. Since my aim here is the limited one of showing the possible relevance and fruitfulness of a Strawsonian approach in epistemology, it will be sufficient to work with a generic understanding of the two competing views that brings out most clearly some of the intuitions motivating each side. Both internalists and externalists, in the sense of the distinction I am going to employ here, agree that knowledge requires more than just true belief, but they differ over what that additional factor consists in and whether the subject of knowledge must be able to have reflective access to it. Let's call whatever is sufficient (in a non-Gettier situation) to turn a true belief that p into knowledge a *warrant* for p.[19] While internalists have variously cashed out the warrant-requirement in terms of reasons, justification, evidence, etc., externalists have favored accounts of warrant in terms of, e.g., reliability, information, and safety. We can ignore these differences for our present purposes and define generic versions of what has come to be called "access internalism" and "access externalism" as follows:

> *Access Internalism (AI)*: A knows that p only if there is adequate warrant for p and that warrant is reflectively accessible to A.
> *Access Externalism (EI):* A knows that p only if there is adequate warrant for p (which warrant need not be reflectively accessible to A).

"Reflectively accessible" here means, very roughly, that A can become aware of the warrant just by reflecting on her own state of mind. Further important distinctions within the internalist and externalist camps are possible, depending for instance on whether reflective access is posited (or denied) with regard to the warrant itself, but also to the warrant's being adequate for knowing that p.[20] These distinctions will not matter for what follows, however.[21]

If the above description of our communicative practice is roughly correct, then an evaluation of AI and AE should start from two aspects of that practice we have highlighted above: First, acceptance is the (defeasible) default. Second, acceptance, at least if we are entitled to it by default, is an implicit knowledge-attribution. Note that we had reached this result without presupposing any specific analysis of the concept of knowledge. In particular, the argument for DAIKA did not depend on any commit-

19. Thanks to Thomas Grundmann for pointing out an error in an earlier definition of "warrant".

20. Cf. Alston 1989 for a classic statement of this distinction.

21. But note that the following argument for AE, if successful, will equally apply to a version of externalism that also denies reflective access to the adequacy of the warrant as a necessary condition for knowledge.

ment to either internalism or externalism. As I will argue now, the way we implicitly attribute knowledge in our communicative practice can be used as the basis for an argument against AI and thus for AE. We start from the following claim about the relation between entitlement (subjective appropriateness) and correctness (objective appropriateness):

(1) If (i) B is default-entitled to accept that p from A, and (ii) B accepts that p from A merely on the basis of A's asserting that p, and (iii) none of the defeaters that would defeat B's entitlement in fact obtains, then B's accepting that p from A is correct (objectively appropriate) (premise).

This claim is meant as an analytic truth: Default-entitlement is defeasible, which means, roughly, that one's acceptance is subjectively appropriate until one becomes aware of a possible defeater. But if in fact there is no defeater, and hence the entitlement will not be defeated, acceptance merely on the basis of someone's assertion is not just subjectively appropriate (appropriate from the subject's perspective), but objectively appropriate (correct) according to the standards that govern our communicative practice.[22]

(2) The fact that A does not have reflective access to a warrant for p does not defeat B's default-entitlement to accept that p from A (premise).

This, of course, is a substantial premise. For the moment, I want to base it on the description of our communicative practice given above which (plausibly enough, it seemed) did not include A's lack of reflective access as a defeater to the default of acceptance. Now the adequacy of this description might be doubted, and I will return to this doubt soon. For now, I will assume that (2) is true as a claim about the standards that govern our communicative practice.

(3) If (i) B is default-entitled to accept that p from A, and (ii) B accepts that p from A merely on the basis of A's asserting that p, and (iii) none of the defeaters that would defeat B's entitlement in fact obtains, then it is (objectively) correct for B to accept that p from

22. I assume here that in order to be default-entitled to accept that p from A, one must not falsely believe there to be a defeater to one's default-entitlement.

A even if A does not have reflective access to a warrant for p (from 1,2).

(4) There are possible cases in which (i) B is default-entitled to accept that p from A, (ii) B accepts that p from A merely on the basis of A's asserting that p, (iii) it is (objectively) correct for B to accept that p from A, and (iv) A does not have reflective access to a warrant for p (from 3).

(5) If B is default-entitled to accept that p from A, and B accepts that p from A merely on the basis of A's asserting that p, B implicitly attributes knowledge that p to A (= DAIKA).

(6) There are possible cases in which (a) it is correct for B to attribute knowledge to A and (b) A does not have reflective access to a warrant for p (from 4,5).

(7) A's having reflective access to a warrant for p is not a necessary condition for the correctness of B's attributing knowledge that p to A (from 6).

In order to turn this into an argument for AE and against AI, we need to connect the conditions under which it is appropriate to attribute knowledge to A to the truth of the claim that A knows that p. The most straightforward way of doing this is by assuming that:

(8) It is correct (objectively appropriate according to the standards of our communicative practice) to attribute knowledge that p to A only if A satisfies all necessary conditions for knowing that p.

From (7) and (8) it follows that:

(9) A's having reflective access to a warrant for p is not a necessary condition for A's knowing that p,

which in turn implies that:

(10) AI is false and AE is correct.

I take this argument to be valid. Premises (1) and (5) follow from the above description of our communicative practice, which I will take for granted now. This leaves only premises (2) and (8) in need of defense against possible objections.

(2) is the claim that lack of reflective access to a warrant is not a defeater to the default of acceptance. This claim can be based on the observation that B does not need to ascertain that A has access to a warrant in order for B to be entitled to accept that p from A. In fact, if B is entitled *by default* to accept that p from A, there is *nothing* A needs to ascertain over and above the fact that A asserted that p.

Against this, it might be objected that, in accepting that p from A in the absence of defeaters, we *presuppose*, and are entitled to presuppose, that A has access to a warrant for p. This objection might be backed by the claim that by asserting that p, A typically presents herself as knowing that p. Since knowledge (according to the objector) requires the reflective accessibility of a warrant, we assume, and may assume, that A has access to a warrant whenever A asserts that p. In effect, the objection claims that (a) it is a necessary condition for it to be appropriate to accept that p from A that A has access to a warrant and that (b) if B is default-entitled to accept that p from A, then B is also default-entitled to assume that A has access to a warrant for p.

Note that this objection presupposes the truth of AI. This is not a problem for the objector, however, since the objection is directed against an argument against AI. So in this stage of the dialectic, the objector is allowed to assume the truth of AI. What is a problem for the objector, however, is that the claim on which the objection is based (namely that we require access to a warrant in every case of appropriate acceptance) is completely *ad hoc* as a claim about our communicative practice. A neutral description of our practice that is not already informed by an internalist conception of knowledge in no way suggests that access to a warrant is a necessary condition for (default-appropriate) acceptance. To see this, consider how the supposed fact that A's access to a warrant is a necessary condition of appropriate acceptance could play out in actual cases of acceptance. First of all, the supposed default assumption (that if A asserts that p, A has access to a warrant for p) will make a difference in the practice only if there are possible defeaters to this default, i.e. if there are cases in which B needs to ascertain, and A needs to manifest, that A has access to a warrant for p. Without the possibility of situations in which the default assumption can be defeated, that assumption would be completely gratuitous. (Otherwise, we might equally posit that acceptance is appropriate only if A's assertion has divine approval, which, however, may be indefeasibly assumed to be present in each case of acceptance.)

Now the obvious, and in fact the only, candidates for situations in which the supposed default assumption of A's access to a warrant is being challenged, and possibly defeated, are situations in which A is required to offer a reason, or some evidence, for the truth of his assertion that p. By offering a reason or evidence in favor of p, so the objector may claim, A shows his access to a warrant for p. If A is unable to offer a reason (or some evidence) for p, this shows that A lacks such a warrant.

But even if this much is granted, it does not follow that access to a warrant is necessary for appropriate acceptance *in the default case* (where no reason-giving is required of A). It does not follow because the reason-giving that is actually required of A for B's acceptance to be appropriate always has the character of a *response* to a challenge. If there is no challenge, it is entirely unclear what an adequate response would have to look like (cf. Williams 2001, Ch. 14). For instance, if A asserts that there is coffee in the kitchen, and B objects that there is no more coffee in the coffee maker, A might respond that there is coffee in a thermos. If A asserts that the wall is blue, and B objects that it looks blue only because of the blue light shining on it, A might respond that the wall looks blue even when the blue light is switched off.

In both examples, it is the objection, or challenge, that indicates the direction an appropriate response will have to take. Without an objection, reason-giving is not only not required, it is even entirely unclear what would count as an adequate reason or as sufficient evidence. If A asserts that the wall is blue and B who can't see the wall right now, but has seen it before, objects that it is not blue, typically it will be sufficient for A to point out that he can see the wall right now and that it *looks* blue. But, as we have just seen, this response will be insufficient if the challenge is that the wall really is white, but there is a blue light shining on it. Again, a different response will be needed if the challenge is that the wall is yellow, but seen in green light, or that A's color vision is malfunctioning, and so on.

It is important to note that the mere *possibility* that the wall is yellow, or that A's color vision is malfunctioning, will not suffice as a challenge that undermines the appropriateness of acceptance. If there is no reason to assume that A's color vision may in fact be malfunctioning, the mere logical and physical possibility of a malfunction will not make it inappropriate for B to accept from A that the wall is blue. In order for there to be a real challenge to the default appropriateness of B's accepting that p from A, there must be some indication that something is wrong with A's assertion that p (cf. Willaschek 2007). In case such a challenge comes up, what is required of A in order for it to be appropriate for B to accept that p from A is that A can respond appropriately to the very challenge that has been raised. If there is no challenge, however, there is *nothing* by way of reason giving or offering evidence that is required of A in order for it to be appropriate for B to accept that p from A. And therefore, even if it is granted that A's giving a reason for p shows that A has reflective access to a warrant for p, from the fact that accepting that p from A in the presence of a relevant challenge is appropriate only if A gives a reason (or offers evidence) for p, it does not follow that A needs to have access to a warrant in cases where it is appropriate *by default* for B to accept that p from A (i.e. in cases where there are no challenges). Rather, since no reason-giving is required in the case of default-appropriate acceptance, and since it is not clear what kind of reason would be required in the absence of a challenge, a general requirement of reflective access (according to which A needs reflective access to a warrant for p in order for it to be appropriate to accept that p from A) cannot be motivated by a description of our communicative practice.

This means that while the suggestion on which the objection against (2) is based (that we attribute access to a warrant by default) may be *compatible* with our communicative practice, it lacks independent support from the neutral description of that practice given earlier. But then, the objection fails, since (2) is entered as a claim about the norms that govern our communicative practice. As we have now seen, as such (2) is plausible and well-motivated, while its denial would be completely ad hoc.

But there still remains premise (8), according to which it is appropriate to attribute knowledge that p to A only if A satisfies all necessary conditions for knowing that p. Against this it might be objected that it can be *pragmatically* appropriate to attribute knowledge that p to A even if A does not satisfy all necessary conditions for knowing that p. According to this objection, a description of a practice in which a concept such as knowledge is attributed can give us no more than the conditions under which it is appropriate to *attribute* that concept. These conditions, however, will depend on the pragmatic point and the practical restrictions of the practice in question. In the case of acceptance, for instance, they may reflect the need for easy and generally successful communication, which would only be hindered by too strict conditions for acceptance. Therefore, it might be appropriate for us to accept what others assert, and thus to attribute knowledge to them, even in situations in which it is possible, although unlikely, that in fact they do not possess knowledge. Hence, the conditions under which communication will generally be successful (and thus the conditions under which attributions of knowledge will be pragmatically appropriate) may not be the same as the conditions under which such attributions are strictly speaking true. Something similar may be said about our practice of attributing responsibility by adopting reactive attitudes: When it comes to attributing knowledge or responsibility, we may be a little lax in our everyday practices—a laxity that is harmless given the purposes of that practice, but fatal in philosophy.

Now I think that already the idea that our standards in philosophy may be somehow constitutionally stricter than those in "ordinary" practices is misguided. After all, in ordinary contexts, someone's life or well-being may depend on whether someone really knows that what they are asserting is true, which rarely is the case in philosophy. So it is not clear why standards for acceptance and knowledge that are strict enough for practical purposes should not be strict enough for philosophy. Something similar can be said for other concepts as well. For instance, it is not clear why standards for attributing responsibility in everyday life should be less strict (e.g. in not requiring indeterminism) than those in philosophy, given that it is only the former that really have an impact on people's lives. Moreover, this objection drives a wedge between the "correct" philosophical account of a concept and the "lax" way in which we use it outside philosophy that threatens to deprive the philosophical analysis of the concept of all practical relevance. After all, why should we care how philosophers analyze some concept such as knowledge or responsibility if this analysis is unrelated to the way in which we actually use this concept—and use it correctly, relative to the standards of our actual practices? And finally, if it is granted that in our actual practices we do *not* require some condition (e.g. indeterminism, reflective access to a warrant) in order to apply a given concept, what could be the basis for the claim that nevertheless the *correct* account of that concept does include this condition? To invoke one's own intuitions about hypothetical cases hardly seems sufficient for this. In conclusion, it seems that the conditions under which we actually attribute a concept, and do so appropriately according to the standards governing the relevant practice, are the best access we have to the truth-conditions of statements in which we explicitly apply that concept, so that the alleged gap between truth-conditions and conditions of appropriate attribution on which the objection depends does not really exist.

I therefore think that the objection against premise (8), too, can be rejected with good reason. But then, our Strawsonian argument for AE will be successful: In our communicative practice, we often implicitly attribute knowledge by accepting what others assert and the conditions under which we do this tell strongly in favor of an externalist account of knowledge.

However, this externalist result must be supplemented by pointing out that there is also an *internalist* element in our practice: In order for B to accept that p from A, in case of a challenge A will often be required to answer the challenge by explicit reason-giving. Sometimes it will be sufficient if someone—A or somebody else—answers those challenges. But in many cases—for instance, if the challenge can only be answered by stating what A himself sees, hears, or remembers—A may be the only person who can give an adequate response to the challenge. And if A indeed can give such a response, A will in many cases have shown to have reflective access to a warrant for p. To be sure, this does not mean that access to a warrant is a necessary condition for knowledge in general. But it might indicate that access to a warrant is a necessary condition for knowledge in many situations in which an assertion, or knowledge-claim, has been challenged. So there is some truth in internalism, even though it is restricted to a special, and, when viewed from the perspective of our communicative practice, rather atypical kind of situation. (This incorporation of an internalist element into a generally externalist conception of knowledge is meant to parallel Strawson's attempt to improve on traditional compatibilism by incorporating a seemingly incompatibilist element, namely a non-consequentialist conception of praise and blame.)[23]

5. *Conclusion*

In this paper, I have suggested that Strawson's indirect and practice-based approach to freedom and responsibility in his classic paper "Freedom and Resentment" can serve as a model for a similar approach in epistemology. I have given a structural description of one fragment of our communicative practice, namely the practice of accepting what others assert. I have argued that, according to the standards that govern that practice, acceptance is the default while rejection requires particular reasons. One

23. As will be obvious, I have not followed Strawson in favoring "reconsiliation" over partisan argument. While Strawson, as I have argued, is primarily interested in offering an improved version of compatibilism and only secondarily, if at all, in arguing against incompatibilism, I have presented an argument for externalism and only added a conciliatory gesture in the end. This may be more a difference in emphasis, though, than in substance.

of these defeaters is lack of knowledge on the side of the asserter, which means that appropriate acceptance, at least in the default case, is an implicit knowledge-attribution. Therefore, the conditions under which we appropriately accept that p allow us to analyze the concept of knowledge that we implicitly employ in the knowledge-attributions that go with acceptance. Finally, I have presented an argument for access externalism on the basis of the connection between acceptance and knowledge-attribution. The main idea behind that argument was that, when we accept that p from A in default situations, that is, without requiring A to give any reasons, we implicitly attribute knowledge to A without requiring A to have access to a warrant. This can be taken to show that the concept of knowledge we implicitly employ in our communicative practice does not include access to a warrant as a necessary condition. Access externalism should be supplemented, however, by an account of the internalist elements in our communicative practice, which become apparent whenever challenges to an assertion are raised and have to be answered – often by the asserter herself. Obviously, the above argument for externalism is not meant to finally settle the long-standing debate between internalist and externalist accounts of knowledge. I hope, however, that it illustrates the potential of a Strawsonian account in epistemology.[24]

References

Alston, William P. 1989: *Epistemic Justification: Essays in the Theory of Knowledge.* Ithaca, N.Y.: Cornell University Press.

Austin, John L. 1956: "A Plea for Excuses". *Proceedings of the Aristotelian Society* 57, 1–30.

Brandom, Robert 1994: *Making It Explicit.* Cambridge, MA: Harvard University Press.

Brown, Jessica 2008: "The Knowledge Norm for Assertion". *Philosophical Issues* 18, 89–103.

Cohen, Stewart 1999: "Contextualism, Skepticism, and the Structure of Reasons". *Philosophical Perspectives* 13, 57–89.

DeRose, Keith 2002: "Assertion, Knowledge, and Context". *The Philosophical Review* 111, 167–203.

24. For valuable comments on earlier versions of this paper I would like to thank Michel de Araujo Kurth, Sebastian Boll, Mikael Janvid, Andreas Maier, Hannes Ole Matthiessen, Andreas Müller, Michael Williams as well as audiences in Cologne and Milan.

Douven, Igor 2006: "Assertion, Knowledge, and Rational Credibility". *The Philosophical Review* 115, 449–485.

Engel, Pascal 1998: "Believing, Holding True, and Accepting". *Philosophical Explorations* 1, 140–151.

Hart, H. L. A. 1948: "The Ascription of Responsibility and Rights". *Proceedings of the Aristotelian Society* 49, 171–194.

Hawthorne, John 2004: *Knowledge and the Lotteries.* Oxford: Clarendon.

Lackey, Jennifer 2007: "Norms of Assertion". *Nous* 41, 594–626.

— 2008: *Learning from Words: Testimony as a Source of Knowledge.* Oxford: Oxford University Press.

Lehrer, Keith 1990: *Theory of Knowledge.* London: Routledge.

Magill, Kevin, 2000: "Blaming, Understanding, and Justification. A Defence of Strawson's Naturalism about Moral Responsibility". In: Ton van den Beld (ed.), *Moral Responsibility and Ontology.* Dordrecht: Kluwer, 183–198.

McKenna, Michael 2005: "Where Frankfurt and Strawson Meet". *Midwest Studies in Philosophy* 29, 163–180.

Pereboom, Derk 2008: "Revising the Reactive Attitudes". In: Michael McKenna & Paul Russell (eds.), *Free Will and Reactive Attitudes: Perspectives on P. F. Strawson's "Freedom and Resentment".* Aldershot: Ashgate Press, 219–234.

Russell, Paul 1992: "Strawson's Way of Naturalizing Responsibility". *Ethics* 102, 287–302.

Stanley, Jason 2005: *Knowledge and Practical Interests.* Oxford: Oxford University Press.

Strawson, Peter F. 1974 [1962]: "Freedom and Resentment". In: *Freedom and Resentment and other Essays.* London: Methuen, 1–25.

Tuomela, Raimo 2000: "Belief versus Acceptance". *Philosophical Explorations* 3, 122–137.

Wallace, R. Jay 1994: *Responsibility and the Moral Sentiments.* Cambridge, MA: Harvard University Press.

Watson, Gary 1987: "Responsibility and the Limits of Evil". In: Ferdinand Schoeman (ed.), *Responsibility, Character, and the Emotions.* New York: Cambridge University Press, 256–286.

Weiner, Matt 2005: "Must We Know What We Say". *The Philosophical Review* 114, 227-51.

Willaschek, Marcus 2007: "Contextualism about Knowledge and Justification by Default". *Grazer Philosophische Studien* 74, 251–272.

Williams, Michael 2001: *Problems of Knowledge.* Oxford/New York: Oxford University Press.

Williamson, Timothy 2000: *Knowledge and Its Limits.* Oxford: Oxford University Press.

Grazer Philosophische Studien
87 (2013), 129–150.

THE DEFEASIBLE STRUCTURE OF ASCRIPTIONS OF RESPONSIBILITY

Claudia BLÖSER
Goethe Universität Frankfurt

Summary

Normally, we can hold persons responsible for their actions without giving explicit reasons for doing so, i.e. our ascriptions of responsibility are justified by *default*. However, an ascription of responsibility can be *challenged* under specific conditions, by adducing reasons that *excuse* or *exempt* a person from responsibility. The aim of the paper is to show how this "default-and-challenge" structure helps to clarify the concept of responsibility. In particular, the distinction between two kinds of challenges will provide a basis for the distinction between two kinds of responsibility-ascriptions, namely the ascription of accountability and the ascription of praise- or blameworthiness.

Introduction

In this paper, I will argue that ascriptions of responsibility possess a "defeasible" or "default-and-challenge" structure. My account takes its starting point from a common fact about our practice of holding each other responsible: Normally, we can hold persons responsible for their actions without having to give explicit reasons for doing so. I refer to this fact by saying that, normally, our ascriptions of responsibility are justified by *default.* However, even in the case of default-justified ascriptions, there are minimal conditions that have to be fulfilled, which I will call *default-conditions.* These include, for example, that the agent must be an adult, since we do not normally ascribe (full) responsibility to children. Still, this default-justified ascription is fallible, and it can be *challenged* under specific conditions, which I will call *challenge-conditions.* These include, for example, excuses such as physical duress or coercion. This default-and-challenge pattern constitutes the *defeasible* structure of ascriptions of responsibility:

(R) If a person P with respect to her action A fulfills default conditions, ascribing responsibility to P for A is appropriate, *unless* there is an indication that some challenge-condition holds.

This account of responsibility as a defeasible concept has distinctive advantages. First, it takes as a starting point our actual practice of ascribing responsibility. Thus the analysis builds on influential accounts such as those developed by Peter Strawson in his article "Freedom and Resentment" (Strawson 1692) and by R. J. Wallace in his book *Responsibility and the Moral Sentiments* (Wallace 1994). These authors also take seriously the fact that holding each other responsible is an integral aspect of our intersubjective practices, and not primarily a metaphysical phenomenon.[1] Second, the account suggested here assigns a central role to the way ascriptions of responsibility can be challenged. The account of challenging reasons has been inspired by R. J. Wallace's account of excuses and exemptions from responsibility. However, our accounts of the role of the challenges differ. In explaining these differences, further merits of the analysis of responsibility as defeasible become apparent. In particular, the distinction between two kinds of challenges to ascriptions of responsibility will help to clarify the concept of responsibility by providing a basis for the distinction between accountability and blameworthiness. Furthermore, the account allows for a unified explanation of moral and legal responsibility. Even if moral and legal contexts differ, it is plausible to assume that ascriptions of responsibility share a common structure in both contexts. The account suggested here highlights the common underlying structure shared by ascriptions of moral and legal responsibility, while also allowing for specific differences. In sum, the analysis of responsibility in terms of a default-and-challenge structure is true to our moral and legal practices of ascribing

1. However, both Strawson and Wallace defend the view that the core of our practice of holding each other responsible is essentially linked to reactive attitudes or particular kinds of *emotions*, such as gratitude, resentment, forgiveness, indignation and guilt. By contrast, my focus will be on *judgments* instead of emotions, for the following reason. What is crucial for holding a person responsible, according to Wallace, is that one believes that it would be appropriate to feel the emotion, not that one actually experiences it. This "appropriateness-condition" is satisfied if a moral obligation has been breached (Wallace 1994, 76). By introducing the appropriateness-condition, Wallace seems to undermine the essential role of reactive emotions. He rather suggests that an ascription of responsibility is justified by a *judgment*, namely the judgment "that a moral obligation you accept has been violated, and there are no exonerating circumstances that you are aware of" (Wallace 1994, 77). As a consequence, I take it that it is judgments and not reactive emotions that are essential for the truth of ascriptions of responsibility.

responsibility, and it provides new philosophical insights into the concept of responsibility.

1. *Defeasible concepts*

In this section, I will introduce the general idea of defeasible ascriptions of responsibility and relate it to the original idea of defeasible concepts introduced by H. L. A. Hart, who first introduced the idea of defeasible concepts in his paper, "The Ascription of Responsibility and Rights" (Hart 1948/49). Starting from an analysis of characteristics of certain legal concepts such as "contract", Hart argues that the application of those concepts, which he calls "defeasible concepts" (cf. Hart 1948/49, 148), cannot be adequately described by specifying necessary and sufficient conditions. Rather, under certain necessary and *normally* sufficient conditions, a defeasible concept can be applied, *unless* there are reasons to challenge the ascription. Hart borrows the word "defeasible" from the law, where "defeasible"

> is used of a legal interest in property which is subject to termination or "defeat" in a number of different contingencies but remains intact if no such contingencies mature. (Hart 1948/49, 148)

According to Hart, there are two ways of calling into question the application of a defeasible concept: First, by a denial of the facts that form the basis of the application ("joinder of issue") or, second:

> [by] a plea that although all the circumstances on which a claim could succeed are present, yet in the particular case, the claim or accusation should not succeed because other circumstances are present which brings the case under some recognized head of exception. (Hart 1948/49, 147f.)

Hart's account of legal concepts clearly exhibits a default-and-challenge structure analogous to (R) even if he doesn't use this terminology: There are *default conditions,* i.e. facts that are normally sufficient for the application of the defeasible concept. However, it is possible in a particular case to call into question whether the concept applies by advancing a "joinder of issue" or by adducing *challenge-conditions*. The main difference between joinders of issue and challenges is that joinders of issue undermine the very basis of the application of the concept, the default conditions, whereas challenges are compatible with the fulfillment of default conditions. Challenges indicate that, although the necessary and *normally* sufficient default-conditions are fulfilled, they are not sufficient for the application of the concept in this particular case.

Hart identifies a defeasible structure not only in the case of legal concepts, but also for concepts traditionally designated as "mental elements" in criminal law, such as *mens rea*, intentionality or voluntariness (Hart 1948/49, 152f.). According to Hart, *mens rea*, i.e. the mental element recognized in criminal law that designates the consciousness of guilt, cannot be understood as a positive concept, but can only be fully explained by reference to a list of possible challenges, such as "mistake of Fact, Accident, Coercion, Duress, Provocation, Insanity, Infancy" (Hart 1948/49, 153). With respect to the concept "voluntary", Hart puts his view especially clearly:

> the word "voluntary" in fact serves to exclude a heterogeneous range of cases such as physical compulsions, coercion by threats, accidents, mistakes, etc., and not to designate a mental element or state; nor does "involuntary" signify the absence of this mental element or state. (Hart 1948/49, 153)

This means that for Hart, the word "voluntary", at least in legal contexts, does not have any positive content, but serves only as the negation of a heterogeneous list of cases of "involuntary" actions. Elements such as the consciousness of guilt and voluntariness are commonly thought of as conditions of responsibility. By characterizing the conditions of responsibility as defeasible, Hart creates a basis for an analysis of responsibility as defeasible.[2] Whereas Hart mostly talks about defeasible *concepts*, I prefer to speak about defeasible *judgments* or *ascriptions* of responsibility. However, these two approaches are, even for Hart himself, closely related: Hart calls responsibility a defeasible concept, because the *appli-*

2. Note that Hart himself introduces defeasibility as providing the basis for a new philosophical analysis not of the concept of responsibility, but of the concept of action. Action sentences, according to Hart, are defeasible, and furthermore, they are primarily used ascriptively, i.e. they don't describe facts but ascribe responsibility. This is the core of Hart's "ascriptivism", which received strong criticism (e.g. Geach 1960, Pitcher 1960). His critics convinced Hart himself that his account was mistaken, and consequently he declined to reprint the paper in his collection *Punishment and Responsibility* (1968). Interestingly, there are recent attempts to take up and develop the insights of Hart's analysis of action (cf. Sneddon 2006, Stoecker 2007). I think, however, that Hart's ideas on defeasibility can be divorced from his ascriptivism. I therefore neglect the details of Hart's ascriptivism, and instead follow some of his critics who argue that the true essence of Hart's analysis is that defeasibility is a feature not of the concept of action, but of responsibility (cf. Pitcher 1960, 235 and Cherry 1974, 104).

cation of the concept *in a judgment* follows a default-and-challenge pattern.

2. *Two kinds of challenges and two aspects of responsibility*

Hart has been rightly criticized for being unclear about the meaning of "responsibility".[3] The term responsibility is used in a variety of ways. Literally, it designates our ability to respond, mostly understood as the ability to answer for our actions. This ability is often called "accountability". It is widely acknowledged that the concept of responsibility has a *prospective* use, namely responsibility in the sense of "duty", and also a *retrospective* use, namely responsibility as praise- or blameworthiness for actions that lie in the past. Thus, there are many possibilities for distinguishing different uses or aspects of responsibility. In this section, leaving the prospective use aside, I propose distinguishing two aspects of responsibility on the basis of the distinction between two kinds of challenges.

The two aspects of responsibility I want to distinguish are *accountability*, on the one hand, and *praise- or blameworthiness*, on the other hand. The ways we *challenge* ascriptions of responsibility in everyday life and in law can motivate this distinction. In characterizing the challenges to ascriptions of responsibility, I will follow R. J. Wallace (cf. Wallace 1994, 118), who argues that there are in principle two ways of challenging ascriptions of responsibility. The two classes of challenges are *exemptions* and *excuses*:[4] *Exemptions* are challenges that point to the fact that a person is not a fully-fledged member of our moral community, such as a child or a person who is mentally ill. These challenging reasons function "globally" insofar as they refer to the agent rather than to some particular act. This distinguishes them from *excuses* like physical constraint or coercion, which function "locally" in relation to a particular act.[5]

3. Pitcher, for example, conjectures that in saying that a person is responsible for her action, Hart means that the person is "deserving of censure or punishment for it" (Pitcher 1960, 230). In a later essay, "Postscript: Responsibility and Retribution", Hart distinguishes and discusses different notions of responsibility (Hart 1968, 210–237).

4. The terminology "exemptions" and "excuses" was originally introduced by Gary Watson (Watson 1987, 260).

5. P. F. Strawson also acknowledges these two different groups of challenges, without thereby distinguishing two notions of responsibility. According to Strawson, a challenge that Wallace calls exemption, "allows that the circumstances were normal, but presents the agent as psychologically abnormal—or as morally undeveloped. The agent was himself; but he is warped or deranged,

Let me discuss the difference between exemptions and excuses in more detail, because this distinction will be the basis for distinguishing the two aspects of responsibility. The rough characterization given so far suggests that exemptions show that an agent is *permanently*, i.e. in all situations, not responsible, whereas excuses show that the agent is *temporarily*, i.e. in a particular situation, not responsible. This is a useful preliminary approximation to what distinguishes exemptions and excuses, as it correctly describes the paradigmatic cases of exemptions like being a child or being mentally ill: In both cases, the agent is considered permanently exempt from responsibility—at least for a considerable stretch of time, i.e. as long as she is a child or mentally deranged. Yet, in Wallace's list of the most important exemptions, there are candidates that do not fit this characterization. The list includes "childhood, insanity or mental illness, addiction, posthypnotic suggestion, behavior control, psychopathy, and the effects of extreme stress, deprivation, and torture" (Wallace 1994, 166). In the cases of stress, deprivation, and torture, it seems that the exemption is only a *temporary* one. So, what characterizes the class of exempting reasons, if it is not the temporal extension? A further idea to distinguish exemptions and excuses could be that exempting conditions are *internal* to the agent, whereas excusing conditions refer to *external* facts. This characterization at least works for exemptions: they point to the fact that the agent lacks certain features that qualify him as an appropriate candidate for responsibility-ascriptions. Later, I will characterize those features in more detail, and I will follow Wallace in describing them as certain mental capacities. Exemptions thus show that the person does not posses the mental capacities that qualify her as an appropriate candidate for responsibility-ascriptions. This interpretation captures the sense in which all the exemptions in Wallace's list can be said to function: Children and the mentally ill are exemptions because they do not posses the relevant capacities during a considerable stretch of time, whereas other exemptions—like extreme stress or torture —undermine the relevant capacities during a certain time.

Before turning to the characterization of excuses, we arrive at a first approximation of the sense of responsibility that is undermined by exemptions: It is responsibility as *accountability*. In saying that a person is account-

neurotic or just a child" (Strawson 1963, 79). The challenges that Wallace calls excuses are those which "do not invite us to see the *agent* as other than a fully responsible agent. They invite us to see the *injury* as one for which he was not fully, or at all, responsible" (Strawson 1963, 77f.).

able, we roughly mean that she has the relevant capacities that make her in principle answerable for her actions.

Next, I will characterize the second class of challenges, excuses, which leads to a second aspect of responsibility. Typical excuses, taken from Wallace's typology of excuses (cf. Wallace 1994, 136–147), are inadvertence, mistake or accident, physical constraint, or coercion, necessity and duress. This list shows that the reasons for excuses are quite diverse. The preliminary idea that excuses are *external* reasons for undermining responsibility does not apply to all excuses. It gives a correct characterization of excuses like physical constraint (e.g. being chained) or coercion (e.g. being threatened by a gun), but not for the case of inadvertence. To cite Wallace's example: If I tread on a person's hand inadvertently, while walking to the refrigerator to get a beer, I have the excuse that I have not anticipated that I would be treading on a person's hand when I made the choice to get a beer (cf. Wallace 1994, 137). In this case, there is no *external* excusing reason; rather, the excuse refers to the fact that I did not *intend* the action, in this case the action of treading on the person's hand. What all excuses have in common is that they show that the agent did not possess the *kind of intention* that would make him responsible for the action (cf. Wallace 1994, 128): Neither the cashier who hands over the money to the thief, nor the person who inadvertently treads on another's hand had the kind of intention (e.g. intending to steal the money or harming someone) that would make them fully answerable for their actions.

Now, we can identify the sense of responsibility that is undermined by excuses: It is responsibility as *praise- or blameworthiness*. If a person has an excuse, she is not (fully) blameworthy for an action that nonetheless violates a valid norm. The same applies to praise: If the person did not posses the right kind of intention, she does not deserve praise for an action that is positively evaluated with respect to a norm.

On the basis of this preliminary understanding of accountability on the one hand and praise- and blameworthiness on the other, let us regard the logical relation between these two aspects of responsibility. Accountability is a necessary condition for praise- and blameworthiness: Only a person who possesses the capacities that allow for the ascription of accountability is an appropriate addressee for praise or blame. Accountability is not identical with (or sufficient for) praise- or blameworthiness: Persons are accountable in virtue of certain mental capacities, whereas praise- or blameworthiness are ascribed to accountable persons in virtue of particular actions that are evaluated with respect to norms. This means that praise-

and blameworthiness require two further necessary conditions besides accountability of the person: First, that the accountable person performed an action that, second, is evaluated with respect to a norm. Yet, this relation between accountability and praise- or blameworthiness also sheds light on the meaning of accountability: Accountability is the normative status of persons who are *possible targets of praise and blame* (and hence possible targets of ascribing praise- or blameworthiness). It is an interesting question whether accountability, as a necessary condition for praise- and blameworthiness, has any application independent of ascriptions of praise- and blameworthiness. An answer to this question would have to draw attention to other attitudes persons have towards each other which presuppose that the other is accountable. One example is mentioned by Kant, who claims that the ability to live according to one's own concept of happiness presupposes accountability. Therefore, young children and the insane cannot live according to their own concepts of happiness, but according to those of others.[6]

To sum up, the distinction between exemptions and excuses motivates the distinction between accountability and praise- or blameworthiness. Thus, I agree with Wallace on the distinction between the two notions of responsibility. However, I suggest reversing his methodological order: Whereas Wallace *first* draws the distinction between two senses of responsibility and *then* argues that there are two kinds of challenges, I suggest that we *motivate* the distinction between the notions of responsibility by considering the kinds of challenges in our practice of ascribing responsibility. Exemptions show that the person is not (or is to a lesser degree) accountable, whereas excuses undermine praise- or blameworthiness.[7]

6. Kant says in the *Metaphysics of Morals*: "I cannot do good to anyone in accordance with *my* concepts of happiness (except to young children and the insane), [...] rather, I can benefit him only in accordance with *his* concepts of happiness" (Translation by Mary Gregor, 203).

7. Wallace himself motivates the distinction by distinguishing between a "dispositional" and an "occurrent" interpretation of his reactive account (Wallace 1994, 70). On the occurrent interpretation, to hold a person responsible is either to experience a reactive emotion because the person has violated a moral obligation or to believe that the emotion would be appropriate. This is an interpretation "of holding a person responsible for some particular moral wrong; it tells us what it is to regard a person as having done something *blameworthy*" (Wallace 1994, 70). According to the dispositional account, to hold a person responsible is to be *susceptible* to reactive emotions in case the person violates a moral norm. This means that one regards the person as "the sort of agent" who is an appropriate addressee for reactive emotions, i.e. an accountable agent. This method of distinguishing between accountability and blameworthiness, however, is only open to an account that assigns reactive emotions the central role. In contrast, the distinction by way of the challenges is open to every account of responsibility

3. *The defeasible structure of ascriptions of accountability and praise- or blameworthiness*

In this section, I will argue that ascriptions of both aspects of responsibility, accountability on the one hand and praise- or blameworthiness on the other, exhibit a defeasible structure. The two aspects are two instances of the general scheme (R) introduced above:

(R) If a person P with respect to her action A fulfills default conditions, ascribing responsibility to P for A is appropriate, unless there is an indication that some challenge-condition holds.

This scheme applied to accountability looks as follows:

(RA) If a person P fulfills default conditions with respect to her actions, holding her *accountable* for her actions is appropriate, unless there is an indication that an exempting reason holds.

What are the default conditions for holding a person accountable? Remember that default conditions are those conditions under which we normally don't have to give reasons for ascribing responsibility. As a general rule, the obtaining of default conditions should be easily observable (cf. Hannes Ole Matthiessen's contribution in this volume). It seems that in order to hold a person accountable by default, no other condition has to be fulfilled except that the person is an adult. If we encounter an adult person, we can take her to be accountable without having to give reasons for this. As indicated before, I follow accounts of responsibility that identify the feature that makes a person accountable with certain psychological capacities.[8] Wallace, for example, characterizes the relevant capacities as "powers of reflective self-control: the general ability to grasp and apply moral reasons and to regulate [one's] behavior by the light of such reasons" (Wallace 1994, 155).[9] Yet, in order to hold an adult person accountable, it is not

that takes seriously the way we call into question ascriptions of responsibility in our moral and legal practice.

8. For other accounts that focus on capacities as conditions for responsibility see e.g. Fischer and Ravizza (Fischer and Ravizza 1998).

9. I want to leave it open how to characterize these capacities in more detail, because I am mainly interested in the structural features of ascriptions of responsibility, not the exact description of the relevant capacities.

necessary to inquire wether the person possesses the relevant capacities. It suffices to see that the person is an adult, because one can suppose that adults normally possess the relevant capacities.

This leads to the question of wether the ascription of accountability goes hand in hand with the ascription of the possession of the relevant capacities. Let me indicate why this is not the case. It is true that "being adult" justifies both the ascription of accountability *and* the assumption that the person possesses certain capacities. Yet, accountability is a *normative status*, whereas the possession of capacities is a psychological fact. It is conceivable that there is a society whose members possess the capacities that could justify holding them accountable, but that there is no normative practice of ascribing responsibility, i.e. accountability and praise- or blameworthiness, in this society. Possessing capacities is a fact that is independent of a normative practice in a way that being accountable is not. It is misleading to describe the ascription of accountability as an ascription of the relevant capacities, because a person possesses the capacities independently of such an ascription, whereas the normative status of being accountable is essentially tied to the practice of ascribing accountability.

Thus, I hold that the ascription of accountability to an adult is justified by default. Still, pointing to some challenging reason, i.e. an exemption, can challenge the ascription. Recall that typical exemptions, as mentioned above, include "childhood, insanity or mental illness, addiction, posthypnotic suggestion, behavior control, psychopathy, and the effects of extreme stress, deprivation, and torture" (Wallace 1994, 166). Now, we can answer the question what their relation to the default conditions is. Following Hart, I suggested that there are "joinders of issue" that call into question the fulfillment of default conditions, whereas "challenges" are compatible with default conditions. Obviously, all candidates in Wallace's list, except childhood, can be regarded as challenges, because they are compatible with the person being an adult. If the person is a child, we are not default entitled to hold her accountable in the first place—default conditions are not fulfilled, i.e. childhood is a "joinder of issue". However, if we are dealing with an adult person, we can normally hold her accountable without giving reasons. Yet, if a challenge comes up, e.g. it turns out that she suffers from mental illness, extreme stress or similar impairments of her mental capacities, we need special reasons for nevertheless holding her accountable.

Having established the defeasible structure for ascriptions of accountability, I now turn to the ascription of praise- or blameworthiness, which also possesses a defeasible structure:

(RPB) If a person P fulfills default conditions, and her action A is evaluated with respect to a valid norm, regarding P as *praise- or blameworthy* with respect to A is appropriate, unless there is an indication that some excusing condition holds.

In the following, I will first describe the default conditions for praise- or blameworthiness, then discuss two issues connected with the fact that an ascription of praise- and blameworthiness concerns the evaluation according to *norms*, and finally turn to the question of possible challenges.

One element of the default conditions for praise- and blameworthiness is implied by the fact that accountability is a necessary condition for praise- and blameworthiness. This means that "being an adult", which is the default condition for accountability, also has to be part of the default conditions for praise- and blameworthiness. What is needed apart from this is that an adult person *performed an action A* that is *evaluated according to valid norms*. Consider a simple example: If you have an appointment with another (adult) person, and she comes far too late, you are by default entitled to blame her. The default conditions are that the person is an adult and that she performed an action—coming too late—that violates the (social) norm that one should be on time.

This example concerns the violation of a norm, and therefore the ascription of blameworthiness, and furthermore the evaluation according to a social – or, arguably, moral—norm. Next, I will discuss those two aspects one after the other: First, we will see how different results of an evaluation lead to praise- or blameworthiness, respectively, and second, we will see that the scheme (RPB) is applicable to different kinds of norms.

The evaluation of a specific action with respect to a norm can lead to three results: negative, neutral or positive. If a person fails to meet a demand expressed by a norm, the person is normally blameworthy. The action can turn out to be a "neutral" action, either because one cannot think of a relevant norm according to which the action is evaluated (at least at first sight, it is difficult to imagine how to normatively evaluate my action of going for a walk in the afternoon), or because the evaluation by a norm qualifies the action neither as forbidden nor as obligatory. As I am interested in praise- and blameworthiness, which is not attributed with respect to neutral actions, I will leave the neutral case aside. In the positive case, a minimal sense of praise might already be appropriate if a person fulfils a valid norm. However, this could also count as an example of the neutral case, or a kind of "positive acknowledgement", which can be expressed in a way not normally associated with "praise". Imagine you are seated on a bus in which all other seats are taken. An old lady gets on the bus and looks around for a place to sit. When you offer her your seat, this may simply be something that is expected of you, but the old lady will normally still express her gratitude. This example shows that there are forms of positively acknowledging morally good actions, even if they do not count as praise in a strong sense. One way to capture the conditions for praiseworthiness in the strong sense would be to say that a person P is praiseworthy for action A, if and only if P is accountable and her action exceeds the demands expressed by a valid norm (and no challenge condition holds).

These considerations make it possible to spell out a criticism regarding Wallace's restriction of ascriptions of responsibility to ascriptions of blame. According to Wallace, "praise does not seem to have the central, defining role that blame and moral sanction occupy in our practice of assigning moral responsibility" (Wallace 1994, 61). Let me briefly indicate why I think this assumption is not adequate for an analysis of responsibility. There are two reasons why one might think that blame is of particular interest in our practice of ascribing responsibility, but I think neither stands up to closer scrutiny. First, being exposed to blame is unpleasant and costly in a way that being praised is not. This might suggest that we attribute a greater importance to the fairness of blame because blame has a greater immediate impact on our emotional household, and we want to avoid misplacing blame. Second, attributions of *legal* responsibility seem to be restricted to the negative case. The centrality of the legal model for ascriptions of responsibility might lead one to think of negative ascriptions as paradigmatic. Nevertheless, neither of these considerations justifies neglecting the positive case for a philosophical analysis of responsibility. First, even if blame has greater immediate emotional consequences than praise, it remains questionable whether it is of greater emotional importance for a person's life on the whole. Positive acknowledgment of appropriate actions and praise for morally good actions are crucial not only for the education of children, but also for sustaining positive moral relations to others and to oneself. To be sure, in the legal context, misplaced blame and punishment do have severe consequences that ought to be avoided. The priority of the negative case in the ascription of *legal* responsibility certainly has to be acknowledged, but this does not warrant generalizing from the legal case to everyday contexts.

If this is correct, it is a virtue of the present account that, in analyzing ascriptions of responsibility in terms of (RPB), it treats negative and positive ascriptions on equal terms. Ascriptions of blameworthiness are based on the fact that an accountable person has performed an action, which is evaluated according to certain norms. This evaluation can yield both negative and positive (as well as neutral) results—there is no compelling reason why negative ascriptions, i.e. blame, should be philosophically more important than the other two. Thus, the account suggested privileges neither positive nor negative ascriptions of responsibility, because they are two instances of the same structure.

So far, it has been left unspecified what kinds of norms are involved in (RPB). Indeed, the suggested analysis of responsibility is meant to be applicable to different kinds of norms, as the formulation (RPB) can be understood as a "scheme", where different kinds of norms can be inserted. In particular, the analysis applies to moral and legal norms. I take it that the main difference between moral and legal responsibility consists in the difference between the relevant *norms*, rather than in any difference in the meaning of the notion "responsibility".[10] Now, if an action is evaluated with respect to *moral* norms, we get *moral* responsibility, whereas if the action is evaluated with respect to *legal* norms, this implies *legal* responsibility. If this is correct, my account succeeds in articulating the common structure of moral and legal responsibility.

Wallace restricts himself to moral responsibility and it is clear from what has been said so far that my account, too, applies to moral responsibility. Now, I will briefly indicate with regard to (RA) and (RPB) how the defeasible structure is also suitable as a menas of describing ascriptions of legal responsibility.

Continental penal codes and the M'Naghten Rules formulate ascriptions of legal accountability in a way that points to a default-and-challenge structure.[11] The striking feature they share is that *only* reasons for

10. This is also Hart's view: The "striking differences between legal and moral responsibility are due to substantive differences between the content of legal and moral rules and principles rather than to any variation in meaning of responsibility when conjoined with the word 'moral' rather than 'legal'" (Hart 1968, 225f.).

11. To cite §20 of the German Criminal Law: "Whoever upon commission of the act is incapable of appreciating the wrongfulness of the act or acting in accordance with such appreciation due to a pathological emotional disorder, profound consciousness disorder, mental defect or any other serious emotional abnormality, acts without guilt" (Translation by the German Federal Ministry of Justice). Wallace cites the M'Naghten Rules: "[T]o establish a defence on the ground of insanity it must be clearly proved that, at the time of committing the act, the

challenging accountability are listed, whereas no positive conditions are included. This is a clear indication that ascriptions of accountability in the law exhibit a defeasible structure: Normally (by default), an adult is legally accountable, and only in exceptional cases can this ascription of responsibility be challenged. Reasons challenging legal accountability are similar to challenging reasons for moral accountability: Both in the continental penal codes and the M'Naghten Rules, mental illnesses count as exemptions.[12] This is an indication that Wallace's account of psychological powers as conditions for accountability can be extended to apply to legal responsibility. The "powers of reflective self-control", which, according to Wallace, encompass "the general ability to grasp and apply moral reasons and to regulate [one's] behavior by the light of such reasons" (Wallace 1994, 155), only have to be understood in a broader way: If one does not merely focus on moral reasons when one considers the ability to act on reasons, but understands the powers of reflective self-control as capacities to comply with normative standards in a broader sense including legal reasons, these powers can be the basis for accountability in a broader sense, i.e. for moral and legal accountability alike.[13]

With respect to (RPB), the ascription of praise- and blameworthiness, it is obvious that the same structure applies to legal responsibility, too. As indicated above, if an action of an accountable person is evaluated with respect to a legal norm, say in court, she is held legally responsible. As in the moral case, there is a legal ascription of praise- and blameworthiness, which expresses itself in legal reward or—more commonly—legal punishment.

To complete the discussion of the defeasible structure of praise- and blameworthiness, we have to take a look at the possible challenges. As discussed above, the challenges are the "excuses", which show that the agent did not possess the right kind of intention in order to be regarded as praise- or blameworthy. In the example mentioned above—the person who comes too late to an appointment—a typical excuse might be that her car had a flat tire and she had to wait until it was fixed. All typical excuses (like inadvertence, mistake or accident, physical constraint, or coercion,

---

accused was labouring under such a defect of reason, from disease of the mind, as not to know the nature and quality of the act he was doing, or, if he did know it, that he did not know he was doing what was wrong". (Wallace 1994, 167f.)

12. Wallace makes the same observation: "Though these rules [the M'Naghten Rules, CB] are meant to formulate conditions of nonliability in the law, they seem equally to express a natural view about the effect of mental illness on moral accountability" (Wallace 1994, 168).

13. Cf. for this suggestion also Willaschek 2010, 578.

necessity and duress) seem to be challenges in the sense that they are compatible with the default conditions (that an adult person performed an action A that is evaluated with respect to norms), but undermine the ascription of blameworthiness. An example for a "joinder of issue", which undermines the fulfillment of default conditions, is that it was not person P who performed the action—it might have looked like that at first sight, but in fact it was person Q.

It is plausible that many of the excuses with regards to blame would also undermine ascriptions of praiseworthiness.[14] Admittedly, "excuse" is only used for the mitigation of blameworthiness, and there is no word for the analogue in the case of praiseworthiness. However, the right kind of intention is important for being praiseworthy, too, and the excuses are precisely those reasons that show that the person did not possess the right kind of intention. If, for example, it turns out that you gave up your seat on the bus only because you wanted to get out at the next bus stop and you didn't notice the old lady at all, her gratitude is not appropriate. This suggests that the lack of proper intention is a challenge to ascriptions not only of blame, but also of praise.

However, there might be asymmetries as to what undermines blame and praise. Susan Wolf, for example, argues that "being psychologically determined to perform good actions is compatible with deserving praise for them, but that being psychologically determined to perform bad actions is not compatible with deserving blame" (Wolf 1990, 79). This means that if a person is so virtuous that she cannot do otherwise than to act morally, this does not undermine praise. Concerning blameworthiness, on the other hand, one might hold that the ability to act otherwise is in fact a condition for blameworthiness. The account of responsibility as defeasible can accommodate asymmetries such as these by noting that the reasons for withdrawing blame might be different from those for withdrawing praise. The crucial point here is that a defeasible structure applies to both, and acknowledging it can help to recognize similarities and differences.

To close the section on challenges, I want to draw attention to two questions that have to be answered by an account that takes the defeasible structure of responsibility-ascriptions seriously: First, the question

14. This is also claimed by Bennett: "It is widely believed, I think rightly, that what stops the performer of a regretted action from being blameworthy is just what stops the performer of a welcomed action from being praiseworthy. Anyway, the two sets of conditions have a large overlap" (Bennett 1980, 15).

of the legitimacy of challenges and second, the question of unrecognized challenges.

Regarding the question of legitimacy, one plausible option is a contextualist position, which implies that the validity of a challenge depends on the specific situation, time and culture. Inadvertence counts as an excuse when stepping on a snail, but not when stepping on a baby.[15] This applies not only to challenges to praise- and blameworthiness, but also to challenges to accountability: In the Middle Ages, being possessed by the devil was generally recognized as an exempting reason, which is not the case today. Also, it seems plausible to assume that at any one time, attributions of responsibility do not follow exactly the same rules in every culture. Therefore, the account suggested here has some weakly relativist consequences. This relativism is weak in the sense that the validity of challenges does not depend on someone's whim, but is grounded in relatively stable social practices. Attributions of responsibility are not the result of arbitrary individual choices, but are governed by the rules of a given social practice, which obligate all participants in the practice.[16]

The second question is how to deal with the fact that there can be challenges that are unknown at a given time. This problem is especially pressing with respect to accountability.[17] A brain disease, for example, that could not be detected fifty years ago, might today count as a reason to exempt a person from being accountable. Yet, fifty years ago, a person would have been considered to be accountable. This means that the possibility of a "gap" between an *ascription* of accountability and the person really *being* responsible can never be excluded. If no exempting reasons can be found even under closest scrutiny at one point in time, one is entitled to ascribe responsibility. However, it may be that a challenge condition exists undiscovered, because the means available at that point in time do not suffice to detect the exempting reason. For this reason, I prefer to talk about the defeasible structure of *ascriptions* of accountability, without thereby implying that the person is without doubt accountable.

15. This is one of Austin's examples (Austin 1961, [orig. 1956], 142).

16. Cf. Willaschek 2010, 574.

17. It seems that ascriptions of praise- or blameworthiness do not suffer from the same epistemic problem. I cannot think of an example of a possible ground for an excuse that cannot in principle be detected at a given time. Therefore, there does not seem to be a gap between ascriptions of praise- or blameworthiness and the person *being* praise- or blameworthy.

4. *The role of challenges in a theory of responsibility*

Up to this point, the defeasible structure of ascriptions of responsibility has been exposed as a procedural feature of our practice of ascribing responsibility. This means that the defeasible structure describes the way in which we in fact proceed in attributing responsibility: If default conditions are fulfilled, we do not have to give reasons for the attribution, but only need to reconsider the ascription in light of challenging reasons. Furthermore, one aspect of this defeasible structure—the challenges—has been used to bring to light a philosophical distinction between two aspects of responsibility, namely accountability and praise- or blameworthiness. After briefly comparing this proposal to Wallace's account, I will further consider the role of the challenges in a theory of responsibility. The central question I will be concerned with is how the negative challenge conditions relate to possible positive conditions for responsibility.

The account presented here accommodates certain elements of Wallace's analysis. The excusing and exempting reasons that Wallace discusses (cf. Wallace 1994, chapters 5 and 6) can be understood as challenge conditions. Therefore, one might have the impression that Wallace already attributes a defeasible structure to ascriptions of responsibility. However, he does not explicitly discuss this question. Rather, he uses the investigation of excuses and exemptions as a means of finding the underlying positive criteria of fairness in ascriptions of responsibility. While important in its own right, this approach does not consider the structural function of excuses and exemptions: Wallace neither discusses the default-and-challenge-structure as a procedural feature of our practice, nor does he regard challenges as means of drawing the distinction between the two aspects of responsibility.

However, Wallace's account points to an important question: Does this defeasible structure, in particular the structure of challenges, reflect exclusively a procedural feature of our practice, while the "real core" of responsibility is accounted for by a set of necessary and sufficient conditions? For Wallace, the conditions for responsibility consist in (a) the possession of powers of reflective self-control and (b) the right kind of intention.[18] H. L. A. Hart, by contrast, takes the radical stance of denying that defeasible concepts can be defined in terms of necessary and sufficient

18. Note that Wallace does not talk about *necessary and sufficient* conditions, but only about accountability conditions and blameworthiness conditions (cf. Wallace 1994, 84).

conditions (Hart 1948/49, 161/162). By advancing this thesis Hart rejects the view that a list of challenges points to the absence of a positive element, which Hart calls the "mental element". If Hart is right, this would mean that the negative conditions, the challenges, are *essential* for the meaning of the defeasible concept. Like Hart, Austin takes this view and puts the thesis very clearly with respect to free agency: "[T]o say that we acted 'freely' [...] is to say only that we acted *not* un-freely [...]. Like 'real', 'free' is only used to rule out the suggestion of some or all of its recognized antitheses" (Austin 1956, 128). According to Austin, we should not assume "that the 'positive' word must be around to wear the trousers; commonly enough the 'negative' (looking) word marks the (positive) abnormality, while the 'positive' word, if it exists, merely serves to rule out the suggestion of that abnormality" (Austin 1956, 140).

Even though the non-definability of defeasible concepts is a central concern for Hart (and Austin), it doesn't stand up to closer scrutiny. There are two reasons Hart gives for denying the existence of positive conditions. The first one is that the list of challenges is open and heterogeneous.[19] However, it seems very plausible that challenges to ascriptions of accountability, as well as challenges to ascriptions of praise or blameworthiness, have some basic features in common, instead of being a random collection of diverse elements. The openness of the list of challenges supports rather than refutes the view that there is a positive element, because otherwise it would be inexplicable why a particular element belongs to the list and why new elements might be included.[20] According to Wallace, excuses point to the fact that a person didn't intend an action, while exemptions point to the fact that a person doesn't possess the relevant psychological capacities to be held responsible for it. These two positive conditions—right intentions and capacities—strike me as plausible positive conditions of responsibility, which Hart mistakenly denies.

However, Hart's second objection against positive conditions illustrates a function of the challenges that Wallace fails to consider—one that high-

19. "[I]t is usually not possible to define a legal concept such as 'trespass' or 'contract' by specifying the necessary and sufficient conditions for its application. For any set of conditions may be adequate in some cases but not in others and such concepts can only be explained with the aid of a list of exceptions or negative examples showing where the concept may not be applied or may only be applied in a weakened form" (Hart 1948/49, 148).

20. Hart does acknowledge this point (the common factor would be "helpful as a summary", "emphasizes the similarities" and may "suggest analogies for the further development of the law" (Hart 1948/49, 150f.)), but he nevertheless insists that this positive condition should not count as a condition for the applicability of the defeasible concept.

lights the importance of the defeasible structure of responsibility ascriptions. The second reason why Hart rejects the positive factor is that in our practice, we don't have to inquire whether a positive condition is fulfilled, but only whether there are challenging reasons.[21] This points to an interesting feature of our practice, which has great pragmatic significance: We don't need direct epistemic access to positive conditions of responsibility such as Hart's "mental elements", but may base our judgments on the absence of challenge conditions.

In concrete cases of ascriptions of responsibility, Hart tells us, we only have *epistemic access* to the fulfillment of the positive conditions via the challenges. Let me call this the "epistemic function" of challenges and illustrate it by considering one of the positive conditions, the psychological capacities. Wallace himself seems to hold that we can ascribe the relevant general abilities to adults by default,[22] but he also mentions that the epistemic access to those powers is a problem, and therefore it is not "always entirely clear which people actually have the powers of reflective self-control" (Wallace 1994, 165). The crucial cases in which we ask whether a person possesses the capacity for reflective self-control at the time of an action are those cases in which the person does *not* exercise this capacity. Whether someone is responsible for what she does depends on whether the person nevertheless *possessed* the capacity. Retrospectively, it is impossible to establish, by empirical observation, if the person possessed the capacity at the time of action, even though she did not exercise it. Therefore, one can only decide about the possession of the relevant capacities by considering challenge conditions.

I want to draw attention to another function of the challenges, which one could call the "grasp-of-degree function". Humans are not purely rational beings who possess reflective self-control in a perfect sense. My claim is that we only understand the capacity for reflective self-control required for moral agency if we know what kinds of negative conditions count as undermining this capacity. More precisely, we only understand what *degree* of reflective self-control is required to count as an accountable

21. "[W]hen we are ascribing an action to a person, the question whether a psychological 'event' occurred does not come up in this suggested positive form at all, but in the form of an inquiry as to whether any of these extenuating defences cover the case" (Hart 1948/49, 163).

22. "I take it that we generally view normal, mature adults as possessing the various general abilities collected under the heading of powers of reflective self-control. These are the sorts of abilities one tends to acquire in the course of a normal upbringing, and in the absence of some specific reason to think otherwise, we presume that the adults we deal with are in possession of these abilities" (Wallace 1994, 163).

agent by considering possible challenges. The concept of accountability must leave room for *some* irrationality—i.e. deficient exercise of the capacity for reflective self-control—because otherwise only perfectly rational beings would be accountable and responsibility for immoral actions would be impossible. Wallace, too, concedes that the capacity for reflective self-control comes in degrees—"it is in the nature of such general capacities that they admit of various levels of development" (Wallace 1994, 159). Because the possession of the relevant capacities is not an all-or-nothing affair, Wallace claims that "a certain *level* of development of these powers (no doubt hard to specify exactly) is an [accountability]-condition of responsibility" (Wallace 1994, 160, my emphasis). Accountability seems to be a "threshold-concept" that can be applied if the person possesses the relevant capacities to a degree beyond a certain level or threshold. However, it seems that this threshold of cognitive competence cannot be specified positively. It is hard to conceive how to characterize the necessary level of normative competence without mentioning what counts as *too little* of this competence. This is why I propose that challenge conditions allow for an understanding of where the threshold for normative competence lies. By specifying mental diseases, for example, the contours of what counts as sufficient possession of the psychological capacities become visible. The "grasp-of-degree function" of the challenges consists in delineating the threshold for distinguishing between capacities that are "enough" for reflective self-control and count as accountable from those that are insufficient.

Conclusion

I argued that ascriptions of moral and legal responsibility can be understood as judgments with a defeasible structure. Ascriptions of both moral and legal responsibility follow a double default-and-challenge-pattern: Given that the agent is an adult (default condition), it is appropriate to hold her accountable; no explicit reason-giving is required for this. In this sense, adults are defeasibly accountable *by default*. However, there are possible *challenges* to the default ascription of accountability: If there is an exempting reason, the agent is not (fully) accountable. If the agent *is* accountable (*default* condition for praise- and blameworthiness), this implies in particular that she is an appropriate addressee for praise or blame, given that she performs an action and this action is evaluated with respect to relevant norms. In this case, the person can be held praise- or blameworthy with respect to her action. Again, no reason-giving is required. Only if there is a valid excuse (*challenge*), will ascriptions of (full) praise- or blameworthiness be defeated.[23]

References

Austin, J. L. 1961 [orig. 1956]: "A Plea for Excuses". In: *Philosophical Papers*. Oxford: Oxford University Press, 123–152.

Bennett, Jonathan 1980: "Accountability". In: Zak van Straaten (ed.), *Philosophical Subjects: Essays Presented to P.F. Strawson*. Oxford: Oxford University Press, 14–47.

Cherry, Christopher 1974: "The Limits of Defeasibility". *Analysis* 34, 101-107.

Fischer, John M. & Ravizza, Mark 1998: *Responsibility and Control. A Theory of Moral Responsibility*. Cambridge: Cambridge University Press.

Geach, Peter T. 1960: "Ascriptivism". *The Philosophical Review* 69, 221–224.

Hart, H. L. A. 1948/49: "The Ascription of Responsibility and Rights". In: Antony Flew (ed.) 1963, *Essays on Logic and Language*. Oxford: Oxford University Press, 145–166.

— 1968: "Postscript: Responsibility and Retribution". In: *Punishment and Responsibility. Essays in the Philosophy of Law*. Oxford: Clarendon Press, 210–237.

Kant, Immanuel 1996: *Metaphysics of Morals* (trans. Mary Gregor). Cambridge: Cambridge University Press.

Pitcher, George 1960: "Hart on Action and Responsibility". *The Philosophical Review* 69, 226–35.

Sneddon, Andrew 2006: *Action and Responsibility*. Dordrecht: Springer.

Stoecker, Ralf 2007: "Action and Responsibility—a Second Look at Ascriptivism". In: Christoph Lumer & Sandro Nannini (ed.), *Intentionality, Deliberation and Autonomy*. Aldershot: Ashgate, 35–46.

Strawson, Peter F. 1963: "Freedom and Resentment". In: Gary Watson (ed.) 2003, *Free Will*. Oxford: Oxford University Press, 72–94.

Wallace, R. Jay 1994: *Responsibility and the Moral Sentiments*. Cambridge, MA: Harvard University Press.

Watson, Gary 1987: "Responsibility and the Limits of Evil. Variations on a Strawsonian Theme". In: Ferdinand Schoeman (ed.), *Responsibility, Character and the*

23. I am grateful for helpful comments, especially from the DDD-group (Claudia Cuadra Carbajal, Mikael Janvid, Hannes Ole Matthiessen and Marcus Willaschek) and Markus Schrenk.

Emotions. New Essays in Moral Psychology. Cambridge: Cambridge University Press, 256–286.
Willaschek, Marcus 2010: "Non-Relativist Contextualism about Free Will". *European Journal of Philosophy* 18(4), 567–587.
Wolf, Susan 1990: *Freedom Within Reason*. Oxford: Oxford University Press.

Grazer Philosophische Studien
87 (2013), 151–155.

COMMENT ON CLAUDIA BLÖSER "THE DEFEASIBLE STRUCTURE OF ASCRIPTIONS OF RESPONSIBILITY"

R. Jay WALLACE
University of California, Berkeley

Claudia Blöser's interesting paper defends the idea that moral and legal responsibility exhibit a defeasible structure. Ascriptions of responsibility to agents are ordinarily justified by default, as long as certain basic conditions are satisfied. But there are further conditions, compatible with the satisfaction of the default standards, that provide a legitimate basis for challenging these ascriptions in particular cases. This "default-and-challenge" structure, Blöser maintains, is essential to the practices of moral and legal accountability. Her aim in the paper is to defend the thesis that responsibility is in this way a defeasible concept, and then to show how attention to the default-and-challenge structure of these practices can help to illuminate hitherto obscure features of them.

There is much that I find convincing in Blöser's treatment of these issues. But I also have a few questions about her account. In my brief remarks, I shall focus on the issue of how exactly the default-and-challenge structure is meant to apply to the cases of moral and legal responsibility; I shall turn at the end to the larger question of whether responsibility can be understood as a defeasible practice if we admit that a unified analysis of its positive conditions can be given. (I shall leave to the side disagreements between Blöser and me about the role of moral sentiments in our practices of responsibility and about the comparative importance of blame vs. praise, as these issues are less germane to the larger themes of this volume.)

Blöser proposes a general framework for understanding responsibility as a defeasible concept. The framework is given by her formula (R), which reads as follows:

> "(R) If a person P with respect to her action A fulfills default conditions, ascribing responsibility to P for A is appropriate, unless there is indication that some challenge-condition holds." (1)

She develops her account by applying the general framework separately to two different aspects of responsibility, accountability and praise- or blameworthiness, suggesting that there might be different default and challenge conditions that serve to specify these two different sides of responsibility. A common and important dimension of the defeasible structure that is allegedly exhibited by responsibility in its different aspects is the idea that the default conditions are strictly compatible with the satisfaction of the challenge conditions (4, 11). To say that a challenge condition obtains, in other words, is not to deny that the agent in question satisfies the default conditions for accountability or praise- and blameworthiness, but to claim that other conditions are present that make it reasonable to challenge the ascription of responsibility to the agent in the situation at hand.

But there are problems that arise when we try to specify more precisely the default and challenge conditions for the cases of accountability and praise- or blameworthiness. Let's start with the latter case. Blöser proposes that the default conditions for praise- or blameworthiness are "that an adult person performed an action A that is evaluated according to valid norms" (12). The challenge conditions here are the ordinary moral excuses, such as inadvertence, mistake, accident, and duress, which function by establishing that the accountable agent did not in fact exhibit the "quality of will" that makes it reasonable to praise or blame them for doing A.

It isn't obvious, however, that the excusing conditions really are compatible with the default conditions in these cases. Take a case where P does A inadvertently—say, P pushes a button on the wall, thinking they are thereby turning on the fan, when in fact their doing so activates a gate at the front entrance, whose movements cause severe damage to the vehicle of a person who is arriving at that moment for the party. According to Blöser's account, the excuse of inadvertence in this example is supposed to be compatible with the satisfaction of the relevant default conditions, including the condition that "P performed an action A, and that the action is evaluated with respect to a relevant norm". But the relevant action description A—the description under which what P did is something that offends against a moral norm—would be something like "causing severe damage to the person or property of another". This, it seems, is not a description that in fact truly applies to any of the things that P intentionally did in pushing the button. Of course, P's pushing the button turned out to cause severe damage to the vehicle that the party guest was driving at the time. But the action was not *intentional* under that description, and so it would be questionable to describe that as something that P *did* or *was doing* at the relevant time, as one of P's *actions* in the strict sense. Or if one wishes to insist that P did in fact perform an action of causing severe property damage to the party guest, the action no longer appears to violate a moral norm under the conditions we have described. In particular, the excuse of inadvertence inhibits blameworthiness precisely because *doing A inadvertently* isn't a case of doing something that is morally objectionable in the first place. So it isn't clear that the challenge conditions in this case really are compatible with the default conditions of blameworthiness that Blöser describes.

In the case of accountability the situation is perhaps different in this respect. The default condition here is supposed to be that the agent is an adult, and this condition is, it seems, generally compatible with the presence of Blöser's challenge conditions. Those conditions include the recognized exemptions from accountability, such as "childhood, insanity or mental illness, addiction, posthypnotic suggestion, behavior control, psychopathy, and the effects of extreme stress, deprivation, and torture." Apart from childhood, these exemptions are all conditions that can literally apply to someone who is an adult, and the compatibility of default and challenge conditions is therefore secured, for the most part. But questions can be raised about Blöser's characterization of the default condition in this case. She herself seems to agree that we can develop a unified positive account of the conditions that make agents morally accountable, proposing that these might be understood in terms of the possession of certain basic forms of normative competence or capacity (10). If this is right, however—and I would of course agree with Blöser in thinking that it is—it suggests a different interpretation of the default conditions of accountability. According to this alternative interpretation, the default condition that renders people accountable in the absence of challenge is not being an adult human being, but being a *morally competent* adult. This is the condition that we naturally assume to be satisfied by those we encounter when we hold them accountable for their actions. Normative competence of this kind, however, is not something that is compatible with the challenge conditions for the case of accountability. The basic capacities for moral understanding and self control, after all, are precisely the conditions that are impaired or absent or underdeveloped in agents who are children, or mentally ill, or subject to addiction or posthypnotic suggestion or behavioral control.

Blöser could avoid this result by simply insisting that the default condition for accountability is being an adult, not being a morally competent adult. She could probably also find a way to tinker with the default condition for praise- and blameworthiness, developing an interpretation on which it could be realized compatibly with the satisfaction of the challenge conditions for these forms of moral status. But the larger question for Blöser's approach is the following. It seems that there are perfectly natural and even plausible ways of characterizing the basic conditions of accountability and blameworthiness that do not exhibit the default-and-challenge structure that Blöser takes to be characteristic of defeasible concepts. In particular, we can understand these conditions as ones that are negated or undermined by the recognized excuses and exemptions, rather than as conditions whose realization is strictly compatible with those challenge conditions. It apparently follows that whether we understand the responsibility concepts to exhibit the default-and-challenge structure will depend on which convention we choose for characterizing the default standards that they involve. But this choice of convention would seem to be a fairly arbitrary matter, insofar as there is no principled basis for preferring one way of characterizing the default conditions over others that are equally available. The defeasible character of our practices of ascribing responsibility then becomes an artifact of the way we decide to describe those practices, rather than something that is genuinely endemic to them.

Blöser draws on Hart's approach to certain legal concepts in developing her account of responsibility as a defeasible concept. As she herself notes, however, it is important to Hart that the concepts he is trying to understand do not lend themselves to analysis in terms of a unified set of necessary and sufficient conditions (20). To say that an action is voluntary, on his approach, is not to say that it exhibits some positive quality that is common to all actions that can be described in these terms, but merely to "exclude a heterogeneous range of cases" that are capable of undermining the ascription of responsibility to the agent. This heterogeneous range of cases is the set of possible challenge conditions for responsibility, and it seems to follow from Hart's basic assumptions that these conditions are in principle compatible with the default conditions for responsibility. If there is no unified positive description that is available of the necessary and sufficient conditions of responsibility, then we have no choice in the matter of whether to describe the default conditions of responsibility in terms that are incompatible with the challenge conditions. We can only say that agents are responsible by default when they are R, *unless* one of conditions a, b, c, d, etc. obtains (where being R is compatible with satisfying one of these challenge conditions). Responsibility is in a certain sense "non-definable", and it is this distinctive feature of it that apparently pushes us toward understanding it in terms of the default-and-challenge structure that Hart develops in his work on defeasibility.

Blöser disagrees with Hart, of course, about the non-definability of responsibility. She shares with several contemporary theorists the conviction that we can give a positive and unified account of the necessary and sufficient conditions of accountability and praise- or blameworthiness, and she contends that this assumption can be married to the idea that these are nevertheless defeasible concepts. But this latter assumption seems to me questionable. Once we accept that there is a positive account available of the conditions of responsibility, we admit as well that there is a correspondingly plausible interpretation of the default conditions of responsibility that rules out the excusing and exempting conditions. The default conditions just are the conditions specified in the positive account: when it comes to accountability, for instance, they would involve *being a morally competent adult*, something that is undermined when the exemptions obtain (e.g. when someone is mentally ill or suffering from severe stress or physical exhaustion). Once we understand accountability in these positive terms, the challenge conditions no longer look to be a heterogeneous grab-bag of possible defeaters, but rather a set of conditions that have something significant in common, namely that they impair or undermine an adult agent's moral competence.

Hart's conviction that responsibility exhibits a default-and-challenge structure seems to be motivated fundamentally by his rejection of a unified positive account of this kind. The question for Blöser is whether she can sustain her interpretation of responsibility as a defeasible practice once she has given up Hart's important assumption that the concept of responsibility resists positive analysis.

Grazer Philosophische Studien
87 (2013), 157–160.

REPLY TO WALLACE

Claudia BLÖSER
Goethe Universität Frankfurt

In his helpful comment, R. J. Wallace raises three interesting questions:

1) Are the default conditions of praise- and blameworthiness compatible with the satisfaction of challenge conditions?
2) What are the default conditions in the case of accountability? In particular, how do the positive conditions relate to the default conditions?
3) How is it possible to combine the idea that there are positive conditions for responsibility with the idea that responsibility is a defeasible concept?

Let us start with the first question. In my proposal, challenge conditions to an ascription of blameworthiness are the ordinary moral excuses, such as inadvertence, mistake, accident, duress. I agree with Wallace that those excuses show that the accountable agent did not exhibit the "quality of will", the intention to violate the norm.

In his comment, Wallace constructs an example showing that an excuse is not compatible with the fulfillment of default conditions, because the excuse points to the fact that the person did not intentionally perform the action, which is referred to in the default conditions: P pushes a button on the wall, thinking she is thereby turning on the fan, when in fact her doing so activates a gate at the front entrance, whose movements cause severe damage to a car. This example shows, according to Wallace, that the excuse "P did A (i.e. 'causing damage to a car') inadvertently" is not compatible with the default conditions "P performed action A and the action is evaluated with respect to a relevant norm", because action A was not intentional under this description and so P did not perform action A in the strict sense.

There are two ways of answering Wallace's objection, both of which help to clarify important aspects of my proposal:

One possible answer is that not *every* objection to an ascription of responsibility has to be compatible with the fulfillment of default conditions. Following H. L. A. Hart, I suggested that there are *joinders of issue* that put the fulfillment of default conditions into question. Wallace's example can be understood as calling attention to a joinder of issue: the fact that the person did not perform action A (at least not in the strict sense, because she did not perform the action intentionally) is a joinder of issue; it shows that default conditions are not fulfilled.

A second answer needs a bit more elaboration. One could ask if *every* excuse points to the fact that P did not perform the action under the description given in the default conditions, i.e. under the description under which the action violates a norm. If all excuses show, as Wallace claims, that the person did not intend the action, it seems that the action-description that fits the person's intention is always different from the action-description that is relevant for the violation of a norm. If this were the case, no excuse would be compatible with the fulfillment of default conditions.

I think we should avoid this consequence in order to rescue the plausible idea behind the claim that excuses are compatible with default conditions. The idea is that the person sees the damage to the car and realizes: "I caused damage to the car, but I didn't intend to do that".

There are three possible ways of adjusting the default conditions in order to answer Wallace's objection:

1) P is praise- or blameworthy for the *consequences* of A, unless there is an excuse, whereby "A" is the action-description under which the action is intentional (in Wallace's example: "pushing the button").
2) P is praise- or blameworthy for *state* A, unless there is an excuse, whereby "state A" is a state in the world which can be brought about non-intentionally (in Wallace's example: "the damage to the car").
3) P is praise- or blameworthy for *action* A, unless there is an excuse, whereby "action A" is intentional under at least one description (in Wallace's example P performed the action of damaging the car, although the action is intentional under another description. The fact that it is not intentional under the description that would make it blameworthy constitutes an excuse.)

Now we turn to the second question: Does the positive condition "being a morally competent adult" belong to the default conditions of accountability? If this were the case, all challenges that refer to mental impairments would be "joinders of issue" (in Hart's sense), i.e. there would be no challenge condition that is compatible with the fulfillment of default conditions.

In my proposal, the possession of the relevant cognitive capacities is a positive condition for accountability, but not part of the default conditions. Wallace seems to think that the choice of characterizing the default conditions is "a fairly arbitrary matter" (4). Yet, there are good reasons for restricting the default condition for accountability to being an adult, so that there is no arbitrariness involved. Default conditions are those minimal conditions under which one can hold persons responsible *without having to give explicit reasons* for doing so. As a general rule, the obtaining of default conditions should be easily observable, as it is normally the case with adulthood. Consequently, the positive condition that a person possesses certain mental capacities cannot belong to the default conditions, because mental capacities are not easily observable. Therefore, there is reason not to identify positive conditions and challenge conditions. Rather, the fulfillment of positive conditions is identical to the fulfillment of default conditions and the *absence of challenge conditions*. Challenges can be understood as undermining the positive conditions, not the default conditions (whereas some challenges—joinders of issue—do so by undermining default conditions).

Finally, let me discuss Wallace's third and most general question of how the claim that there are positive conditions for responsibility can "be married to the idea that these are nevertheless defeasible concepts". Wallace points to the important question of how the positive conditions for responsibility relate to the negative challenge conditions. What is the role of defeasibility if the concept of responsibility has positive necessary and jointly sufficient conditions?

Wallace rightly points out that I don't share H. L. A. Hart's motivation for defeasibility, the non-definability of responsibility. Rather, my motivation is the way we *use* the concept of responsibility in our practice. We don't inquire into the fulfillment of the positive conditions—the possession of relevant mental capacities and the agent's intention—but we are entitled to hold a person responsible if no challenges obtain. Yet, is this defeasible structure of ascribing responsibility merely a pragmatic feature of our practice? As I elaborate towards the end of the fourth section of my paper, I see two irreducible functions of negative conditions for responsibility: First, they have an "epistemic function"—as the positive conditions are empirically unobservable, one has epistemic access to the obtaining of the positive conditions only via the absence of challenge conditions. Second, the "grasp-of-degree function" refers to the fact that without a grasp of the possible challenge conditions we could not understand what degree of reflective self-control (the relevant mental capacity) a person has to possess in order to count as accountable. Only the specific challenges give content to the abstract idea of reflective self-control as a mental capacity that is a necessary condition for responsibility. In sum, even if I agree with Wallace that there are positive conditions for responsibility, I argued that the negative challenge conditions stand in a complementary relation to the positive conditions in a way that makes them indispensable for an understanding of the concept of responsibility.

Grazer Philosophische Studien
87 (2013), 161–176.

CAN A SPASM CAUSE AN ACTION? AN ARGUMENT FOR RESPONSIBILIST THEORIES OF ACTION[1]

Katarzyna PAPRZYCKA
University of Warsaw

Summary

According to causalism, actions are events caused in the right way by appropriate mental states. According to responsibilism, attributions of actions are attributions of responsibility. The notion of action is understood as a complement to the notion of non-action, which is in turn delineated by the presence of defeating conditions. I argue that causalism has a problem in answering the title question negatively. The fact that a spasm causes the arm to rise does not compete with a possible *additional* causal process (with the appropriate mental etiology) that leads to (and overdetermines) the very arm rising.

According to the intentionalist theories of action, actions are events that have a special origin. On the causal theory of action, which is paradigmatic for this approach, actions are those events that have been caused in the right way by appropriate mental states. According to the responsibilist theories (of which H. L. A. Hart's 1951 theory is an example), to attribute an action is to attribute responsibility for events or states of the world. Such attributions are characteristically defeasible—the notion of action is thus understood as a complement to the notion of non-action, which is in turn delineated by the presence of defeating conditions (e.g. spasms, ticks, etc.).

In this paper, I present an argument for the responsibilist accounts of action that is reminiscent of the logical connection argument. The datum

1. The work on the paper has been made possible in part by an NCN grant (DEC-2012/05/B/HS1/02949). I regret that I was unable to attend the conference but I am grateful to the organizers for the invitation. I want to thank especially Claudia Blöser for a very careful reading of the final version of the paper.

for the argument is the immediacy with which we infer that an action of raising an arm, for example, has not occurred given that the agent's arm was hit by a spasm (which caused the arm to rise). This datum is easily explained by responsibilism, according to which there is a logical connection between undefeated defeating conditions and non-actions. I argue that it cannot be so easily explained by the causal theory of action. In fact, it looks like the causal theorist either needs to buttress his position by the responsibilist account or else has to accept the paradoxically looking claim that one can intentionally raise an arm caused by a spasm.

In §1 I sketch the distinction between the two types of theories and show them to have a common root in Aristotle's remarks on what is voluntary. In §2 I sketch Hart's version of responsibilism and point out some advantages of responsibilist theories (§3). In §4, I explain the responsibilist challenge to the causal theorist.

1. *Two types of action theories*

There are two very general ways of looking at action. According to intentionalism, actions are performances that have a special origin. On the causal theory of action, which could be seen to be paradigmatic for this approach, an action is an event that is caused in the right way by appropriate mental states (Brand 1984; Davidson 1963; 1973; Mele 1992; 2003; Searle 1983). But even many of the challengers to the causal theory share the basic intuition. On the ever more popular agent-causal views (Chisholm 1976; Lowe 2008; O'Connor 2000), an action is an event that also has a special origin—it must be caused by the agent. Volitionalist approaches (e.g. Ginet 1990) likewise follow this general line of thinking. What is characteristic about the intentionalist theories is that in order to answer the question whether an agent's performance[2] is an action, one must investigate, for example, whether it was caused in the right way.

According to responsibilism, by contrast, performances by skilled and competent agents are taken to be actions by default. It is only in special circumstances (when conditions that defeat responsibility attributions are present) that agents are taken off the hook, so to speak, and their performances are not counted as actions. This kind of approach to action has

2. The use of the term 'performance' here is theoretical—it is constructed in such a way as to encompass both actions and non-actions—the winkings and the blinkings, the arm raisings and the arm risings, the fallings off the stairs and the runnings down the stairs, etc.

been proposed by H. L. A. Hart (1951), and unfortunately much forgotten since (though see Paprzycka 1997; 2008; Sneddon 2006; Stoecker 2001; 2007).

These two general types of theories of action could be seen to have a source in Aristotle's remarks on the voluntary. Aristotle says:

> What comes about by force or because of ignorance seems to be involuntary. What is forced has an external origin, the sort of origin in which the agent or victim contributes nothing—if, e.g. a wind or human beings who control him were to carry him off.[3]

These remarks can be—and have been—taken to support both views. However, there is a tension between these two theories that is already evident in this quotation. Aristotle clearly recognizes that there are certain circumstances that interfere with our agency, like being pushed by someone or something, being physically forced to do something by someone or something, etc. Aristotle describes those cases as ones where the agent contributes nothing.

Aristotle's account is suggestive of a certain picture of what it means for a performance to be a mere happening rather than an action:

(N_e) The agent's φing was a mere happening (non-action) iff "external forces" caused him to φ.

This may be thought to generate a corresponding picture of what it means for a performance to be an action:

(A_i) The agent's φing was an action iff "internal forces" caused him to φ.

(N_e) captures the central thought of responsibilism while (A_i) captures the central thought of intentionalism. The ideas of "internal forces" and "external forces" are treated as metaphors that need to be elaborated more fully.[4]

---

3. Aristotle, *Nicomachean Ethics*, trans. Terence Irwin (Indianapolis: Hackett, 1985), 1110a1–4.

4. The distinction is not (as suggested by the form of words Aristotle sometimes uses) between forces outside and inside the agent, for there can be the wrong kind of forces inside the agent (spasms, e.g.), and there may be the right kind of outside forces (e.g. when someone helps an old person through the street). See also Frankfurt (1988).

The logical relationship between (A_i) and (N_e) is far from clear. It might appear that the claims are equivalent. Closer inspection, however, shows that this is not so—not unless the following claims are true:

(A-N) a performance is an action just in case it is not a mere happening (non-action),

(i-e) "internal forces" caused α to φ iff "external forces" did not cause α to φ.

The former claim is the least problematic of the two: we can view the concepts of action and non-action as complementary (relative to a class of performances). Given (A-N), we can establish that what follows from (N_e) is:

(A_e) the agent's φing was an action iff it was not caused by "external forces."

Analogically, what follows from (A_i) is:

(N_i) the agent's φing was a mere happening iff it was not caused by "internal forces."

What is puzzling, however, is whether (i-e) is true. According to (i-e), causation by "internal forces" precludes causation by "external forces." *Prima facie* it is not clear why these two types of forces should exclude one another. Why could they not jointly cause the performance?

Responsibilism provides an answer to this question. It begins with a substantive account of what it means for "external forces" to cause an agent's performance (N_e) and then explains what it means for the agent to act by appealing to the absence of such forces (A_e). From its point of view, the idea of "internal forces" causing the performances is a hypostatization of the absence of such causation by "external forces." In other words, the responsibilists take (i-e) to be providing a reductive definition of what it means for the "internal forces" to be in operation. The proper theoretical work is done by the idea of the absence of "external forces." The notion of action is thus understood as a complement to the notion of non-action (of a mere happening). Non-actions in turn are understood in terms of the presence of defeating conditions (e.g. spasms, ticks, etc.).

Causalism, on the other hand, begins with a substantive account of what it means for "internal forces" to cause an agent's performance (A_i). It thus cannot adopt the responsibilist interpretation of (i-e). In accepting the claim (N_i), that it is the lack of causation by "internal forces" that explains why a performance is a mere happening rather than an action, causalism opens itself to the possibility that an action can be caused by "external forces," for the performance could be determined by both types of causal processes. This is the core of the responsibilist challenge (§4), to which we will turn after a brief reminder of Hart's theory of action (§2) and some of its advantages (§3).

2. *H. L. A. Hart's theory of action*

Hart argued that the concept of action is essentially a normative and a social concept that presupposes accepted rules of conduct. A good analogy is the concept of property. Just as it does not make sense to think that a statement like "Smith owns this piece of land" is a sentence that is "concerned wholly with an individual" (Hart 1951, 161), so statements like "Smith did it" likewise cannot be understood as being about one individual only. According to Hart, the main thrust of action statements is to attribute ("ascribe" in Hart's language) responsibility for certain events or states of the world[5] to individuals on the basis of generally accepted rules of conduct.

On Hart's view, action claims are ascriptive rather than descriptive.[6] They are never true or false; they are appropriate or inappropriate in view of relevant conditions. Transposed from the formal into the material mode, there are no actions in the world. Our distinction between actions and mere happenings is not ontological but normative. It is to be made in terms of the appropriateness of ascribing responsibility for events or states of the world (when we intuitively think of them as actions) and the inappropriateness of ascribing responsibility for

5. It is not exactly clear on Hart's account what ontological category the variable x ranges over in the expression 'α is responsible for x'. Some critics (e.g. Pitcher 1960) have charged Hart with the view that the variable ranges over actions, thus rendering Hart's account circular. But, most of the time (except for a non-committal statement on the first page of his paper), Hart is quite careful not to talk this way. (For details, see Paprzycka 1997, ch. 2. See also Sneddon 2006; Stoecker 2007.)

6. Hart's ascriptivism has been a source of additional problems (see e.g. Geach 1960; Paprzycka 1997; Sneddon 2006; Stoecker 2007).

events or states of the world (when we intuitively think of them as mere happenings).

The structure of action attribution is characteristically defeasible. First, there are, in Hart's terminology, positive conditions that establish the prima facie applicability of the responsibility attribution. When attribute to John the action of breaking the window, the positive conditions might include John's arm moving in such a way that the glass is broken. Second, there are negative (defeating) conditions that defeat the prima facie appropriateness of ascribing responsibility to the agent. Such conditions include John's arm moving because of a spasm, say, or John's being pushed by someone. When we learn that somebody pushed John and that John smashed the window as a result, we will no longer attribute responsibility to John for breaking the window. It will thus be inappropriate to say that John's breaking the window was his action.

It should be pointed out, however, that defeating conditions can themselves be defeated. Suppose that John ordered, or even coerced, the person to push him so that the window is broken. Such a condition defeats the original defeating condition. As a result, it is reasonable to hold John to be responsible for breaking the window after all. He did it in an unusual way but he did break the window.

This structure allows us to understand the difference between actions and mere happenings or between it being appropriate and it being inappropriate to ascribe responsibility to an agent. It will be inappropriate to ascribe responsibility to the agent if either no positive conditions are present or while the positive conditions are present some (undefeated) defeating condition occurs. It will be appropriate to ascribe responsibility to the agent only if the positive conditions occur and no (undefeated) defeating conditions are present.

Hart's project is to understand the nature of action by getting a better understanding of the structure in particular of the negative (defeating) conditions. He is extremely skeptical about the intentionalist project and suggests that any concept that aspires to distinguishing between actions and mere happenings in fact does so only insofar as it can claim to capture the notorious variety of negative conditions. He says:

> These positive-looking words 'intention', etc., if put forward as necessary conditions of all action only succeed in posing as this if in fact they are a comprehensive and misleadingly positive-sounding reference to the absence of one or more of the defences, and are thus only understandable when interpreted in the light of the defences, and not vice versa. Again, when we are

> ascribing an action to a person, the question whether a psychological 'event' occurred does not come up in this suggested positive form at all, but in the form of an inquiry as to whether any of these extenuating defences cover the case. (1951, 163).

In this passage, Hart gives expression to the characteristic responsibilist view that the concept of "internal force causation" is to be understood in terms of the absence of certain defeating conditions ("defences"). In other words, claim (i-e) is to be taken as a reductive definition of the concept of "internal force causation."

3. *The charm of responsibilism*

While it is beyond the scope of this paper to go into the details of responsibilist positions, I want to mention certain immediate advantages of the accounts especially vis a vis intentionalist conceptions of action.

The general structure of responsibilist accounts can be perhaps cast in the following way.[7] Our attributions of actions of φing to agents presuppose that we take the agents to be in control over φing. When α is in control of φing and φs, α's φing is an action.

Normally we take ourselves to be—and indeed are—in control of various ordinary activities (raising arms, moving feet, reaching for glasses, pouring milk, running, writing, etc.). Arguably the range of activities that we are in control of will depend on the individual—some of us can juggle, dance or raise arms in graceful ways, some of us cannot dance, cannot speak French, and may be incapable of raising our arms. However, the very application of the concept of action in our social lives presupposes that the range of activities that we are in control of overlaps quite a bit. The understanding of the idea of what it is to be in control of φing includes at the very least that the agent is capable of reliably fulfilling the task to φ (and the task not to φ).[8]

7. This is very tentative and vague. I develop some of the concepts mentioned here at a greater length in (Paprzycka 1997). In particular, I argue that the concept of being in control of is to be understood in terms of reasonable normative expectations, and I show how defeating conditions affect the reasonableness of such expectations. However, for one, I do not doubt that there are other ways of developing these thoughts. Moreover, for the purposes of this paper, the development of the whole theoretical machinery would obscure the main argument rather than making it more intelligible.

8. A. Baier (1971) has sketched an approach to action where the idea of a task plays a central role.

Defeating conditions—or Hart's negative conditions—are conditions that affect the agent's control over an activity. When someone breaks a leg, she is no longer in control of running or even walking briskly. When someone acquires a tick, he cannot be relied upon to wink as a sign to start a revolt.

The heart of the responsibilist account involves understanding these key concepts, what it is for the agent to be in control of φing and how various conditions can affect this control. Once the responsibilist demonstrates that most agents indeed are in control of φing, where 'φ' ranges over "common" action types, he entitles himself to the characteristic feature of responsibilist theories, viz. that such action types lie within the agentive purview by default. With respect to them, we are guilty of being agents until proven innocent, so to speak.[9] According to the responsibilist, one does not need to demonstrate any special origin for a performance to count as action as long as it is a performance of a type that falls within the range of those that are within the agent's power or control. Of course, such judgments are defeasible—they are sensitive to the occurrence of any circumstances that affect the agent's control over those types of actions.

It is thus that spontaneous actions (actions done for no reason), for example, present no special problem for the responsibilist. There is no need to find underlying reasons for one's singing in the shower, no need for momentary desires, no need for intentions-in-action. The agent's particular state of mind is largely irrelevant. The agent may be engrossed in thoughts about something completely different. He may be singing because it is his habit, or perhaps because he hears a radio playing a tune, or perhaps really for no reason. According to the responsibilist there is nothing wrong in any of these suggestions. If he just happens to be singing in the shower, it is his action unless something untoward happens. If it turns out, for example, that an evil scientist manipulates the agent's vocal cords in ways that result in the characteristic sounds escaping through the water vapor, that would count as a defeating condition and the characteristic sounds would no longer qualify as something of which the person is an agent. But it is a theoretical mistake to try to postulate metaphysical constructs like "proximal intention," "intention-in-action," "volition," etc. to cover the absence of the defeating conditions. There simply is

9. The thought that some performances acquire the status of actions (indeed intentional actions) by default is present in R. Brandom's (1994) account (see esp. pp. 257ff). While Brandom officially adheres to a causal account of action, this thought makes him a potential responsibilist.

no need to do it as long as one has a good account of what counts as a non-action.

Likewise wayward causal chain cases do not present any special problems for the responsibilist.[10] Examples such as Davidson's (1973) mountaineer case fall into the same bag with other non-actions. They do not present any special problem or indeed any special category for the responsibilist. Recall that the nervous mountaineer becomes nervous because he intends to let go of his partner (attached to a rope) but this intention makes him so nervous—his palms begin to sweat, he begins to shake—that the rope slides out of his fingers. The problem for the causalist is that there appears to be the requisite origin for agent's releasing the rope—its cause appears to be the intention to let go of the rope. The responsibilist will take the releasing of the rope as an action of the mountaineer by default (releasings of ropes as well as holdings on to ropes are the sort of action that it is within the mountaineer's power to perform). However, in this case there is a defeating condition. The extreme nervousness (palm sweating, hands shaking), never mind what caused it, defeats the prima facie attribution of responsibility to the agent because it shows that he was not in control of such activities after all.

For similar reasons, the responsibilist is open to the idea of letting in as actions cases that are notoriously problematic for the intentionalist because the requisite "internal forces" seem to be missing. This has been claimed to be so in case of arational actions (Hursthouse 1991), habitual actions (Pollard 2003; 2006), nonintentional actions (Chan 1995), unintentional omissions (Smith 1984; 1990), as well as mistakes and slips (Peabody 2005).

4. *The responsibilist challenge*

So far I have presented some reasons for thinking that a responsibilist account might be worthwhile considering. Let me now turn the tables and suggest that there is a reason to favor responsibilism.

10. I am only speaking here of the so-called antecedential wayward causal chain cases, of which Davidson mountaineer example is paradigmatic. From a responsibilist perspective, the first question in action theory is the question what the difference between an action and a non-action is. It is only later that the question of what makes some actions intentional is taken up. The antecedential wayward causal chain cases affect the judgment of whether an action was performed. The consequential wayward causal chain cases are cases where the action has been performed but the waywardness affects the issue whether the action has been intentional.

The central thought behind the responsibilist theories is that there is a logical connection between the presence of (undefeated) defeating conditions and mere happenings. When a spasm hits one's arm, the resulting movement is not an arm raising, a voting, or a showing of one's courage; it is simply *not* an action. This can be couched in a claim drawn from (N_e):

(1) If a spasm causes an arm to rise, *ceteris paribus* the arm rising is not an action.[11]

The challenge to the causalist is to explain why (1) holds.

The causalist answer will presumably invoke the fact that the arm rising was not caused by an appropriate mental state, proximate intention say (see Mele 1992; 2003; Mele & Moser 1994; for similar views see Brand 1984; Thalberg 1984).[12] He might make us look at the spasmatic arm rising and make us acknowledge that no intention is doing the causing (though it is hard to conceive how this could be accomplished while keeping our responsibilist intuitions at bay). But even if we acknowledge this in a particular case, we should worry that the causalist cannot exclude the possibility that the spasm is *also* caused by an intention after all. An arm rising in a spasm is a causal process: its effect is the rising of the arm, and its cause is a certain neural activation. But the causal effect—the rising of the arm could be *overdetermined*—it could have another cause: the agent's intention. Since the intentionalist is committed to the claim that actions are actions in virtue of their intentional etiology, he would have to say that the rising of the arm in such an overdetermined case is an action. This is strongly counterintuitive.

Let us consider how Mele and Moser (1994) handle Davidson's mountaineer case. They suggest that the case presents no problem to the causal account because the mountaineer's letting go of a rope is not proximally caused by an intention but rather by his state of nervousness. The question that the responsibilists are posing is: on what basis are we excluding causation by an intention?

Granted, it may of course turn out—in the mountaineer case—that after the intention to let go of the rope causes the state of nervousness,

11. The *ceteris paribus* clause is important, since we need to remember that the logical relations advocated on the responsibilist account are defeasible (see also footnote 14).

12. I am focusing here on a certain version of the causal theory of action. I believe, however, that the challenge is quite general and that it affects most versions of what I have called the intentionalist approach to action.

it expires. Thereafter, the state of nervousness takes over and causes the releasing of the rope and of the partner attached to it (Fig. 1).

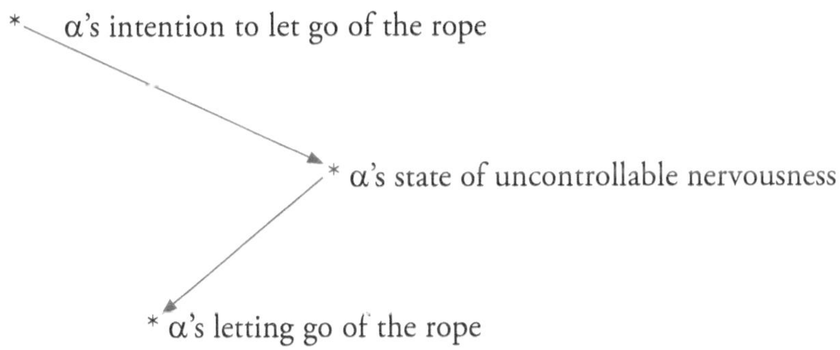

Fig. 1. *The structure of Davidson's mountaineer case as reconstructed by Mele and Moser (1994)*

However, might it not also happen that the picture be rather different? Rather than expiring the intention may continue to be at work, it may be a little "surprised" by sweaty palms' cooperation but it may continue to cause the behavior:

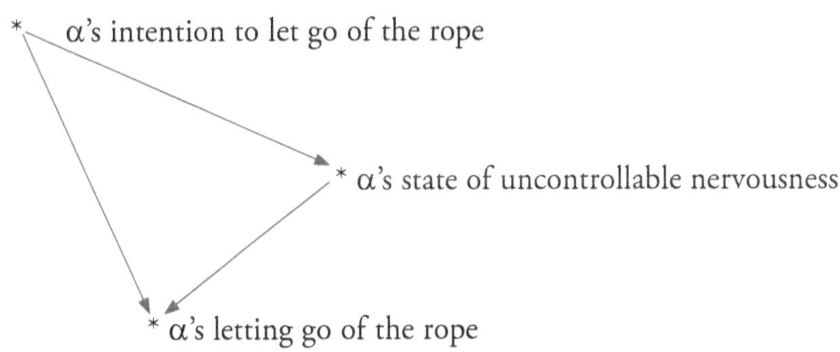

Fig. 2. *An alternative structure of the mountaineer case*

In other words, the intention causes the mountaineer to be so nervous that he uncontrollably lets go of his rope but at the same time the intention causes the letting go of the rope. The effect is causally overdetermined.

In such a case, however, the causalist should say that α's letting go of the rope is an action since it was proximally caused by the intention. The fact that it was caused by something else too—even if it was an uncontrollable state of nervousness—is of no consequence.

The responsibilist, by contrast, argues that such a situation is incoherent. We simply cannot even begin to envisage an agent who intentionally performs an action caused by an uncontrollable state of nervousness. There is a logical conflict between the uncontrollable state of nervousness and actionhood (and *eo ipso* any suggestion of the movement being intentional).[13]

Mele and Moser actually consider another case, where they do allow the intention to operate in conjunction with a state of nervousness. Let us consider it too, though it should be clear that the case differs substantially from the Davidsonian mountaineer case. G. M. Wilson (1989) speaks about a weight-lifter whose intention causes a state of nervousness but that very state is in fact necessary for the weight-lifter to do what he intends (to lift a very heavy weight). In Wilson's case, the agent succeeds in part because the nervous state of his body is conducive to the attainment of his goal. In Davidson's original case, the state of the agent's body is also conducive to the attainment of his goal but it is moreover such that the agent completely loses control over what he does. Were he to decide, or were he to be ordered, not to let go of his partner, he would have let go of him anyway. This is not the case in Wilson's story. The nervousness does not function as a defeating condition, it does not affect the control over the movements in the way it does in the mountaineer case.

Mele and Moser diagnose Wilson's case differently. They think that the problem in the mountaineer case concerns the fact that there is no direct connection between intention and behavior, while in Wilson's case there is a connection between intention and behavior.

This, however, does not alleviate the worry as we posed it. Since it is possible for an intention to do the causal work together with a state of nervousness, on what grounds are we excluding a case where an agent intentionally performs a movement caused by an uncontrollable spasm?[14]

13. In his (2003) book, Mele considers a number of variations on the mountaineer case that differ from one another in the extent to which the movement (the letting go of the rope) is caused by the intention and by the nervousness. But in all of the cases, the uncontrollable nervousness is seen to stand in conflict and so to exclude the intention. Here is a representative illustration, where Mele speaks of an agent, Clem, who is not performing an action of loosening his grip on the rope because "no intention of his is playing this role; Clem's nervousness prevents that by temporarily depriving him of control over the motions of his hands" (p. 60).

14. But might a spasmatic movement (arm rising) not be an agent's action after all? Suppose that an amicable neuroscientist identifies just the neural activation required for the production

The responsibilist puts forward the following question to the causalist: Is it possible for an intention to cause an arm rising in a spasm? If the causalist gives a negative answer then the responsibilist triumphs because she will argue that the causalist must appeal to the responsibilist conceptual resources in order to substantiate the impossibility claim. If the causalist gives a positive answer then the responsibilist triumphs again because the causalist account is thus shown to lead to the acceptance of an incoherent case as an example of an action by the agent.

5. *Conclusion*

We started with a datum: when an arm rises because of a spasm, we immediately infer that the arm rising is not an action. This datum is easily explained by responsibilism, according to which there is a logical connection between (undefeated) defeating conditions and non-actions. It is much more problematic to explain the datum on the causal theory of action. The fact that a spasm causes the arm to rise *prima facie* does not compete with a possible *additional* causal process that leads to (and overdetermines) the very arm rising. This additional process *could* after all have the appropriate sort of mental etiology. If that were so then the causal theorist should conceive it as a possibility that a spasm cause an action, which seems to contradict the datum.

While the challenge as presented is directed at the causal theory of action, it can be extended to intentionalist theories of action more generally. The challenge is to use the resources of the theory in question—independently of the responsibilist ones—to explain why the occurrence of a defeating condition (such as a spasm) precludes a performance from counting as an action.

---

of a spasmatic arm rising. He constructs a little apparatus wired up to an agent, John, in such a way that when a red button is pressed, the appropriate neurons are activated, causing a sudden arm rising. John being a curious person he is, upon learning about the functioning of the button, immediately wants to try it out. He presses the button, causing a jerky rising of his own arm. Is this an action of John's? The responsibilist will answer positively. This is because the defeating power of the defeating condition (the spasm) has now been defeated. John is in control over that condition. The details of the case are not as important now as the realization that the structure of such a case is very different from the cases we have been considering so far. Moreover, such cases are in fact problematic for the causalist because they appear to resemble their diagnosis of the original mountaineer case. The intention causes the button depression but is no longer doing any work from then onwards.

My suspicion is that the problem can be put to rest once causalist (and, more generally, intentionalist) theories recognize their place in the conceptual space of action theory. They are best thought of as theories designed to answer not the problem of action (what is the difference between an action and a mere happening?) but rather the problem of the intentionality of action (when is an action intentional?). The thought that the notion of intentional action is the key in particular to the understanding of the notion of action has been an unfortunate dogma in contemporary action theory and has rightly come under fire. In fact, much of the theoretical pressure on the concept of intentional action derives from the perceived need for the concept of intentional action to ground the concept of action. It is useful in this context to remind oneself of Austin's remark:

> I sit in my chair, in the usual way—I am not in a daze or influenced by threats or the like: here it will not do to say either that I sat in it intentionally or that I did not sit in it intentionally… (Austin 1961, p. 190)

In contrast to causalism (and intentionalism more generally), responsibilism is designed first and foremost to answer the problem of action. By showing that the concept of action can be understood independently of the concept of intentional action, responsibilism offers a good background for work on the concept of intentional action, which should be devoid of pressures to stretch the concepts.

References

Austin, J. L. 1970: "A Plea for Excuses". In: *Philosophical Papers.* London: Oxford University Press, 175–204.

Baier, Annette 1970: "The Search for Basic Actions". *American Philosophical Quarterly* 8, 161–170.

Brand, Myles 1984: *Intending and Action. Toward a Naturalized Action Theory.* Cambridge, MA: The MIT Press.

Brandom, Robert 1994: *Making It Explicit.* Cambridge, MA: Harvard University Press.

Chan, David K. 1995: "Nonintentional Actions". *American Philosophical Quarterly* 32, 139–152.

Chisholm, Roderick M. 1976: *Person and Object.* La Salle, IL: Open Court.

Davidson, Donald 1963: "Actions, Reasons, and Causes". Reprinted in: *Essays on Actions and Events.* Oxford: Clarendon Press, 1980, 3–19.
— 1973: "Freedom to Act". Reprinted in: *Essays on Actions and Events.* Oxford: Clarendon Press, 1980, 63–81.
Frankfurt, Harry 1988: "The Problem of Action". In: *The Importance of What We Care About.* Cambridge: Cambridge University Press, 69–79.
Geach, Peter T. 1960: "Ascriptivism". Reprinted in: *Logic Matters.* Berkeley, CA: University of California Press, 1972, 250–254
Ginet, Carl 1990: *On Action.* Cambridge: Cambridge University Press.
Hart, H. L. A. 1951: "The Ascription of Responsibility and Rights". In: Anthony Flew (ed.), *Essays on Logic and Language.* Oxford: Blackwell, 145–166.
Hursthouse, Rosalind 1991: "Arational Actions". *Journal of Philosophy* 88, 57–68.
Lowe, E. Jonathan 2008: *Personal Agency. The Metaphysics of Mind and Action.* Oxford: Oxford University Press.
Mele, Alred R. 1992: *Springs of Action.* Oxford: Oxford University Press.
— 2003: *Motivation and Agency.* Oxford: Oxford University Press.
Mele, Alred R., & Moser, Paul K. 1994: "Intentional Action". *Nous* 28, 39–68.
O'Connor, Timothy 2000: *Persons and Causes. The Metaphysics of Free Will.* Oxford: Oxford University Press.
Paprzycka, Katarzyna 1997: *Social Anatomy of Action. Toward a Responsibility-Based Account of Agency.* Ph.D. Dissertation, University of Pittsburgh.
— 2008: "Sneddon on Action and Responsibility". *Polish Journal of Philosophy* 2, 69–88.
Peabody, Kay 2005: "Trying Slips: Can Davidson and Hornsby Account for Mistakes and Slips?". *Philosophia* 35, 173–216.
Pitcher, George 1960: "Hart on Action and Responsibility". *The Philosophical Review* 69, 226–235
Pollard, Bill 2003: "Can Virtuous Actions Be both Habitual and Rational". *Ethical Theory and Moral Practice* 6, 411–425
Pollard, Bill 2006: "Explaining Actions with Habits". *American Philosophical Quarterly* 43, 57–68
Searle, John R. 1983: *Intentionality. An Essay in the Philosophy of Mind.* Cambridge: Cambridge University Press.
Smith (Milanich), Patricia G. 1984: "Allowing, Refraining, and Failing. The Structure of Omissions". *Philosophical Studies* 45, 57–67
Smith, Patricia G. 1990: "Contemplating Failure: The Importance of Unconscious Omission". *Philosophical Studies* 59, 159–176
Sneddon, Andrew 2006: *Action and Responsibility.* Dordrecht: Springer Academic Press.
Stoecker, Ralf 2001: "Agents in Action". *Grazer Philosophische Studien* 61, 21–42.

Stoecker, Ralf 2007: "Action and Responsibility—A Second Look at Ascriptivism". In: Christoph Lumer & Sandro Nannini (eds.), *Intentionality, Deliberation and Autonomy: The Action-Theoretic Basis of Practical Philosophy*. Aldershot: Ashgate, 35–46.

Wilson, George M. 1989: *The Intentionality of Human Action*. Stanford, CA: Stanford University Press.

Grazer Philosophische Studien
87 (2013), 177–195.

AUTONOMOUS BY DEFAULT. ASSESSING "NON-ALIENATION" IN JOHN CHRISTMAN'S CONCEPTION OF PERSONAL AUTONOMY

Michael QUANTE
Westfälische Wilhelms-Universität Münster

Summary
The condition "identification-with" plays a prominent role in contemporary hierarchical analyses of personal autonomy. Objections to these accounts have prompted refinements of the hierarchical analysis and the notion of identification within them. John Christman, having developed such a more fine-grained hierarchical analysis over the last twenty years, has argued recently that the condition of identification-with should be replaced by a condition of non-alienation in such accounts. In this paper, this theoretical move is criticized and the thesis is defended that we should base accounts of personal autonomy on a default-and-challenge structure in general instead of replacing "identification-with" by "non-alienation".

> What ensures that we accept our love without equivocation, and what thereby secures the stability of our final ends, is that we have confidence in the controlling tendencies and responses of our own volitional character.
>
> Harry G. Frankfurt

Over the last twenty years, John Christman has developed a comprehensive conception of personal autonomy that starts from Harry G. Frankfurt's and Gerald Dworkin's higher-order-theories. In doing so he has oriented his work towards the problems that arise for Frankfurt's account. A crucial advancement of Christman's conception consists in integrating a historical component that takes the process of acquiring beliefs and desires within a person's biography into account for the assessment of the person's autonomy (see Christman 1991 and 1993). Beyond this, Christman's conception reacts to further developments within the debate about personal autonomy: Even though he still groups himself with the individualist camp, his newest conception is meant to capture also the social dimension of human persons, which is treated under the heading of relational autonomy. Thereby he incorporates central insights of the communitarian critique of individualist conceptions of autonomy, although he seeks to stay within the framework of liberalism. Finally, it is worth noting that Christman tries to guard his conception against the objection of being too intellectualist or rationalist, by including the affective and the bodily dimension of human persons. It is particularly this last aspect by which Christman seeks to dismantle the charge that a higher-order-theory is too demanding, that it asks too much of the finite subjects human beings simply are, and that it leads to the ethically inacceptable result that many decisions and indications of wishes by human beings, which we intuitively recognize as expressions of their autonomy and respect prima facie, do not count as autonomous. In other words, a conception of personal autonomy that is too demanding in the end yields an encroaching paternalistic practice and at the same time provides a philosophical justificatory basis for it (cf. Beauchamp 2005, 317–321 or Taylor 2009, chaps. 3 and 4).

Against this general background of the debate about personal autonomy and the developments of John Christman's conception that are to be located within that debate, I here want to deal with an aspect that comes up especially in the newest statement of his view: The replacement of the condition of "identification-with" that is central to Frankfurt's account by the condition of "non-alienation."[1] To do so, I will first briefly reconstruct Christman's conception of personal autonomy as it is presented in his *The Politics of Persons* (1). Then I will trace his critique of the condition of "identification-with" and his alternative condition of "non-alienation" (2). Finally, I will critically examine Christman's proposal and suggest why it is more promising to model personal autonomy in general on a conception of default-and-challenge (3).

1. By the "newest statement" of Christman's conception of personal autonomy I mean the one he develops in *The Politics of Persons*. For reasons that will become clear in the course of my analysis I include Christman's discussion of the relation between "identification-with" and "alienation," as it is presented in an earlier essay (Christman 2001).

1. *Christman's conception of personal autonomy in* The Politics of Persons

The emphasis of his account is, as Christman puts it, "more on the conditions of authenticity rather than competence" (Christman 2009, 155). My contribution is focused on the conditions of authenticity only insofar as it is within them that the replacement of "identification-with" by "non-alienation" takes place. Since many other aspects relevant to or problematic about a conception of personal autonomy are blinded out in the following, it is irrelevant for the purposes of this contribution that the "account of competence" Christman presents here is, according to his own assessment, "clearly incomplete" (Christman 2009, 155).

As a summary of conditions of personal autonomy, which he up to that point develops in much detail by dealing with criticism of higher-order-theories of personal autonomy, Christman offers the following conception:

> [A]utonomy can be specified as obtaining if the following conditions hold (as elaborated in the previous discussion): Relative to some characteristic C, where C refers to basic organizing values and commitments, autonomy obtains if:
>
> (Basic Requirements—Competence):
> 1. The person is competent to effectively form intentions to act on the basis of C. That is, she enjoys the array of competence that are required for her to negotiate socially, bodily, affectively, and cognitively in ways necessary to form effective intentions on the basis of C;
> 2. The person has the general capacity to critically reflect on C and other basic motivating elements of her psychic and bodily make-up; and
>
> (Hypothetical Reflection Condition—Authenticity):
> 3. Were the person to engage in sustained critical reflection on C over a variety of conditions in light of the historical processes (adequately described) that gave rise to C; and
> 4. She would not be alienated from C in the sense of feeling and judging that C cannot be sustained as part of an acceptable autobiographical narrative organized by her diachronic practical identity; and
> 5. The reflection being imagined is not constrained by reflection-distorting factors. (2009, 155)

It is important to note that this is an account of *personal* autonomy since the historical (or biographical) dimension is integrated therein (via conditions 3 and 4) and that not being alienated is a necessary condition for a person being personally autonomous relative to some characteristic C.

Furthermore, one minor clarification is in order: Although presented as necessary conditions only this set of conditions is, as Christman himself states, "meant generally as sufficient conditions for autonomy" (Christman 2009, 156).

In the non-technical "prose" following this definition of personal autonomy Christman describes his conception this way:

> Autonomy involves competence and authenticity; authenticity involves non-alienation upon (historically sensitive, adequate) self-reflection, given one's diachronic practical identity and one's position in the world. (Christman 2009, 155)

It is evident that Christman's recent conception relies heavily on this condition of non-alienation and, thereby, on the conception of "alienation" which is in the background. Therefore in the next section of this paper I will go into the details of this part of Christman's conception of personal autonomy.

2. *From questions of identity to questions of alienation*

In a footnote, Christman himself characterizes the strategy he follows in developing his account of personal autonomy further this way:

> What I have done is urge that we shift our focus, from what identity *is* to conditions in which it is importantly constricted; that is from questions of identity to questions of alienation. (Christman 2009, 214 fn. 11)

Therefore it is helpful to have a look at his objections against the condition of "identification-with" at first, before going into the details of his condition of "non-alienation".

2.1 *Christman's critique of the condition of "identification-with"*

Christman's critique of conceptions of personal autonomy that refer to a condition of identification can be summarized in the following two points: first, he holds that the condition of identification is ambiguous, for it oscillates between the mere recognition that a certain trait applies to me, and the positive valuation of the fact that the trait in question applies to me (see Christman 2009, 143 and Christman 2001, 203).[2] Second,

2. In the following I will refer to mere recognition without an evaluative dimension by *identification-as* and to a form of recognition that expresses an evaluative self-relationship by

he takes this condition, when it is understood in the former sense, to be too weak to guarantee personal autonomy, for in that case an evaluative self-relationship would be lacking (Christman 2001, 203). On the other construal the condition would be too strong, since it would require a "wholehearted endorsement" (ibid., 202 fn. 44) that would make for "full[.] identification-with" (ibid., 2003; see Christman 2009, 143f.). In contrast, Christman takes the condition of non-alienation he proposes to be both stronger, for mere recognition without an evaluative component is insufficient (Christman 2001, 203), and weaker, because it allows not only for cases of wholehearted endorsement in which I fully identify with one of my traits as guaranteeing autonomy (Christman 2009, 143f. and Christman 2001, 202).

Christman's reflections are not directed primarily against attempts at explicating the condition of identification in the sense of a purely theoretical self-ascription (= identification-as) of a trait; this is why we shall disregard this line in the demarcation of his account. The point he deems central is that the evaluative reading some conceptions of personal autonomy give of the condition of identification makes for too strong requirement. This he takes to lead to a situation in which human beings are in principle confronted with an excessive demand due to such a conception of autonomy, and in which some cases are ruled out as cases of autonomy, even though we would normally recognise them as instances of personal autonomy and respect them accordingly.

If this critique is to be successful as a justification of Christman's alternative proposal to replace the condition of identification-with by the condition of non-alienation, then it must be possible to show, first, that his conception does not suffer from such an ambiguity of its central criterion, and second, that it can sidestep the effect of excessive demand the criticised conceptions are reproached for.

2.2 *Christman's condition of "non-alienation"*

We should note first that Christman's critique of conceptions of personal autonomy that work with a condition of identification in the sense of endorsement (= identification-with) is given to misunderstanding. In some places it seems as though he wants to introduce his condition of

identification-with. For a discussion of the distinction between "identification-as" and "identification-with" in the context of personal autonomy see Quante 2002, chap. 5 and Quante 2007a, chaps. 7–9.

non-alienation as an alternative to endorsement. But in some more explicit places it becomes clear that he wants it to be understood as an alternative to the demand of wholehearted endorsement:

> Alienation is a stronger reaction; it involves feeling constrained by the trait and wanting decidedly to *repudiate* it. (Christman 2009, 143f.; see Christman 2001, 203).

Thereby he commits to a very strong reading of Frankfurt's conception, which can be evidenced in Frankfurt's texts, but that does not adequately represent Frankfurt's position.[3] Now I do not want to deal with the question whether Christman's critique is based on the best possible interpretation of Frankfurt's work. But this ambiguity in Christman's stage-setting is also systematically relevant, for it entails three ambiguities of his own conception.

(i) In analogy to the oscillation between "endorsement" and "wholehearted endorsement" we have identified in Christman's characterisation of the conception he criticises, his own conception implies an oscillation between "alienation" and "deep alienation." This leads to an ambiguity in his condition of "non-alienation," for it is unclear whether this is to exclude only cases of deep alienation or also weaker forms of alienation. Alienation consists in a person's not wholeheartedly confirming a trait, deep alienation requires, by contrast, a vehement negative evaluation that destroys the functional unity of a person. Thus both "mere" and "deep" alienation can function as the opposite concepts of "wholehearted" or "full" identification-with. But only deep alienation is supposed to be incompatible with autonomy.

This ambiguity makes it difficult to comprehend exactly how Christman's replacement strategy is meant to work. If "non-alienation" only excludes cases of deep alienation but still admits for less serious cases of alienation, then the condition in question is actually one of non-(deep alienation). This condition is not coextensive with the condition of wholehearted identification, for the latter also excludes weaker cases of alienation. If we instead interpret the condition of non-alienation as excluding all

3. This impression arises in particular if one neglects the contextual thrust of Frankfurt's reflections. The strong formulations regarding a decided identification-with and wholeheartedness (especially in Frankfurt 1988, chaps. 5, 7, 8, and 12) serve to answer the problem of regress. They are not meant as an analysis of the everyday standard conditions under which human persons normally exercise their autonomy.

cases of alienation, we get a very strong requirement. But such a strong requirement could not evade the charge of excessive demand Christman puts forth against the condition of wholehearted identification. A systematically charitable reading would therefore have to interpret Christman's condition of non-alienation in the sense of non-(deep alienation).

(ii) Another ambiguity lies in Christman's characterisation of non-alienation as "reflective." Characterising a situation of non-alienation as "non-reflective" can either mean that the subject in question has in fact not engaged in critical reflection. But Christman intends "reflective" to cover two different sorts of case. On the one hand this condition is fulfilled by an actual reflection on the part of the subject which is qualified further in other parts of the conception. On the other hand, this condition can also be regarded as fulfilled, according to Christman, if this reflection is undertaken hypothetically and ascribed counterfactually to the subject by an interpreter who wants to assess the subject's personal autonomy.

At first we could understand Christman's proposal as saying that a positive achievement that is actively attained by the subject was replaced by the absence of a factor that blocks autonomy. But now this explication of "reflective" makes clear that a situation of not being alienated is only compatible with personal autonomy if the subject has undergone a process of reflection or if an onlooker has assumed such a process of reflection counterfactually.[4] This eliminates the advantages of Christman's strategy concerning the charge of excessive demand with respect to the conception that works with a condition of identification-with.

(iii) Finally we should point to another source of ambiguity ensuing from the fact that Christman does not, at least not at the surface of his conception, require a positive condition to be fulfilled, but only the absence of a certain state. This mode of talking, according to which a subject does not identify with a trait that applies to itself, can either mean that no evaluative judgement is made (= identification-as). Or it can mean that the subject —factually or counterfactually—reaches a negative evaluative judgement and thus identifies negatively with the trait in question. In the latter case we are lead to the question, already granted, whether this negative attitude

4. This ambiguity is grounded in Christman's uncommented move from the requirement of an *absence* of alienation (= not to be alienated), as it is formulated in the fourth element of his definition, to the requirement of a—factual or counterfactual—*exclusion* of alienation (= reflective non-alienation).

needs only to fulfil the condition of alienation or even the condition of deep alienation so that the personal autonomy of the subject is not given with respect to this trait.

Summarizing our discussion so far, we can first note that Christman's condition of reflective non-alienation carries some ambiguities, too. Particularly the oscillation between "alienation" and "deep alienation" creates problems analogous to those he makes out in the condition of identification-with, which he takes to oscillate between "endorsement" and "wholehearted endorsement." Even if we grant that the latter ambiguity can be traced back to Frankfurt's conception, we will have to note at this point that Christman inherits this problem in virtue of his own strategy.

In view of our other question we have to grant, secondly, that Christman's condition of the absence of "deep alienation" is in fact not open to the charge of excessive demand. To the contrary, it rather attracts the charge of formulating to weak a condition of personal autonomy. Were we to require the absence of all forms of "alienation," it would not be possible to see why Christman is less open to the charge of excessive demand and to the empirical inadequacy of his conception of personal autonomy than are proponents of a conception which implies the positive requirement that a subject must "fully" (Christman 2001, 202) identify with the trait in question in order to count as autonomous.[5]

Frankfurt and Christman agree about the requirement of an evaluative identification-with that manifests itself in the factually or counterfactually ascribed exercise of the capacity of critical self-evaluation. This is why in both conceptions this critical self-evaluation equally functions as a conceptual test for deciding whether or not a subject is personally autonomous with regard to a certain trait. There is further agreement among them about the absence of deep ambivalence (Frankfurt) or deep alienation (Christman) being a necessary condition of this personal autonomy. But it is controversial how the two conceptions treat all the cases in between the extremes of deep alienation on the one hand and wholehearted endorsement on the other. Christman is aware of the fact that "non-alienation" and "identification-with" are no complete opposites. But the way he introduces his condition on the basis of criticising the condition of identification-with covers the grey area of the cases in between wholehearted

5. By "empirical inadequacy" I here mean that the required condition is principally impossible to fulfil by finite subject such as human persons.

endorsement and deep alienation, for he continuously infers from the negation of the strong reading of identification-with to the absence of a strong form of alienation, i.e. to non-(deep alienation). But this skips cases in which the complexity and finitude of human persons shows up in everyday contexts.[6]

3. *"Non-alienation" versus "identification-with": a useful opposition?*

Our analysis of Christman's proposal shows that his strategy does not yield any immediate advantages for determining personal autonomy, which could be understood as reactions to his two critical points (ambiguity of the condition, overly demanding effects of the conception). It remains to be inquired whether Christman's proposal of replacing the condition of identification-with by a condition of non-alienation in conceptions of personal autonomy does make sense from other perspectives. To answer this question we have to get rid of the ambiguities we pointed out above in Christman's condition of non-alienation. We shall thus assume in what follows, firstly, that only the case of "deep alienation" is incompatible with personal autonomy; secondly, I assume that the absence of alienation is to be grounded in a critical reflection that is either carried out by the person in question or undertaken hypothetically by an onlooker, thus I assume that it is to be understood as non-alienation. If I am not mistaken, this is best in line with Christman's answer to the question whether the person in question is autonomous with respect to a certain characteristic where he takes the condition that "the person does not feel deeply *alienated* from it upon critical reflection" to be the "proper test for the acceptability of the characteristic in question" (Christman 2009, 143; see also 153).[7]

Departing from these two assumptions we will now, in a first step, identify a number of critical points against Christman's proposal. In a second step, we will assess Christman's overall strategy.

6. This dialectical situation is similar to the quarrel between compatibilists and incompatibilists in the free will debate in which complex cases are blinded out in favour of extreme positions; see Quante 2007b.

7. The formulation of the third and fourth conditions in Christman's conception entails that the case of counterfactually ascribed reflection is also to be included.

3.1 *Critique of Christman's proposal of replacement*

Firstly, one can object to Christman's condition of non-alienation that it provides too weak a requirement, as "non-alienation" is defined only as the absence of "deep alienation."[8] This excludes only those cases in which a person

> is unable to present a minimally settled sense of herself to others in practical discourse. (Christman 2001, 203)

He is surely right to say that

> we all contain some measures of internal conflict and complexity, and an attitude of ironic acceptance of the tensions of our own psyches is inevitable and perhaps healthy in a multidimensional and perplexing world. (ibid., 203)

Even if this repudiates the excessive and unrealistic requirement of wholehearted identification-with, which not only Christman imputes to his opponents, it does not entail that only a massive psychic defect, in the sense of the incapacity meant above, excludes the possibility of personal autonomy. This would only be the case if personal autonomy were conceived of as the capacity of rational decision and action, which again does not match the comprehensive conception of personal autonomy. The distinction will lie within the range of psychic constellation that can be characterized as non-deeply alienated. And Christman's construction does not provide criteria for determining this distinction more precisely.

Secondly, the concept of "critical self-reflection" is problematic." In the case of reflection that is factually carried out, the personality of the individual in question is involved and the factual absence of deep alienation, which from the perspective of the interpreter of the situation as a whole must count as inadequate, can be traced back to disturbing factors that are excluded as inadmissible in view of the condition Christman includes in his overall conception. In this case his overall conception would not turn out to be too weak, even though the decisive work is not done by the condition of non-alienation.

8. As in this paper I exclusively deal with this proposal of replacement, I will leave aside the other aspect of Christman's condition of authenticity, which he intends to solve problems that arise for Frankfurt's conception. But it is to be recognized particularly that Christman urges with the fifth condition of his conception that the critical self-reflection, which is a part of the condition of non-alienation, has to meet further conditions (see Christman 2009, 146 and 162).

In the case of hypothetical critical reflection we have to distinguish between two cases, since the evaluative standard of this counterfactual deliberation will either be the psychic structure of the individual in question or it must consist in general assumptions that are presumed to be plausible.[9] On the first variation, we have the same situation we had in the case of a critical reflection that is factually carried out and that, from the perspective of the interpreter, leads to a false negative result (non-alienation appears where alienation would be adequate). On the second variation, the standard is detached from the psychic structure of the individual so that the reference to the personality and thereby the biographical aspect of autonomy impends to get lost. It is hard to reconcile this result with the overall design of Christman's conception of personal autonomy (for this condition of adequacy of his conception of personal autonomy see Christman 2001, 201f.).

Thirdly, and especially in view of the history of the concept of alienation, it is to be criticised that Christman reduces "alienation" to a category of individual psychology.[10] Even if we agree with his goal to integrate an affective or emotional component into the conception of personal autonomy in this way, we have to see why this could not also be integrated in the condition of identification-with. Nor is it understandable why Christman dismisses the social psychological dimension of alienation. In Christman's account, too, the absence of alienation in the sense of an individual psychic experiential state does not determine by itself whether a person can count as autonomous with regard to one particular aspect of their personality. Rather, an intersubjective comprehensibility (see Christman 2009, 239) of this psychic reaction is required and this yields the possibility of intersubjective critique, even if the ambiguity of hypothetical self-reflection pointed out in the second objection makes it impossible to determine more precisely the standards of such an external critique within Christman's own conception.

Christman explicitly justifies his proposal to replace the condition of identification-with by the condition of non-alienation by saying that this avoids ambiguities and weaknesses of conceptions that seek to explicate personal autonomy in terms of the condition of identification-with. Thus it is not inappropriate, *fourthly*, to voice the objection that no

9. Besides indispensable standards of rationality this will presumably also include assumption about the structure of needs and about desires that are grounded in the human form of life and are thus normally given.

10. For a good account of the complexity of the concept of alienation see Jaeggi 2005.

such progress is detectable. For, on the one hand, the centre-piece of the condition of identification-with, i.e. critical self-reflection, is obviously also implied in Christman's condition of non-alienation, as non-alienation is understood as the result of factual (or a hypothetically ascribed) critical self-evaluation that needs to be stable across certain contexts and occasions.

On the other hand, the semblance of theoretical progress can be rendered as an effect of the ambiguity of Christman's critique of the conception of identification-with. As we saw in the second section of this contribution, Christman equates "identification-with" with "wholehearted endorsement" (Christman 2001, 202 fn. 44). Even if some of Frankfurt's formulations do not at any rate exclude this interpretation, it is obvious that this requirement would be far too strong and would in fact have effects that are gravely excluding and legitimize paternalistic infringements. It has been pointed out and criticised above that the inversion of this argument targeted on the condition of non-(deep alienation) would equally go too far and would formulate too weak a requirement. At this point I want to take my critique one step further and show by means of a conceptual distinction that the condition of identification-with can be formulated in a more differentiated and adequate way than Christman assumes and than it has been done in some of the received conceptions of personal autonomy. But when we do this, the apparent theoretical advantage of Christman's proposal dissolves.

It is uncontroversial that it must be about identification-with, since a "mere acknowledgement" (Christman 2001, 203; see also Christman 2009, 143) is insufficient as a condition of personal autonomy.[11] This is an evaluative judgement that, according to Christman, encompasses cognitive and affective aspects. Three results of such critical self-evaluation are conceivable: (1) an affirmative evaluation, (2) an adverse evaluation, and (3) an explicit suspension of judgement or the evaluation that the content is neutral.[12] Despite the worries discussed above we here accept Christ-

11. Presumably, one will also have to rely on such "mere acknowledgement," which is here termed "identification-as," in an analysis of personal autonomy. This is the case if (and insofar as) this theoretical stance of first-personal self-reference is a necessary element of propositionally constituted self-consciousness. At least if the matter is propositionally constituted identification-with, Christman speaks about judgements throughout, this practical self-relationship is connected with a theoretical self-reference.

12. This third case is not without further qualifications to be equated with "identification-as" as a purely theoretical attitude, as this is a practical attitude that either suspends the evaluative judgement for the moment or arrives at the result of evaluative neutrality. So in both cases the

man's assumption that it is irrelevant whether such a judgement is in fact rendered by the individual in question in the context of critical reflection or whether it is ascribed counterfactually in the context of hypothetical reflection; thus we do not in the following need to distinguish between these two variants. However, we have to introduce a distinction of cases with respect to each of the three possible results of a critical self-evaluation. Regarding the affirmative judgement we have to distinguish between a mere or prima facie endorsement (1.1) and wholehearted endorsement (1.2) that excludes tensions or ambivalences. Accordingly, with respect to the adverse judgment we have to distinguish between mere rejection (2.1) that corresponds to Christman's concept of alienation, and a deep rejection (2.2) where the judgement destroys the person's integrity and capacity to act (Christman's "deep alienation"). In view of the third case we have to differentiate the neutral judgement (3.1) that a trait is deemed evaluatively irrelevant and the neutrality of the suspension of judgement (3.2) where a person leaves it (yet) open how they evaluate the trait in question.[13]

Christman imputes to the Frankfurtian position that it posits case (1.2) as a necessary condition for personal autonomy and he then rightly rejects this as an excessive demand. But his counterproposal to treat the absence of deep alienation (case 2.2) as sufficient for personal autonomy, suffers from the reverse error of positing too low a threshold. As seen above, Christman and Frankfurt agree that case (1.2) is sufficient for personal autonomy and case (2.2) is sufficient for personal heteronomy. What is less clear, as Christman's own critique of the ambivalences of those conceptions that work with a condition of identification-with attests already,

---

evaluative, i.e. the practical dimension is at issue, whereas it is completely lacking in the case of a purely theoretical identification-as in the sense of a merely cognitive self-ascription of a trait. The question that is crucial in the philosophy of self-consciousness, whether personal self-relationships always include a practical dimension or whether there exist also forms of purely theoretical personal self-consciousness, cannot be dealt with at this stage. If one denies the possibility of a purely theoretical personal self-relationship, then identification-as is only conceivable as a variation of the third case. Furthermore it is important not to equate the two variants of the third case with the pathological state in which a person is incapable of taking an evaluative stance about themselves and their states or traits.

13. It is important not to identify case (3.2) with the ambivalence of a person both Christman and Frankfurt address. Ambivalence means that a person arrives at differing judgements concerning a trait so that they do not exhibit a stable psychic structure in that respect. If this instability entails functional disorder, ambivalence can endanger the autonomy of a person. The indecision often referred to in this context can also mean the suspension of a judgement illustrated in case (3.2), which can also lead to functional disorder.

is whether such conceptions would treat case (1.1) as sufficient and case (2.1) as compatible with personal autonomy.

To my mind this result suggests the following conclusion: The capacity to form an evaluative self-relationship and to render an evaluative judgement is crucial for personal autonomy (see Quante 2007a, chaps. 8 and 9).[14] Whether this occurs in the affirmative, the adverse or in a form that attests neutrality, is irrelevant for the question of personal autonomy. This capacity for critical self-evaluation is a necessary condition that is exercised factually under appropriate circumstances or that has to be ascribed counterfactually and in a controlled way, i.e. with reference to the biography of the person in question.[15] The result of deep alienation is surely incompatible with personal autonomy, here we can agree with Christman *and* Frankfurt, but this is not because of the content of the judgement but because of the disturbing effects it elicits as a psychic state in the subject in question.

If one takes this, in contrast to Frankfurt's and Christman's, more fine-grained conception of critical self-evaluation as a basis, it becomes apparent that Christman's proposal to improve on Frankfurt's conception by replacing the condition of identification-with by the condition of non-alienation does not work. This is because, first, he takes the false opposition between "wholehearted identification" and "deep alienation" as his starting point and does thus not take the crucial middle ground between these two extremes into account.[16] On the other hand, the remedial proposal is

14. In "Freedom of the will and the concept of a person," his first essay in this field, Frankfurt already speaks of a "capacity for reflective self-evaluation" (Frankfurt 1988, 12). There, in the context of discussing the case of the unwilling addict, he touches upon the possibility of "identification and withdrawal" (ibid., 18) as modes of evaluation. But it remains unclear in Frankfurt whether the act of evaluation, independent of its result, is sufficient for a person to count as autonomous with respect to their (her?) first order desires (given the absence of other factors that inhibit autonomy). In this regard, my proposal at this point goes beyond Frankfurt's conception.

15. As will become clear instantly, this ascription should be conceptualized as default-position and not as a result of critical examination.

16. A paradigm example of this is Christman's statement: "Even if our identities are in flux and our value commitments conflicting, and even though we are full of ambivalences and unresolved tensions, we are autonomous only if we can say that our decisions flow from us as the author of that ongoing struggle to negotiate those conflicts and tensions. Decisions and desires that fail to bear the proper relation to that ongoing personal project of character development that reflective agents are all engaged in, count as external and alienated and do not manifest autonomy in a crucial way" (2008, 156). Obviously Christman does not demand the total absence of "ambivalences and unresolved tensions" but neither does he offer criteria

set on the wrong level, since the relevant measure for personal autonomy is the capacity for critical self-evaluation which Christman's condition of non-alienation also implicitly makes use of. At this stage of theorizing, this much we can note, no progress has been obtained. Therefore I disagree with Christman when he stresses the advantages of his strategy as follows:

> In this way, I avoid the question of whether I wholeheartedly endorse the factor as a personal ideal, but I also do not simply accept my addictions or constraints with equanimity. (Christman 2008, 158)

It is simply not sufficient for a conception of personal autonomy to shy away from the extremes of mere acceptance (= identification-as) and wholehearted identification-with; if we really want to make philosophical progress we will have to enter the middle ground between these extremes and try to give a philosophically illuminating description of the overall structure we can find here. As I will point out now very briefly this should be done by following the general scheme of default-and-challenge.

3.2 *Autonomous by default: a radical alternative*

Christman's basic strategy is to replace a positively phrased condition for personal autonomy ("identification-with") with a negative condition ("non-alienation"). Basically, this seems to be the right track, as we can thus replace a positively characterized catalogue of necessary and sufficient conditions with a criterion that points to factors that endanger autonomy, without having to come up with a comprehensive list of these factors. Thereby we can accommodate the fact that "personal autonomy" is a negative concept in the sense that we do not dispose of a list of necessary and sufficient conditions that could function as criteria, but we are in a position to identify concrete challenges that either prevent or render inadequate an ascription of personal autonomy. Even though with this statement I approve of Christman's general strategy, I think the implementation of this strategy by integrating the condition of non-alienation as a "conceptual test" (Christman 2009, 153) for the ascription of personal autonomy is not expedient. Beyond the objections I have raised in detail against the elaboration of the condition of non-alienation,

---

which might help to determine where the crucial border lies beyond which personal autonomy is destroyed by alienation.

I want to close with two general deliberations I can here only sketch programmatically.

1. What speaks against the use of the concept of alienation as an ersatz for the condition of identification-with is that alienation is thus reduced to a factor of individual psychology. It is, however, implausible to claim that a person who reaches a negative evaluation of a trait that constitutes them thereby forfeits their personal autonomy with respect to this trait. This intuition may become plausible if one assumes the person in question not to have the chance to get rid of this trait. Put this way, the source of the incompatibility does not lie in the negative judgement, but in the assumption—which indeed needs to be examined in itself—that autonomy and determinism are incompatible.[17] Or the intuition is grounded in the negative judgement's having effects which undermine the person's capacity to act. But then it is the effect and not the negative judgement in itself, which constitutes the incompatibility with personal autonomy. Taken by itself, critical self-evaluation is an expression of personal autonomy even if it yields a negative result with respect to a particular trait, but it is not a sign of a lack of personal autonomy.[18]

Consequently, nothing is gained by limiting the concept of alienation to a factor of individual psychology for determining personal autonomy. But one looses grip of a conception that could be suitable as a social philosophical category for critically capturing societal framework conditions in which it is systematically made hard or even impossible for human beings to develop and exercise the capacities necessary for personal autonomy, especially the capacity for critical self-evaluation.[19] If it is clear that the distinction between personal autonomy and heteronomy does not coincide with that between alienation and non-alienation (in the sense of

17. Christman himself refers to this intuition: "If, while feeling alienation and self-repudiation of this sort, a person is unable to rid herself of the characteristic in question, she is heteronomous in relation to it" (2009, 144). For a detailed analysis of this intuition and the condition "unable to rid of" within the framework of an analysis of personal autonomy see Mele's discussion of sheddable and unsheddable attitudes (Mele 1995, 153–173).

18. The way of speaking Christman also adopts, according to which a person is personally autonomous with respect to a trait, can be misleading at this point. As long as the phrase "with respect to" is understood in the sense of "being the object of critical self-evaluation," a negative evaluation and personal autonomy are compatible with one another.

19. A complex conception of alienation, one that equally encompasses the individual psychological and the social philosophical dimensions, is to be found, for instance, in Karl Marx; see Quante 2011b.

individual psychology), then by adopting Christman's strategy we loose a powerful category of critical social philosophy without drawing profit in the analysis of personal autonomy.[20] As Kim Atkins (2008, 124 f.) states, that a

> relational approach to autonomy aims at distinguishing between reasons that one really wants to have and those that are the result of uncritically internalized social norms. Oppressive socialization can interfere with autonomy at three different levels: the formation of one's beliefs, desires, values, emotions, and attitudes, including attitudes to oneself; the development of the competencies necessary for autonomy; and the ability to make autonomous decisions or to act on them. A relational theory of autonomy responds to all three levels of interference by aiming at unifying the first-, second-, and third-personal perspectives of selfhood.

As I see it a non-reduced complex concept of alienation which takes into account both the level of individual psychological states and the level of social institutions and arrangements can help to spell out such a 'unifying' conception of personal autonomy. Therefore, as far as Christman intends to integrate the insights of the relation-autonomy-accounts into his conception of personal autonomy he should not give away such a thick concept of alienation.

2. The general lesson to learn from Christman's proposal is the insight that one should not only take account of the character of the concept of autonomy as a negative concept on the level of particular conditions, but that one should abandon the formulation of positive conditions from the outset. This is why the formulation of the fourth condition in Christman's conception is more to the point than the substantial explication that follows it is.

The analysis of Christman's proposal does not reveal the negative finding that the negatively formulated condition of non-alienation does point to a positive list of conditions that are demanded in this test, because it entails the requirement of being the result of critical reflection. It also suggests the suspicion that we have to do without this kind of explication of an authenticity condition and confine ourselves to naming the general preconditions human beings fulfil as a general rule and under normal

20. A promising attempt to preserve the critical function of the concept of alienation in the debate about personal autonomy is offered by Oshana 2005.

circumstances.[21] The default-condition, set as the normal case, forms a solid basis for the counterfactual elements an explication of personal autonomy cannot renounce without succumbing to the danger of excessive demand or over-intellectualization of personal life. The task of philosophy, and also the task of empirical sciences, has to consist in identifying the circumstances under which human persons do not exercise this capacity for personal autonomy in particular cases, in particular contexts or even permanently; this includes the circumstances under which human beings cannot even develop this capacity for personal autonomy, we need only think of the field of socialisation and education. Not only the bestowing of the sort respect we owe to autonomous persons, but also the ascription of personal autonomy as a complex set of capacities has to be conceived in terms of the model of default-and-challenge. The fulfilment of the required conditions has to be presupposed as the normal default-position that can be challenged and examined in each individual case, if doubts or critique can be established with sufficient reasons. From these challenges there emerges a part of the complex nexus that makes up the personal autonomy of human persons. The philosophical inclination is to leave this structure of default-and-challenge and to give in to the temptation of developing a positive conception of personal autonomy that promises to indicate necessary and sufficient conditions of personal autonomy. But if we cannot be certain ever to have identified all conceivable challenges, we cannot presume that we have completely come to terms with the complex nexus underlying human personal autonomy. It is decisive not to view this as a general threat in the sense of a philosophical scepticism that must be dismantled in general before our practice of ascribing personal autonomy can be recognized as justified.

The general lesson to draw from Christman's proposal is that we should not build individual negatively formulated criteria into a positive conception of personal autonomy, but that we should arrange the conception of personal autonomy as a whole along the lines of the model of default-and-challenge. The autonomy of our practice of ascribing personal autonomy and of the respect for personal autonomy consists in our reliance on this practice, even though we are not capable of explicating the complex structure of its foundation comprehensively. Viewed thus, the exercise, ascription, and recognition of personal autonomy are ultimately based on trust.

21. This structure is taken into account by all those conditions posited by Christman that require minimal standards or the "absence of neuroses and other debilitating pathologies" (2001, 201) and "normal" functioning (ibid.).

References

Atkins, Kim 2008: *Narrative Identity and Moral Identity*. London: Routledge.

Beauchamp, Tom L. 2005: "Who Deserves Autonomy, and Whose Autonomy Deserves Respect?". In: James Stacey Taylor (ed.), *Personal Autonomy*. Cambridge: Cambridge University Press, 310–329.

Christman, John 1991: "Autonomy and Personal History". *Canadian Journal of Philosophy* 21, 1–24.

— 1993: "Defending Historical Autonomy: A Reply to Professor Mele". *Canadian Journal of Philosophy* 23, 281–290.

— 2001: "Liberalism, Autonomy, and Self-Transformation". *Social Theory and Practice* 27, 185–206.

— 2008: "Why Search for Lost Time? Memory, Autonomy, and Practical Reason". In: Kim Atkins & Catriona Mackenzie (eds.), *Practical Identity and Narrative Agency*. London: Routledge, 146–166.

— 2009: *The Politics of Persons*. Cambridge: Cambridge University Press.

Frankfurt, Harry G. 1988: *The Importance of What We Care About*. Cambridge: Cambridge University Press.

Jaeggi, Rahel 2005: *Entfremdung. Zur Aktualität eines sozialphilosophischen Problems*. Frankfurt am Main: Campus Verlag.

Mele, Alfred R. 1995: *Autonomous Agents. From Self-Control to Autonomy*. New York: Oxford University Press.

Oshana, Marina A. L. 2005: "Autonomy and Self-Identity." In: John Christman & Joel Anderson (eds.), *Autonomy and the Challenges to Liberalism*. Cambridge: Cambridge University Press, 77–97.

Quante, Michael 2002: *Personales Leben und menschlicher Tod*. Frankfurt am Main: Suhrkamp Verlag.

— 2007a: *Person*. Berlin: de Gruyter.

— 2007b: "Autonomy for Real People". In: Christoph Lumer & Sandro Nannini (eds.), *Intentionality, Deliberation and Autonomy. The Action-Theoretic Basis of Practical Philosophy*. Aldershot: Ashgate Publishing Company, 209–226.

— 2011a: "In Defence of Personal Autonomy". *Journal of Medical Ethics* 37, 597–600.

— 2011b: "Recognition as the Social Grammar of Species Being in Marx". In: Heikki Ikäheimo & Arto Laitinen (eds.), *Recognition and Social Ontology*. Leiden: Brill, 239–267.

Taylor, James Stacey 2009: *Practical Autonomy and Bioethics*. London: Routledge.

Grazer Philosophische Studien
87 (2013), 197–215.

ON THE OPEN TEXTURE OF LAW

Frederick SCHAUER
University of Virginia

Summary
H. L. A. Hart and others have argued that law is open-textured. It is in the nature of law, they say, that it necessarily possesses an open texture going beyond the open texture of the language in which legal rules are written. But when we examine the question of open texture in light of Hart's claim that the open texture of law entails the necessary defeasibility of legal rules, we discover that Hart and his followers are mistaken. Both the alleged open texture of law *qua* law and the defeasibility of legal rules are contingent features of certain legal rules in certain legal regimes, but neither are necessary components of the nature of law or the nature of rules.

1. *Introduction*

In *The Concept of Law*, H. L. A. Hart famously claimed that the law is *open-textured* (Hart 1994, 123, 128–36). Hart borrowed the term from his Oxford colleague Friedrich Waismann (Waismann 1945), whom he duly acknowledged as the inspiration for the conclusion that law as well as language is open-textured. But is Hart's claim correct? Waismann argued that *language* is necessarily open-textured, but is there an open-texture to law distinct from, or at least going beyond, the open-texture of the language in which legal rules are written? Hart seemed to believe so, but it is not at all clear that Hart was right in so believing. Nor is it apparent that Hart and others are correct in maintaining that law's open texture produces the necessary defeasibility of legal rules. For even if law is open-textured, it does not follow for law, as it may follow for language, that the uncertainty generated by an instance of open texture—an unprovided-for or unregulated case (Hart 1994, 272)—is necessarily an occasion for revising an existing legal rule and thus making law, as Hart explicitly maintained (Hart 1994, 272). Indeed, resistance to precisely such revision may well be what characterizes rules. If that is so, then Hart's claims that law's defeasibility follows from its open texture and that law is necessarily and essentially defeasible may both be mistaken. Or so I shall argue here.

2. *Waismann on the open texture of language*

I begin with a *précis* of Waismann's basic idea. Arguing against the logical positivist credo that meaning was a function of verifiability (Ayer 1946), Waismann observed that even the most precise and carefully delimited empirical terms might nevertheless produce uncertainty in the face of unforeseen and virtually unimaginable instances. Because language cannot anticipate all possible occurrences in all possible worlds, he argued, there persists the ineliminable potential that a definition of an empirical concept bounded in all now-foreseeable dimensions can break down in the face of unforeseen and unforeseeable events. To illustrate the phenomenon, Waismann observed that if we attempted to verify the statement, "There is a cat next door," no amount of seeing, touching, or patting the cat to verify that it was indeed a cat could foreclose the logical possibility that the creature we thought was a cat according to all of the existing criteria of catness might then grow to gigantic size, or die and then come back from the dead. Were such eventualities to occur, Waismann argued, the existing criteria for application of the term would collapse. An uncertainty that had not previously existed would arise precisely because of the appearance of the unexpected, and it is central to Waismann's idea of open texture that the possibility of the unexpected, at least for material object statements, can never completely be foreclosed.

At about the same time that Waismann was writing about open texture, J.L. Austin captured the identical idea even more vividly. Austin asked us to imagine a creature that appeared to be a goldfinch according to the existing definition of what it is to be a goldfinch, but which then proceeded to explode, or quote Virginia Woolf (Austin 1946, 160). Under such circumstances, he says, "we don't know what to say." It is precisely the lack of knowing what to say (or do) in the face of the unforeseen and unforeseeable that Waismann originally called, in German, "*Die Porosität der Begriffe*" (the porosity of concepts), and then, at the suggestion of W.B. Kneale (Waismann 1945, 121), relabeled in English as "open texture." Thus, as Stewart Shapiro puts it in summarizing Waismann's idea,

"*P* exhibits *open-texture* if there are possible objects *p* such that nothing in the established use of *P*, or the non-linguistic facts, determines that *P* holds of *p* or that *P* fails to hold of *p*. In effect, *Pp* is left open by the use of language, to date." (Shapiro, 2011).

As Waismann explicitly stressed, open texture is not to be confused with vagueness (Waismann 1945, 122). Some terms are indeed vague in that they are indeterminate with respect to known (existing or currently imaginable) applications. It takes no great foresight to understand that some collections of things may or may not be *heaps*, that certain kinds of behavior may or may not be *kind*, or that a car traveling at 90km/hour on a particular stretch of highway may or may not be traveling *quickly*. In such cases, we perceive now that some applications of the term are indeterminate. But open texture is different. It is the *possibility* of vagueness—the *potential* vagueness—of even those terms that appear to have no uncertainties with respect to known or imagined applications. We could list all of the existing criteria for something being a goldfinch, and thus the term "goldfinch" would not be vague for any of the known existing goldfinches and non-goldfinches in the world. But because such a precise and non-vague definition of "goldfinch" would not likely contain the criteria of "does not explode" or "does not quote Virginia Woolf," the occurrence of the previously unimagined would render the hitherto non-vague term newly vague with respect to that application. And because such a possibility could never entirely be eliminated for empirical concepts, Waismann maintained, attempting to define the meaning of such concepts in terms of verifiability was destined to failure.

3. *Hart and the open texture of the law*

In analyzing the operation of legal rules, Hart purported to adopt Waismann's idea and adapt it to law. Hart claimed that rules necessarily possess "a fringe of vagueness or 'open texture'" (Hart 1994, 123), and he attributed the idea to Waismann (Hart 1994, 297). But it is not obvious that Hart and Waismann were talking about the same thing. One problem is that Hart's language is ambiguous as between the view that vagueness and open texture are distinct, as Waismann argued, and the view that "open texture" is for Hart simply a synonym for "vagueness." Perhaps he is merely following the common practice of using the "*x* or *y*" locution to say that *y* is an alternative and possibly better way of saying *x*, as when I describe my dog as "my pet, or my cherished companion."

Although Hart's language is susceptible to that interpretation, a more plausible reading is that Hart did see vagueness and open texture as different, but not in the same way as Waismann. After introducing the term "open texture," Hart defines it as the fringe area of a term with clear and unclear—core and fringe (or core and penumbra)—applications. Thus, a man who is two meters in height is clearly tall, and a man who is one and one half meters is clearly not tall, and so a man who is in the area of uncertainty—1.85 meters, say—exists in the fringe of the term "tall." And the same applies to terms less pervasively vague than "tall"—that is, to terms which, unlike "tall," are determinate for most of their known applications. Take "wine," for example. Its extension is quite precise, such that the vast majority of substances, and even the vast majority of potable liquids, are easily classified as wine or not wine. But whether non-alcoholic wine is wine at all is not so clear. Consequently, we can say that non-alcoholic wine is located in the relatively small fringe of a term with a large core of settled meaning—a term containing, overwhelmingly, clear cases of application or non-application.

That "open texture" was to Hart the label not for potential vagueness but for the *actual* vagueness surrounding the determinate applications of partially non-vague terms becomes even more plain when we examine his introduction of the now-famous example of a rule prohibiting vehicles in the park (Hart 1994, 129; Schauer 2008). For most of the "paradigm, clear cases," the application of the term is straightforward, and Hart offers "motor-cars, buses, and motor-cycles" as examples of such clear cases. But with respect to an electrically propelled toy motor-car, he says, the application of the term "vehicle" is no longer straightforward. Accordingly, with respect to the question whether the no-vehicles-in-the-park rule applies to the electrically propelled toy motor-car, Hart continues, the law can be seen to have exhibited its open texture. He then goes on to say that in such cases we "confront the issues at stake and [...] then settle the question by choosing between the competing interests in the way that best satisfies us. In doing so we shall have rendered more determinate our initial aim, and shall incidentally have settled a question as to the meaning, for purposes of this rule, of a general word." (Hart 1994, 129). "The open texture of the law means that there are, indeed, areas of conduct which must be left to be developed by courts or officials striking a balance, in the light of circumstances, between competing interests which vary in weight from case to case." (Hart 1994, 135). And although, in theory, a judge could weigh the competing interests and then decide, taking into account all of the competing substantive reasons as well as the reason for having a rule, to apply the rule, Hart was later quite explicit that in all such cases of applying or not applying a rule to facts not subsumed under the existing rule, "the judge both makes new law and applies the established law which both confers and constrains his law-making powers" (Hart, 1994, 272).

4. *The open texture of law and the open texture of language*

Hart's explication of the open texture of legal rules is as interesting as it is important, but Hart may be less explaining or using Waismann's idea than he is modifying it. Of course many terms do have cores of settled meaning and fringes of now-debatable applications. What Hart said about the term "vehicle" in a legal rule holds also for most terms. And it holds even when those terms are not components of prescriptive rules. In numerous contexts, there are core and fringe applications of "bus," "run," "blue," and "dead," for example, and so the core and fringe feature of most of the words in any language will be part of the language of legal rules as well. Waismann's point, however, is different. It is that even terms with *no* currently known fringes may still develop such fringes in the face of currently unforeseeable applications, and that this possibility can never completely be eliminated. The claim of language's open texture is thus a claim about (empirical) language's inevitable potential uncertainty, and it is this idea that Hart seeks to transfer to legal decision-making.

In one respect Hart is plainly correct. Law is inevitably potentially uncertain just because language is inevitably potentially uncertain. Legal rules are ordinarily canonically written in language, and are typically (or perhaps necessarily) understood in language even when, as is often the case in common law systems, they may have no single formal canonical inscription in a book of statutes, regulations, or constitutional provisions. Because legal rules are thus language-dependent, the properties of language in general are present with respect to legal rules expressed in language. More particularly, the phenomenon of open texture, as identified by Waismann, must be a feature of all legal rules.[1] To illustrate, imagine a legal

1. For purposes of this article, I assume that Waismann is basically correct. My question is not whether Waismann is, ultimately, right, but what, if Waismann is right, this says about law.

rule pertaining to goldfinches—say, a rule declaring the goldfinch to be an endangered species and thus protected against hunting, capturing, and the like. The rule would specify what could or could not be done with or to goldfinches, and, because "goldfinch" is a term with no special legal meaning, might then implicitly or explicitly incorporate the ordinary meaning of "goldfinch" then present in the language. But if someone were charged with violating the law by, say, capturing an exploding goldfinch, the very uncertainty of whether such a creature was a goldfinch at all would make the legal consequences of the capture *pro tanto* uncertain as well.

If Waismann's idea is sound, then open texture is indeed an ineliminable feature of law, but it is ineliminable in law precisely because it is ineliminable in language. As long as law is written and understood in language, then the characteristics of language infuse law as well. Law is thus open-textured, and necessarily so, just because of the ineliminable open texture of language, but this conclusion does not yet suggest that legal open texture is any more than, or any less than, the open texture of the terms in which the law is written and understood.

5. *Is the open texture of law more than the open texture of its language?*

The open texture of language thus produces open texture in law, but this conclusion is neither startling nor particularly interesting. Insofar as language is open-textured, it follows that *any* use of language is *pro tanto* open-textured. Law is thus open-textured, but so too are novels, theatrical productions, everyday conversations, restaurant menus, and the instructions I give to the automobile mechanic. If Waismann is right, then the phenomenon of open-texture pervades language use, and Austin's exploding goldfinch can appear and make the immanent open texture of language present and problematic in *any* use of language, including but by no means limited to legal language.

Hart, however, seems to make a broader claim, as his examples demonstrate. The important difference for our purposes between Austin's exploding goldfinch and Hart's electrically propelled toy motor-car is that we can not only imagine the latter, but can also describe it with existing linguistic tools. A toy electric motor-car does not exemplify the open texture of language, and so for it to be an example of the open texture of law, Hart must have had in mind a feature of law distinct from the open texture of language.

That there is something about law, or more precisely about legal rules, that seems to Hart analogous to the open texture of language, but which is not simply the open texture of language, is suggested by the no-vehicles-in-the-park example. The no-vehicles-in-the-park rule is a straightforward example of a rule. Many rules, including this one, are presently both under- and over-inclusive with respect to their background justifications (Alexander & Sherwin 2001; Schauer 1991). Consider the typical highway speed limit. The speed limit is a rule, designed to serve the background justification of fostering highway safety. But we know now that a designated speed limit aimed at ensuring safe driving will excessively limit some experienced and safe drivers under ideal conditions who are in fact driving safely, albeit above the speed limit. And by reaching some instances of safe driving, the rule reaches beyond its background justification, and is accordingly over-inclusive. Conversely, some forms of unsafe driving—driving just below the limit in snow and ice, for example, or an inexperienced driver's driving right at a high motorway limit—are not covered by the speed limit rule. The rule is thus under-inclusive to the extent that some behaviors covered by the rule's background justification of ensuring safety are not covered by the rule itself. But neither such over- nor under-inclusion represents open-texture in either Waismann's or Hart's senses, because neither involves a confrontation with what was previously unexpected or undecided. For all of the reasons of predictability and consistency, among others, that we use rules, the speed limit rule is knowingly adopted with full-knowledge of its under- and over-inclusion, and with, ideally, full appreciation of the fact that achieving the virtues of rule-based decision-making involves enduring the vices of a rule's under- and over-inclusiveness.

In other instances, however, the tokens of under- or over-inclusiveness may not be imagined by the rule-makers at the time a rule is made, and thus not anticipated in selecting the language of the rule. Such instances are presumably what Hart had in mind when he used the example of the toy electric motor-car (Bix 1993, 17–35). He considered it an example of legal open-texture because a particular application of a rule was not settled by the language of the rule, as it would have been had the rule-maker specified that the prohibited vehicles were of a certain size, or propelled in a particular way, or capable of carrying a designated number of passengers. But in Hart's example, the extension of the rule is not so limited, extending to anything that is a "vehicle." And because we do not know whether the toy electric motor-car is a vehicle, we do not know whether it contravenes the no-vehicles-in-the-park rule.

The mere fact that a new occurrence is not covered by a rule, however, need not produce the same "we don't know what to say" response that the exploding goldfinch occasions with respect to the previous criteria for proper use of the word "goldfinch." The rule could have carefully defined "vehicle" in all then-known directions, and could also have said that anything not a vehicle according to that definition would not be covered by the rule. And the rule could accomplish this goal with then-existing linguistic resources. Were the rule to be formulated in this way, and if, say, the rule defined a vehicle in a way that limited vehicles for the purpose of the rule as being of a certain size, or having the capacity to hold a certain number of human passengers, then the toy electric motor-car would simply not have been covered by the rule, even though this particular application was not imagined at the time the rule was written and enacted. But if the rule, as in Hart's example, is specified simply in terms of "vehicles," then the presence of the toy electric motor-car might well be an example of the limited foresight or imagination of the particular drafters of a particular rule, but little more than that. If the term "vehicle," standing alone, is indeterminate with respect to toy electric motor-cars, then we have an example of the open texture of language as manifested in a legal rule, but not an example of a feature of law going beyond the open texture of language. And if the term "vehicle," standing alone, is determinate with respect to toy electric motor-cars (assuming that toy electric motor-cars *are* vehicles), then this is like the speed limit—an application lying within the scope of the rule but not serving the rule's background justification. This, to repeat, is a familiar (and often intentional) feature of rules, but does not generate the quandary or uncertainty that characterizes open texture.

6. *On the possibility of closure rules*

As noted above, rules may contain closure provisions, excluding (or, in theory, including) all applications not plainly encompassed by the rule. And as Hart observed (Hart 1994, 272), Jeremy Bentham imagined and discussed just this kind of rule, one with its own specified closure. For Bentham, who notoriously abhorred the idea of judicial legislation, a gap in the law was not the occasion for judicial gap- filling, but for legislative action, albeit legislative action prompted by the a proposal from the judge. Bentham, with his penchant for neologisms, called this the "suspensive" power or "sistitive" function, whereby a judge would suspend execution of the law pending legislative revision (Postema 1986, 434–439). For present purposes, however, the issue is not principally about the strategy to be followed when a legal rule does not plainly cover some occurrence in the world. Rather, Bentham shows that a set of rules can in theory provide a closure or default rule specifying what is to happen in *all* events not plainly covered by the existing rules (Gardner 2001, 212). Consider the implicit closure rule of the Anglo-American criminal law, according to which all behavior not clearly prohibited by an enacted legal prohibition is permitted. Or consider a hypothetical rule of private law, pursuant to which claimants could recover against defendants only if an explicit rule authorized such recovery, and only if the claimant's actual claim clearly fell within such an explicit rule. In all other cases, the claim would fail. This might well be a bad rule, neglecting to account for the fact that in private law an uncompensated wrongfully caused injury is as regrettable as compensation where there is no injury or wrong. But the justice or injustice of the rule is a side issue. What is important is simply that a closure or default rule is entirely possible.

Any closure rule would, of course, remain subject to the open texture of the language of the closure rule itself. But if the closure rule's language were determinate, then there is no reason why law would necessarily be compelled to face a situation in which the law simply runs out, in the way that language runs out when confronted with the exploding goldfinch. Indeed, Hart appears to concede as much, in his posthumously published "Postscript," when he is describing Bentham's approach (Hart 1994, 272). By characterizing Bentham's proposal—a form of closure rule—as an alternative to judicial discretion, Hart implicitly concedes that there are systemic options for law other than judicial discretion or judicial law-making. In so conceding, however, Hart sets himself at odds with what he, earlier in *The Concept of Law*, appears himself to have maintained, and sets himself at odds with what others have said about legal defeasibility. And it is to this that we now turn.

7. *The possibility of non-defeasibility*

With the foregoing analysis in mind, consider Hart's claim that a rule with an "unless" clause can still be a rule (Hart 1994, 136). This itself seems uncontroversial. A rule that is specified in "If A, then ϕ, unless B" form is merely a different way of formulating a rule with multiple conditions for its application, as in "If A and not-B, then ϕ" (Schauer 1991, Stone 1985, 68–73).[2] Moreover, using an "unless" clause is sometimes a method of formulating a genuine reason-providing but still non-absolute rule. In American constitutional law, for example, a governmental classification by race is unconstitutional *unless* the government can justify such a classification by a "compelling interest" where it is understood that a compelling interest is a heightened standard of justification substantially stronger than that minimally necessary—a mere "rational basis"—typically needed to justify ordinary legislative classifications (*Loving v. Virginia* 1967). But neither using an "unless" clause to formulate a rule with multiple conditions for its application nor using one to express a non-absolute rule genuinely implicate the idea of open texture. The latter is, to be sure, a way of accommodating for the possibility that the details of all potential overrides cannot fully be anticipated in advance, but still differs from the case in which specific law confronts the genuinely unexpected. Making rules defeasible and using a vague standard for defeat is a way of managing the uncertainty of the future, but is different from the case in which a non-vague rule confronts the genuinely unexpected.

Although intentional vagueness to manage an uncertain future is more or less straightforward, Hart makes a stronger and more problematic claim when he maintains not only that a rule with an "unless" clause is still a rule, but also that the list of "unlesses" cannot be exhaustively specified in advance (Hart 1994, 136; MacCormick 1974, 117). In this he marks a position now quite common in the legal literature. Richard Posner, for example, insists that courts *always* (the word is crucial) retain the power to append "ad hoc exceptions" at the moment of application even to existing, precise, and exceptionless rules (Posner 1988, 834f.). Similarly, Richard Tur argues that courts *necessarily* have the power to set aside the indications of rules in the service of equity or justice when applying the rule would produce an unjust result or a one at odds with the rule's background justification (Tur 2001), Ronald Dworkin has described the list of legal principles as "numberless," (Dworkin 1977, 43f.), and Neil MacCormick has offered a slightly more qualified version (MacCormick 1995) of the same claim. And although Ronald Dworkin's later insistence that there is a "real" rule existing behind the formal words of a written rule is mysterious (Bix 1993, 34f.), the heart of his argument is the view, related to those

2. I put aside burden-of-proof considerations, which may make the two formulations more different than they would be absent such considerations (Chapman 1998; Finkelstein 1999).

just set out, that written rules are necessarily defeasible in the service of the real rule lurking in the background (Dworkin 1986).

Thus a new argument is now before us—that law's open texture is not merely the open texture of law's language, and not simply the conventional claim that legal rules, like all rules, *can* be treated as defeasible,[3] but that legal rules are *necessarily* defeasible. The claim is not that treating legal rules as defeasible is desirable, useful, or common, but that it is in the nature of rules or the nature of law that legal rules are necessarily and thus invariably defeasible. In this respect, Dworkin, Posner, and Tur may go beyond Hart's claim, at least if we interpret Hart's claim as being limited to cases that are legally unregulated. This may be in some tension with Hart's text here, for Hart's claim about "unless" seems not limited to such cases. But if Hart is instead understood as limiting his claim about unless to the cases not regulated by the law, then his claim is more modest than the more expansive ones—claims about law and judges and not just about rules—of Dworkin, Posner, Tur, and many others.

To be distinct from the defeasibility occasioned by the open texture of language, *legal* defeasibility must exist within the area of linguistic determinacy. Were it otherwise, we would simply be rehearsing in legal context the issues of linguistic open texture and consequent linguistic indeterminacy. Thus the claims of Dworkin, MacCormick, Posner, and Tur, among others, and suggested by Hart in asserting the impossibility of listing in advance all of the possible "unlesses," are best understood as claims positing defeasibility even in the face of linguistic determinacy. Consider, to take the obvious example, the case featured by Ronald Dworkin, the 1889 decision of the New York Court of Appeals in *Riggs v. Palmer*. In *Riggs*, Elmer Palmer's grandfather had named Elmer is his will, but was contemplating changing the will, to Elmer's disadvantage. In order to accelerate his inheritance, Elmer killed his grandfather with poison. He was eventually caught, charged with murder, tried, convicted, and imprisoned. But Elmer argued that he was still entitled to inherit his grandfather's estate, relying on the New York Statute of Wills, which provided, to oversimplify, that anyone named as a beneficiary in a will would inherit upon the death of the testator. Importantly, the Statute provided no relevant exceptions to that rule, and the judges who thought Elmer should inherit and even

3. Indeed, there is a vast literature exploring the logic of legal defeasibility (Hage 2005; Prakken 1997; Sartor 1995; Stelmach & Brożek 2006), but that literature attempts to model and analyze defeasibility when it exists in a legal system, rather than addressing the question whether the existence of such defeasibility within a legal system is (or is not) a legal or logical necessity.

those who thought he should not agreed that the rule as written was clear and did not contain grounds for an exception.

The judges who thought that Elmer should lose were in the majority, relying on the "no man should profit from his own wrong" principle to produce that outcome. But it is important that there was agreement among *all* the judges that a literal application of the rule would allow Elmer to inherit. This was not, therefore, a case of linguistic vagueness, ambiguity, or open texture in Waismann's sense. The language was clear. It is just that the clear language happened to produce an unfortunate and seemingly unfair result. But is such a result an indication of the open texture of law *qua* law? Is it an example of the necessary defeasibility of legal rules?

Riggs illustrates the distinction between a rule that gives no answer and a rule that gives a bad answer, and precisely this distinction undercuts the claim of necessary defeasibility. The rule in *Riggs* did not contain an "unless" clause, and thus we might conclude, or Hart might have concluded, that *Riggs* presents a situation not envisaged when the rule was drafted. And we might also conclude that the situation presented by *Riggs* is one in which a previously unimagined situation shows how a hitherto unneeded and unanticipated "unless" clause might have been a good idea. Yet even if that is so, the rule without the "unless" clause is still capable of generating a clear outcome, albeit a morally (in this case) unpalatable one. Consequently, the existence of hypothetical "unless" clauses whose addition would have prevented an unfortunate outcome is insufficient to make the case that legal rules are necessarily defeasible. If there is such a case to be made, essentially a claim that all of the rules in a system should have open-ended "unless" clauses, it must be a moral or policy claim rather than a logical or linguistic one. A rule that ill serves its background justification in a particular case is still a rule capable of producing an outcome, and whether such an outcome should be tolerated when it is unsound as a moral or policy matter is different from whether such an outcome presents an "exploding goldfinch" type of genuine uncertainty.

8. *On the grounds for defeasibility*

When the New York court concluded in *Riggs* that Elmer could not inherit because of the "no man shall profit from his own wrong" principle, it treated the most directly applicable legal rule as defeasible in the service

of blocking of an important public works project. And in *United States v. Locke*, a statute setting a filing deadline of "prior to December 31" was upheld even when its literal application resulted in the arguably unfair exclusion of a claim filed on December 31 by someone who assumed, not unreasonably, that the statute really meant to say "on or prior to December 31."

There are numerous other examples, in the United States and elsewhere, and it would be mistaken to describe the defeasibility of legal rules as a universal or even overwhelmingly common feature of legal decision-making. Although legal decision-makers sometimes treat rules as defeasible, frequently they do not. Often they treat the literal language of a rule formulation as conclusive, and refrain from adding exceptions at the moment of application, overriding the indications of rules in the service of justice or equity or efficiency, or modifying rules at the moment of application. Such non-defeasibility may not be wise, but it is both possible (Baker 1977, 38) and widespread. Rule-formulations have meanings distinct from the background justifications lying behind the rules and distinct from what the best (or even a good) rule-free outcome in some particular instance would be. Although treating rules as defeasible is widespread in many legal systems, examples like those just offered show that rules are often applied as written—treated as non-defeasible—even when what seem to be valid defeating conditions are present. Fuller may have been empirically sound in pointing out, *contra* Hart, that treating rules as defeasible is ubiquitous in many modern common law systems, but, even as a descriptive matter, it is hard to defend the position that a legal system without widespread and legitimate defeasibility is for that reason no legal system at all.

Moreover, non-defeasibility is hardly without justification. The arguments for rules are familiar, and most of the arguments for rules in general are arguments for treating rules as non-defeasible. When the designers of some decision-making environment are distrustful of judges and other legal decision-makers who might be biased, corrupt, incompetent, ill-equipped for the job, or just very rushed, then the designers might want to constrain those decision-makers by rules rather than granting wide discretion. Indeed, when distrust is at its acme, decision-makers may not be granted the authority to decide when some application of a rule is ridiculous or absurd, let alone unfair, inequitable, unjust, or inefficient. It is easy to see that it would be absurd to exclude the truck used as a war memorial from the park, but the real question is whether and when some class of officials should be empowered to decide which applications are absurd and which are not. Moreover, rules also serve to allocate decision-making responsibility. To treat a rule as non-defeasible is often simply to decide that some but not other officials will have the power to cancel, override, amend, or modify an existing rule. And insofar as rules also bring the advantages of certainty, predictability, settlement, and stability for stability's sake, treating the rules as defeasible comes at the sacrifice of each of these values, even though of course it brings the potential advantages of fairness, equity, and, in theory, reaching the correct result in every instance.

9. *The contingency of defeasibility*

It now becomes apparent that the traditional defenses of the necessary defeasibility of legal rules—whether Hart's, or Posner's, or MacCormick's, or Tur's—mostly rest on a certain view about the powers and abilities of judges. Few people would maintain that police officers or ordinary bureaucrats, for example, should have the power to revise the rules that constrain them when those rules appear to indicate a poor outcome in a particular case. And if that is so, then the view that defeasibility in the hands of judges is required by the Rule of Law while defeasibility in hands of others is not turns out to be a view about the capacities of judges within particular legal systems. So long as we can imagine something properly called a legal system in which the power of rule revision and rule override is not entrusted to judges, then we can imagine something properly called a legal system in which defeasibility is somewhat or even largely absent.

Defeasibility is thus not a property of rules at all, but rather a characteristic of how some decision-making system will choose to *treat* its rules. The Wittgensteinian maxim that rules do not determine their own applications reminds us that how a rule will be treated is not something inherent in the rule itself. If the plain or literal (but not necessarily the ordinary language) meaning of a rule can indicate an outcome, it is a function not of the rule but of how the rule will be treated whether that indicated outcome is to be taken as conclusive, presumptive, or even, at the extreme, as having no weight in itself, being but a totally transparent (to its background justification, or to the all-things-considered best outcome) heuristic or rule of thumb. The question of defeasibility is not a question about what is *in* a rule, but is rather a question about how what is in a rule, or about how what a rule says, is to be treated, and this is not, and can never be, something that can be determined by the rule itself.

The question of defeasibility is thus exposed as descriptive and prescriptive, but neither logical nor conceptual. It is logically and conceptually possible for rules to be interpreted, understood, applied, and enforced according to the literal meaning of the component language of their formulations. Whether in this or that legal system they are in fact so treated is a descriptive question, and it turns out, as the examples above illustrate, that as a descriptive matter defeasibility is less universal in actual legal systems than we might have thought, even in the legal systems in which we might have most expected it to exist.

With respect to the prescriptive question, whether the literal meaning of a rule-formulation will be treated as what the rule indicates, and whether what the rule indicates will be treated as conclusive, are questions that cannot be answered by reference to the moral goals of particularized justice. Those goals exist, to be sure, as Plato, Aristotle, and countless successors have argued. But so too do the Rule of Law goals that might be thought of as the goals of generalized justice, or aggregate justice, or systemic justice. And as long as those non-particularistic goals have a place in our moral and prescriptive reasoning, then we cannot conclude, the actual practices of some parts of some legal common law legal systems notwithstanding, that the defeasibility of legal rules is a necessary part of all legal systems, or that the defeasibility of rules in general is a necessary part of all decision-making environments. Defeasibility may well be a desirable component of some parts of some legal systems at some times, but it is far from being an essential property of law. And if law is not necessarily defeasible, then law is not open-textured in Waismann's sense, nor even in Hart's sense. Insofar as language is open-textured, then so too, necessarily is law. But if law's language exhausts the open texture of law, and thus when law's language does not exhibit language's open texture, there is no residual open texture of law at all.[4]

4. Earlier versions of this paper have been presented at Duke University, Albert-Ludwigs-Universität-Freiburg, and the University of Palermo. I am grateful for comments and assistance from James Boyle, Bruno Celano, Daniel Gruschke, Hannes Matthiessen, Ralf Poscher, and Andrew Stumpff. And special thanks to Michel de Araujo Kurth for his penetrating and valuable comments on the penultimate draft.

References

Alexander, Larry, & Emily Sherwin 2001: *The Rule of Rules: Morality, Rules, and the Dilemmas of Law.* Durham, North Carolina: Duke University Press.

Ayer, A. J. 1946: *Language, Truth and Logic.* London: Victor Gollancz, Ltd., 2d. ed.

Austin, J. L. 1946: "Other Minds". *Proceedings of the Aristotelian Society* (Supp.) 20, 148–187.

Baker, Gordon P. 1977: "Defeasibility and Meaning". In: Peter M.S. Hacker & Joseph Raz (eds.), *Law, Morality, and Society: Essays in Honour of H. L. A. Hart.* Oxford: Clarendon Press, 26–57.

Bix, Brian 1993: *Law, Language, and Legal Determinacy.* Oxford: Clarendon Press.

Chapman, Bruce 1998: "Law Games: Defeasible Rules and Revisable Rationality". *Law and Philosophy* 17, 443–480.

Dworkin, Ronald M. 1977: *Taking Rights Seriously.* London: Duckworth.

— 1986: *Law's Empire.* Cambridge, MA: Harvard University Press.

Finkelstein, Claire Oakes 1999: "When the Rule Swallows the Exception". In: Linda Meyer (ed.), *Rules and Reasoning: Essays in Honour of Fred Schauer.* Oxford: Hart Publishing, 147–175.

Fuller, Lon L. 1958: "Positivism and Fidelity to Law—A Reply to Professor Hart". *Harvard Law Review* 71, 630–672.

— 1969: *The Morality of Law* (revised edition). New Haven: Yale University Press.

Gardner, John 2001: "Legal Positivism: 5 ½ Myths". *American Journal of Jurisprudence* 46, 199–227.

Hage, Jaap 2005: *Studies in Legal Logic.* Dordrecht: Springer.

Hart, H. L. A. 1958: "Positivism and the Separation of Law and Morals". *Harvard Law Review* 71, 593–629.

— 1994: *The Concept of Law*, 2d ed. Penelope A. Bulloch & Joseph Raz (eds.), Oxford: Clarendon Press.

Loving v. Virginia 1967: 388 U.S. 1.

MacCormick, Neil 1974: "Law as Institutional Fact". *Law Quarterly Review* 90, 102-129.

— 1995: "Defeasibility in Law and Logic". In: Zenon Bankowski, Ian White, & Ulrike Hahn (eds.), *Informatics and the Foundations of Legal Reasoning.* Dordrecht: Kluwer, 99–117.

Posner, Richard A. 1988: "The Jurisprudence of Skepticism". *Michigan Law Review* 86, 827–858.

Postema, Gerald J. 1986: *Bentham and the Common Law Tradition.* Oxford: Clarendon Press.

Prakken, Henry 1997: *Logical Tools for Modelling Legal Argument: A Study in Defeasible Reasoning in Law*. Dordrecht: Kluwer.
Riggs v. Palmer 1889: 22 N.E. 188 (N.Y.).
Sartor, Giovanni 1995: "Defeasibility in Legal Reasoning". In: Zenon Bankowski, Ian White, & Ulrike Hahn (ed.), *Informatics and the Foundations of Legal Reasoning*. Dordrecht: Kluwer, 119–158.
Schauer, Frederick 1991: *Playing By the Rules: A Philosophical Examination of Rule-Based Decision-Making in Law and in Life*. Oxford: Clarendon Press.
— 1991: "Exceptions". *University of Chicago Law Review* 58, 871–904.
— 2004: "The Limited Domain of the Law". *Virginia Law Review* 90, 1909–1956.
— 2008: "A Critical Guide to Vehicles in the Park". *New York University Law Review* 83, 1109–1134.
Shapiro, Stewart 2011: "The Open-Texture of Computability" (unpublished).
Stelmach, Jerzy & Bartosz, Brożek 2006: *Methods of Legal Reasoning*. Dordrecht: Springer.
Stone, Julius 1985: *Precedent and Law*. Sydney: Butterworths.
Tennessee Valley Authority v. Hill 1978: 437 U.S. 153.
Tur, Richard 2001: "Defeasibilism". *Oxford Journal of Legal Studies* 21, 355–368.
United States v. Kirby 1868: 74 U.S. (7 Wall.) 482.
United States v. Locke 1985: 471 U.S. 84.
Waismann, Friedrich 1945: "Verifiability". *Proceedings of the Aristotelian Society (Supp.)* 19, 119–47, and in A.G.N. Flew (ed.), *Logic and Language (First Series)*. Oxford: Basil Blackwell (1951), 117–44.

Grazer Philosophische Studien
87 (2013), 217–257.

SELECTED THEMATIC BIBLIOGRAPHY OF WORK ON DEFEASIBILITY IN PHILOSOPHY AND RELATED DISCIPLINES

Michel de ARAUJO KURTH
Goethe Universität Frankfurt/Main

This is a bibliography of work on defeasibility from many different fields of philosophy and various related disciplines. In many cases the specialized discussions surrounding the concept of defeasibility are known only to experts who work in the respective areas (such as philosophy of law, epistemology, logic etc.). Given this situation, the primary aim of this bibliography is to facilitate exchange across discipline borders.

To collect the bibliographical data, several bibliographies and databases were used. In some cases survey papers of experts made it possible to decide which work should and which should not be included in this bibliography (for instance, use was made of the following articles in the Stanford Encyclopedia of Philosophy: 'Non-monotonic Logic', 'Defeasible reasoning', 'Logic and artificial intelligence'). Since the author himself has a background in law, legal philosophy and practical philosophy in general, he relied on his own experience with respect to these fields. But in many other cases this bibliography is not 'smarter' than the digital databases which were used for its construction (in particular: PhilPapers, Philosopher's Index, SSRN, JSTOR, Hollis-Harvard University). When a piece of literature was especially hard to come by and the author had no possibility of reading it for himself, the decision was based upon reading the abstract or upon the title alone.

Although all work on defeasibility I could find was included in this bibliography, it seems very likely that many relevant titles will have eluded my attention. In any case, I do not want to claim that this bibliography on defeasibility is complete.

In case a title fell under more than one section heading within the bibliography, it was brought under the heading that seemed most germane. This means that readers interested in one area may find relevant titles also in neighboring sections.

Even though this work is the product of one limited mind, I hope that it can be a helpful guide to those who want to learn more about work on defeasibility, particularly form research fields other than their own.

1. Ethics, moral philosophy, moral psychology, practical reasoning, deontic logic . . . 216
2. Philosophy of law, legal reasoning, AI and law . . . 220
3. Free will, responsibility and philosophy of action . . . 228
4. Philosophy of science . . . 229
5. Metaphysics and philosophy of religion . . . 230
6. Epistemology . . . 230
7. Philosophy of language and linguistics . . . 235
8. Formal logic and formal epistemology . . . 236
9. Philosophy of logic, informal logic, argumentation heory . . . 243
10. Philosophy of mind and philosophy of cognitive science . . . 246
11. Artificial intelligence and computer science . . . 247

1. *Ethics, moral philosophy, moral psychology, practical reasoning, deontic logic*

Adshead, Gwen (2003): "Measuring Moral Identities: Psychopaths and Responsibility", in: *Philosophy, Psychiatry, & Psychology* 10 (2), 185–187.

Alchourrón, Carlos Eduardo (1993): "Philosophical Foundations of Deontic Logic and the Logic of Defeasible Conditionals", in: J. J. Meyer, R. J. Wieringa (eds.), *Deontic Logic in Computer Sciences. Normative Systems Specifications*, New York: Wiley & Sons, 43–84.

— (1996): "Detachment and Defeasibility in Deontic Logic", in: *Studia Logica* 57 (1), 5–18.

Asher, Nicholas; Bonevac, Daniel (1996): "Prima facie obligation", in: *Studia Logica* 57 (1), 19–45.

— (2005): "Free choice permission is strong permission", in: *Synthese* 145 (3), 303–323.

Asscher, Joachim (2008): "The moral distinction between killing and letting die in medical cases", in: *Bioethics* 22 (5), 278–285.

Belzer, Marvin; Loewer, Barry (1993): "Absolute Obligations and Ordered Worlds", in: *Philosophical Studies* 72 (1), 47–70.

Björnsson, Gunnar; Almér, Alexander (2009): "Contextualism, assessor relativism, and insensitive assessments", in: *Logique Et Analyse* 52 (208), 363–372.

Bonevac, Daniel (1998): "Against conditional obligation", in: *Noûs* 32 (1), 37–53.

Bonevac, Daniel (2004): "Reflection without Equilibrium", in: *The Journal of Philosophy* 101 (7), 363–388.
Bratman, Michael (1979): "Practical Reasoning and Weakness of the Will", in: *Noûs* 13 (2), 153–171.
Brink, David (1994): "Moral conflict and its structure", in: *The Philosophical Review* 103, 215–247.
Broome, John (1999): "Normative requirements", in: *Ratio* 12, 398–419.
— (2004): "Reasons", in: R. Jay Wallace; Michael Smith; Samuel Scheffler; Philip Pettit (eds.), *Reason and Value: Essays on the Moral Philosophy of Joseph Raz*, Oxford: Oxford University Press, 28–55.
Carlos A., Oller (2006): "Obligaciones prima facie y derrotabilidad", in: *Análisis Filosófico* 26 (1), 147–155.
Chisholm, Roderick M. (1963): "Contrary-to-Duty Imperatives and Deontic Logic", in: *Analysis* 24, 33–36.
— (1964): "The Ethics of Requirement", in: *American Philosophical Quarterly* 1, 147–153.
Dancy, Jonathan (1983): "Ethical particularism and morally relevant properties", in: *Mind* 92, 530–547.
— (1991): "An ethic of prima facie duties", in: Peter Singer (ed.), *A Companion to Ethics*, Cambridge, Mass.: Blackwell Publishers, 219–229.
— (1993): *Moral Reasons*, Cambridge, Mass.: Blackwell Publishers.
— (2000): "The particularist's progress", in: Brad Hooker; Margaret Little (eds.), *Moral Particularism*, Oxford: Oxford University Press, 130–156.
— (2004): *Ethics without Principles*, New York: Oxford University Press.
— (2009): "Moral particularism": in: Edward Zalta (ed.), *The Stanford Encyclopedia of Philosophy*, Stanford University. Available online at http://plato.stanford.edu/entries/moral-particularism/.
Eglin, Peter (1979): "Resolving Reality Disjunctures on Telegraph Avenue: A Study of Practical Reasoning", in: *The Canadian Journal of Sociology* 4 (4), 359–377.
Ferguson, Kenneth G. (2003): "Monotonicity in Practical Reasoning", in: *Argumentation* 17 (3), 335–346.
Frohock, Fred M. (1972): "Reasoning in Politics", in: *The Journal of Politics* 34 (4), 1028–1061.
Gans, Chaim (1986): "Mandatory rules and exclusionary reasons", in: *Philosophia* 615, 373–394.
Geach, P.T. (1960): "Ascriptivism", in: *Philosophical Review* 69 (2), 221–225.
— (1966): "Dr. Kenny on Practical Inference", in: *Analysis* 26 (3), 76–79.
Gibbard, Allan (1990): *Wise Choices, apt Feelings: A Theory of normative Judgement*, Oxford: Clarendon Press.

Girill, T. R. (1978): "On the Defeasibility of Duties", in: *Journal of Value Inquiry* 12, 197–209.

Goble, Lou (2009): "Normative Conflicts and the Logic of 'Ought'", in: *Noûs* 43 (3), 450–489.

Goldman, Alan H. (1998): "Rules and Moral Reasoning", in: *Synthese* 117 (2), 229–250.

Henden, Edmund: (2006): "The Role of All Things Considered Judgments in Practical Deliberation", in: *Philosophical Explorations* 9, 295–308.

Holton, Richard (2002): "Principles and Particularism", in: *Proceedings of the Aristotelian Society* Suppl. vol. 76, 191–208.

Hooker, Brad; Little, Margaret (Eds.) (2000): *Moral Particularism*, Oxford: Oxford University Press.

Horty, John F. (1994): "Moral dilemmas and nonmonotonic logic", in: *Journal of Philosophical Logic* 23 (1), 35–65.

— (2003): "Reasoning with moral conflicts", in: *Nous* 37, 557–605.

— (2007): "Reasons as defaults", in: *Philosopher's Imprint* 7 (3), 1–28.

— (2012): *Reasons as Defaults*, Oxford: Oxford University Press.

Horty, John F.; Belnap, Nuel (1995): "The deliberative stit: a study of action, omission, ability, and obligation", in: *Journal of Philosophical Logic* 24, 583–644.

Hurtig, Kent (2007): "On prima facie obligations and nonmonotonicity", in: *Journal of Philosophical Logic* 36 (5), 599–604.

King, Matt (2008): "Robert Audi, Practical Reasoning and Ethical Decision", in: *Ethics* 118 (4), 717–721.

Kompa, Nikola (2004): "Moral particularism and epistemic contextualism: Comments on Lance and little", in: *Erkenntnis* 61 (2/3), 457–467.

Lance, Mark; Little, Margaret (2004): "Defeasibility and the Normative Grasp of Context", in: *Erkenntnis* 61 (2/3), 435–455.

— (2007): "Where the laws are", in: Russ Shafer-Landau (ed.), *Oxford Studies in Metaethics. Volume 2*, Oxford: Oxford University Press, 149–171.

— (2008): "From particularism to defeasibility in ethics", in: Matjaa Potrc; Vojko Strahovnik; Marc Lance (eds.), *Challenging Moral Particularism*, New York: Routledge Publishers, 53–74.

Little, Margaret (2000): "Moral generalities revisited", in: Brad Hooker; Margaret Little (eds.), *Moral Particularism*, Oxford: Oxford University Press, 276–304.

— (2001): "On Knowing the 'Why': Particularism and Moral Theory", in: *The Hastings Center Report* 31 (4), 32–40.

McKeever, Sean; Ridge, Michael (2006): *Principled Ethics: Generalism as a Regulative Ideal*, Oxford: Oxford University Press.

— (2007): "Turning on default reasons", in: *Journal of Moral Philosophy* 4 (1), 55–76.

Morreau, Michael (1996): "Prima Facie and Seeming Duties", in: *Studia Logica: An International Journal for Symbolic Logic* 57 (1), 47–71.
Pacuit, Eric; Parikh, Rohit; Cogan, Eva (2006): "The logic of knowledge based obligation", in: *Synthese* 149 (2), 311–341.
Patton, Thomas E. (1956): "Reasoning in Moral Matters", in: *The Journal of Philosophy* 53 (17), 523–531.
Pietroski, Paul (1993): "Prima facie obligations, ceteris paribus laws in moral theory", in: *Ethics* 103, 489–515.
Pollock, John L. (1986): "A Theory of Moral Reasoning", in: *Ethics* 96 (3), 506–523.
Prakken, Henry (1996): "Two approaches to the formalisation of defeasible deontic reasoning", in: Studia *Logica* 57, 73–90.
Prakken, Henry; Sergot, Marek (1996): "Contrary-to-Duty Obligations", in: *Studia Logica* 57 (1), 91–115.
Raz, Joseph (2000): "The truth in particularism", in: Brad Hooker; Margaret Little (eds.), *Moral Particularism*, Oxford: Oxford University Press, 48–78.
— (2006): "The Trouble with Particularism (Dancy's Version)", in: *Mind* 115 (457), 99–120.
— (ed.) (1978): *Practical Reasoning*, Oxford: Oxford University Press.
Richardson, Henry (1990): "Specifying norms as a way to resolve concrete ethical problems", in: *Philosophy and Public Affairs* 19, 279–310.
Robins, Michael H. (1983): "Practical Inference, Necessity and Defeasibility", in: *Indian Philosophical Quarterly* 10, 405–424.
— (2010): "Are some prima facie duties more binding than others?", in: *Utilitas* 22 (1), 26–32.
Ross, David (1930): *The Right and the Good*, Oxford: Oxford University Press.
Schroeder, Mark (2009): "A matter of principle", in: *Nous* 43, 568–580.
— (2011): "Holism, weight, and undercutting", in: *Nous* 45, 328–344.
Searle, John (1980): "Prima-facie obligations", in: Zak van Straaten (ed.), *Philosophical Subjects: Essays Presented to P. F. Strawson*, Oxford: Oxford University Press, 238–259.
Skourpski, John (1997): "Reasons and reason", in: Garret Cullity; Berys Gaut (eds.), *Ethics and Practical Reason*, Oxford: Oxford University Press, 345–368.
Sosa, Ernest (1994): "Moral Relativism, Cognitivism and Defeasible Rules", in: *Social Philosophy and Policy* 11 (1), 116–138.
Väyrynen, Pekka (2004): "Particularism and Default Reasons", in: *Ethical Theory and Moral Practice* 7 (1), 53–79.
— (2011): "Moral particularism", in: Christian B. Miller (ed.), *Continuum Companion to Ethics*, London; New York: Continuum Books, 247–260.

Vorobej, Mark (2006): "Defeasibility, trust, and the priority thesis", in: *Dialogue* 45 (4), 755 –761.
Walton, Douglas N. (2007): "Evaluating Practical Reasoning", in: *Synthese* 157 (2), 197–240.
White, Heath (2006): "Desires in Practical Reasoning", in: *Philosophical Studies: An International Journal for Philosophy in the Analytic Tradition* 129 (2), 197–221.

2. *Philosophy of law, legal reasoning, AI and law*

Alchourrón , Carlos Eduardo (2013): "On Law and Logic", in: Jordi Ferrer Beltrán; Giovanni Battista Ratti (eds.), *Logics of Legal Requirements. Essays on Legal Defeasibility,* Oxford: Oxford University Press, 39–52.
— (1991): "Condicionalidad y la representación de las normas jurídicas", in: C. Alchourrón; E. Bulygin (eds.), *Análisis lógico y derecho,* Madrid: Centro de Estudios Constitucionales, 267–269.
— (2000): "Sobre Derecho y Lógica", in: *Isonomía* 13, 11–33.
Alchourrón, Carlos Eduardo; Bulygin, Eugenio (1971): *Normative Systems*, New York: Springer Verlag (Library of exact philosophy, 5).
— (1996): "Norma Jurídica", in: E. Garzón Valdés; F. Laporta (eds.), *El Derecho y la Justicia. Enciclopedia Iberoamericana de Filosofía*, Madrid: Trotta.
Alexy, Robert (1979): "Zum Begriff des Rechtsprinzips", in: *Rechtstheorie,* Beiheft (1), 59–87.
— (1985): "Rechtsregeln und Rechtsprinzipien", in: *Archiv für Rechts- und Sozialphilosophie*, Beiheft NF 25, 13–29.
— (2000): "Prakken, Henry (1997), Logical Tools for Modelling Legal Argument. A Study of Defeasible Reasoning in Law", in: *Argumentation* 14 (1), 65–72.
— (1978): *Theorie der juristischen Argumentation: die Theorie des rationalen Diskurses als Theorie der juristischen Begründung*, Frankfurt am Main: Suhrkamp.
— (1994): *Theorie der Grundrechte*, Frankfurt am Main: Suhrkamp.
Atiyah, Patrick S.; Summers Robert S. (1987): *Form and Substance in Anglo-American Law. A Comparative Study of Legal Reasoning, Legal Theory and Legal Institutions*, New York: Oxford University Press.
Atria, Fernando (2013): "Legislation and Adjudication", in: Jordi Ferrer Beltrán; Giovanni Battista Ratti (eds.), *Logics of Legal Requirements. Essays on Legal Defeasibility,* Oxford: Oxford University Press, 327–361.
Bankowski, Z. (Ed.) (1995): *Informatics and the foundations of legal reasoning*, Dordrecht; Boston: Kluwer Academic Publishers.
Bayón, Juan Carlos (2000): "Derrotabilidad, Indeterminación del Derecho y Positivismo Jurídico" in: *Insomonía 13,* 88–117.

Bayón, Juan Carlos (2001): "Why is legal reasoning defeasible?", in: A. Soeteman (ed.), *Pluralism and Law, Dordrecht; Boston: Kluwer Academic Publishers, 327*–346.

Beltrán, Jordi Ferrer; Ratti, Giovanni Battista (2013): "Defeasibility: An Introduction", in: Jordi Ferrer Beltrán; Giovanni Battista Ratti (eds.), *Logics of Legal Requirements. Essays on Legal Defeasibility,* Oxford: Oxford University Press, 1–10.

— (2013): "Defeasibility and Legality. A Survey", in: Jordi Ferrer Beltrán; Giovanni Battista Ratti (eds.), *Logics of Legal Requirements. Essays on Legal Defeasibility,* Oxford; Oxford University Press, 11–38.

— (eds.) (2013): *Logics of Legal Requirements. Essays on Legal Defeasibility,* Oxford: Oxford University Press.

Berman, Mitchell N. (2003): "Justification and Excuse, Law and Morality", in: *Duke Law Journal* 53 (1), 1–77.

Bermejo, Juan Manuel Pérez (2013): "Principles, Conflicts, and Defeats: An Approach from A Coherentist Theory", in: Jordi Ferrer Beltrán; Giovanni Battista Ratti (eds.), *Logics of Legal Requirements. Essays on Legal Defeasibility,* Oxford: Oxford University Press, 288–308.

Bex, Floris; Prakken, Henry; Reed, Chris; Walton, Douglas N. (2003): "Towards a formal account of reasoning about evidence: Argumentation schemes and generalizations", in: *Artificial Intelligence and Law* 11 (2-3), 125–165.

Bix, Brian (1991): "H.L.A. Hart and the Open Texture of Language", in: *Law and Philosophy*, 51–72.

— (2013): "Defeasibility and Open Texture", in: Jordi Ferrer Beltrán; Giovanni Battista Ratti (eds.), *Logics of Legal Requirements. Essays on Legal Defeasibility,* Oxford: Oxford University Press, 193–201.

Boonin, Leonard G. (1966): "Concerning the Defeasibility of Legal Rules", in: *Philosophy and Phenomenological Research* 26 (3), 371–378.

Borowski, Martin (Ed.) (2010): *On the nature of legal principles. Proceedings of the special workshop "The Principles Theory" held at the 23rd World congress of the International Association for Philosophy of Law and Social Philosophy (IVR), Kraków, 2007 (ARSP Beiheft 119),* Stuttgart: Franz Steiner Verlag.

Brożek, B. (2004): *Defeasibility of Legal Reasoning*, Zakamyce: Kantor.

— (2008): "Revisability versus Defeasibility', in: *Northern Ireland Legal Quarterly* 59 139–47.

Caracciolo, Ricardo (2006): "Normas derrotables: La concepción de Carlos de Alchourrón", in: *Análisis Filosófico* 26 (1), 156–177.

— (2013): "Acts, Normative Formulations and Defeasible Norms", in: Jordi Ferrer Beltrán; Giovanni Battista Ratti (eds.), *Logics of Legal Requirements. Essays on Legal Defeasibility,* Oxford: Oxford University Press, 209–224.

Celano, Bruno (2013): "True Exceptions: Defeasibility and Particularism", in: Jordi Ferrer Beltrán; Giovanni Battista Ratti (eds.), *Logics of Legal Requirements. Essays on Legal Defeasibility,* Oxford: Oxford University Press, 268–287.

Chapman, Bruce (1998): "Law Games: Defeasible Rules and Revisable Rationality", in: *Law and Philosophy* 17 (4), 443–480.

— (1998): "Law, Incommensurability, and Conceptually Sequenced Argument", in: *University of Pennsylvania Law Review* Vol. 146, 1487–1528.

— (2008): "Pluralism in Tort and Accident Law: Toward a Reasonable Accommodation, in: Gerald J. Postema (ed.), *Philosophy and the Law of Torts,* New York: Cambridge University Press, 276–322.

— (2013): "Defeasible Rules and Interpersonal Accountability", in: Jordi Ferrer Beltrán; Giovanni Battista Ratti (eds.), *Logics of Legal Requirements. Essays on Legal Defeasibility,* Oxford: Oxford University Press, 401–417.

Cherry, Christopher (1974): "The Limits of Defeasibility", in: *Analysis* 34 (3), 101–107.

Chiassoni, Pierluigi (2013): "Defeasibility and Legal Indeterminacy", in: Jordi Ferrer Beltrán; Giovanni Battista Ratti (eds.), *Logics of Legal Requirements. Essays on Legal Defeasibility,* Oxford: Oxford University Press, 151–181.

Coval, S.C.; Smith, J.C. (1982): "Rights, Goals, and Hard Cases", in: *Law and Philosophy* 1 (3), 451–480.

Duarte, D'Almeida (2007): "Description, Ascription, and Action in the Criminal Law", in: *Ratio Juris* 20 (2), 170–195.

Duarte, David (2011): "Linguistic Objectivity in Norm Sentences: Alternatives in Literal Meaning", in: *Ratio Juris* Vol. 24, 112–139.

Dworkin, Ronald (1967/1978): "Model of Rules I", in: Ronald Dworkin (ed.), *Taking Rights Seriously,* Cambridge: Harvard University Press, Ch. 2, 14–46 (first published in: University of Chicago Law Review 1967).

Edmundson, William (1993): "Rethinking exclusionary reasons: a second edition of Joseph Raz's 'Practical Reason and Norms'", in: *Law and Philosophy* 12, 329–343.

Epstein, Richard E. (2005): "The Not So Minimum Content of Natural Law", in: *Oxford Journal of Legal Studies* Vol. 25, 219–255.

Ferrer Beltrán, Jordi; Ratti, Giovanni Battista (2010): "Validity and Defeasibility in the Legal Domain", in: *Law and Philosophy* (5), 606–626.

Fields, Lloyd (1996): "Psychopathy, Other-Regarding Moral Beliefs, and Responsibility", in: *Philosophy, Psychiatry & Psychology* 3 (4) 261–277.

Friedman, R.D. (1998): "Logic and Elements", in: *Notre Dame Law Review* 73, 575–602.

Fuller, Lon (1958): "Positivism and Fidelity of Law. A reply to Professor Hart", in: *Harvard Law Review* 71, 630–672.

Gordon, Thomas F. (1993): "The pleadings game: Formalizing Procedural Justice", in: *Proceedings of the Fourth International Conference on Artificial Intelligence and Law*, 10–19.

— (1995): *The pleadings game: An artificial intelligence model of procedural justice*, Dordrecht; Boston: Kluwer Academic Publishers.

Governatori, Guido; Palmirani, Monica; Riveret, Régis; Rotolo, Antonio; Sartor, Giovanni (2007): "Variants of Temporal Defeasible Logics for Modelling Norm Modifications", in: *Proceedings of Eleventh International Conference on Artifical Intelligence and Law*, New York: ACM, 155–159.

Governatori, Guido; Rotolo, Antonino (2008): "A computational framework for institutional agency", in: *Artificial Intelligence and Law* 16 (1), 25–52.

Guastini, Riccardo (2006): "Variaciones sobre temas de Carlos Alchourrón Riccardo Guastini y Eugenio Bulygin: Derrotabilidad, lagunas axiológicas e interpretación", in: *Análisis Filosófico*, 26 (2), 277–293.

— (2013): "Defeasibility, Axiological Gaps, and Interpretation", in: Jordi Ferrer Beltrán; Giovanni Battista Ratti (eds.), *Logics of Legal Requirements. Essays on Legal Defeasibility*, Oxford: Oxford University Press, 182–192.

Günther, Klaus, (2006): "Hirnforschung und strafrechtlicher Schuldbegriff", in: *Kritische Justiz*, 39 (2), 116-132.

— (1988): *Der Sinn für Angemessenheit. Anwendungsdiskurse in Moral und Recht*, Frankfurt am Main: Suhrkamp.

— (2005): *Schuld und kommunikative Freiheit: Studien zur personalen Zurechnung strafbaren Unrechts im demokratischen Rechtsstaat*, Frankfurt am Main: Klostermann.

Hacker, P. M. S. (1977): "Harts Philosophy of Law", in: P. M. S. Hacker; Joseph Raz (eds.) *Law, Morality and Society. Essays in Honour of H. L. A. Hart*, Oxford: Clarendon Press, 1–26.

Hage, Jaap (2010): *Reasoning with rules. An essay on legal reasoning and its underlying logic*, Dordrecht, Boston: Kluwer Academic Publishers.

— (1996): "A Theory of Legal Reasoning and a Logic to Match", in: *Artificial Intelligence and Law*, 199–273.

— (2003): "Law and Defeasibility", in: *Artificial Intelligence and Law* 11, 221–243.

— (2005): *Studies in Legal Logic*, Dordrecht: Springer.

Hage, Jaap; Peczenik, Aleksander (2000): "Law, Morals, and Defeasibility", in: *Ratio Juris* 13, 305–25.

Hansen, Jörg (2006): "Deontic logic for prioritized imperatives", in: *Artificial Intelligence and Law* 14, 1–34.

Hart, H. L. A. (1948-49/1951): "The Ascription of Responsibility and Rights", in: Anthony Flew (ed.) *Logic and Language*, Oxford: Blackwell, 145–166 (first published in: *Proceedings of the Aristotelian Society* 1948-9).

Hart, H.L.A. (1958): "Positivism and the Separation of Law and Morals", in: *Harvard Law Review* 71, 593–629.

— (1961/1994): *The Concept of Law*, 2. ed., New York: Oxford University Press.

— (1968): "Legal Responsibility and Excuses" in: Herbert, L. A. (ed.), *Punishment and Responsibility*, Oxford: Oxford University Press 28–53.

Helm, Paul (1968): "Defeasibility and Open Texture", in: *Analysis* 28, 173–175.

Hernández, Rafael Marín (2013): "Defeasible Properties", in: Jordi Ferrer Beltrán; Giovanni Battista Ratti (eds.), *Logics of Legal Requirements. Essays on Legal Defeasibility*, Oxford: Oxford University Press, 137–150.

Honoré, A. (1977): "Real Laws", in: P. Hacker; J. Raz (eds.), *Law, Morality and Society*, Oxford: Clarendon Press, 99–119.

Horty, John F. (2011): "Rules and reasons in the theory of precedent", in: *Legal Theory* 17, 1–33.

Hruschka, Joachim (1991): "Verhaltensregeln und Zurechnungsregeln", in: *Rechtstheorie* 22, 449–460.

— (2005): "Justification and Excuses: A systematic Approach", in: *Ohio State Journal of Criminal Law* 2, 407–413.

Jackson, B.S. (1998): *Law, Fact and Narrative Coherence*, Liverpool: Deborah Charles Publications.

Kowalski, Robert A.; Toni, Francesca Toni (1996): "Abstract argumentation", in: *Artificial Intelligence and Law* 4 (3-4), 275–296.

Loui, Ronald P. (1995): "Harts Critics on Defeasible Concepts and Ascriptivism", in: *Proceedings of the 5th International Conference on Artificial Intelligence and Law*, ACM Press, 21–30.

Lyons, David (1999): "Open Texture and the Possibility of Legal Interpretation", in: *Law and Philosophy* 18, 297–309.

MacCormick, Neil (1996): "Defeasibility in Law and Logic", in: Zenon Bankowski et. al. (ed.), *Informatics and the Foundations of Legal Reasoning*, Dordrecht; Boston: Kluwer Academic Publishers, 99–117.

— (2007): *Institutions of law. An essay in legal theory*, Oxford; New York: Oxford University Press.

Manero, Juan Ruiz; Atienza, Manuel (2013): "Rules Principles and Defeasibility", in: Jordi Ferrer Beltrán; Giovanni Battista Ratti (eds.), *Logics of Legal Requirements. Essays on Legal Defeasibility*, Oxford: Oxford University Press, 238–253.

Maranhão, Juliano S. A. (2013): "Defeasibility, Contributory Conditionals, and Refinement of Legal Systems" in: Jordi Ferrer Beltrán; Giovanni Battista Ratti (eds.), *Logics of Legal Requirements. Essays on Legal Defeasibility*, Oxford; Oxford University Press, 53–76.

Marmor, Andrei (1999): "The Separation Thesis and the Limits of Interpretation", in: *Canadian Journal of Law and Jurisprudence* 12, 135–150.

Marmor, Andrei (2005): *Interpretation and Legal Theory*, 2. ed., Oxford, Portland: Hart Publishers.
Mendonca, Daniel (2013): "Exceptions", in: Jordi Ferrer Beltrán; Giovanni Battista Ratti (eds.), *Logics of Legal Requirements. Essays on Legal Defeasibility*, Oxford: Oxford University Press, 202–208.
Moore, Michael (1989): "Authority, law, and Razian reasons", in: *Southern California Law Review* 62, 827–896.
Moreso, José Juan (2013): "Legal Defeasibility and the Connection between Law and Morality", in: Jordi Ferrer; Giovanni Battista Ratti (eds.), *Logics of Legal Requirements. Essays on Legal Defeasibility*, Oxford: Oxford University Press, 225–237.
Moreso, José Juan; Navarro, P.; Redondo, M.C. (2000): *Lliçons de filosofía del dret*, Barcelona: Ediuoc.
Morscher, Edgar (2009): *Kann denn Logik Sünde sein? Die Bedeutung der modernen Logik für Theorie und Praxis des Rechts*. Wien: Lit Verlag.
Nash, Jonathan Remy (2013): "Legal Defeasibility in Context and the Emergence of Substantial Indefeasibility", in: Jordi Ferrer Beltrán; Giovanni Battista Ratti (eds.), *Logics of Legal Requirements. Essays on Legal Defeasibility*, Oxford: Oxford University Press, 377–400.
Nitta, Katsumi; Shibasaki, Masato (1997): "Defeasible reasoning in japanese criminal jurisprudence", in: *Artificial Intelligence and Law* 5 (1–2), 139–159.
Panaccio, Charles-Maxime (2011): "In Defence of Two Step Balancing and Proportionality in Rights Adjudication", in: *Canadian Journal of Law and Jurisprudence* Vol. 24, 109–128.
Peczenik, Aleksander (1989): *On Law and Reason*, Boston; Dordrecht: Kluwer Academic Publishers.
— (1996): "Jumps and logic in the law", in: *Artificial Intelligence and Law* 4 (3-4), 297–329.
— (2000): "Scientia iuris - an unsolved philosophical problem", in: *Ethical Theory and Moral Practice* 3 (3), 273–302.
Perry, Stephen (1987): "Judicial obligation, precedent, and the common law", in: *Oxford Journal of Legal Studies* 7, 215–257.
— (1989): "Second-order reasons, uncertainty, and legal theory", in: *Southern California Law Review* 62, 913–994.
Petroski, Karen (2008): "The public face of presumptions", in: *Episteme* 5 (3), 388–401.
Prakken, Henry (1997): *Logical Tools for Modelling Legal Arguments. A Study of Defeasible Reasoning in Law*, Dordrecht, Bosten: Kluwer Academic Publishers.
Prakken, Henry (2008): "A formal model of adjudication dialogues", in: *Artificial Intelligence and Law* 16 (3), 305–328.

Prakken, Henry; Sartor, Giovanni (1996): "A dialectical model of assessing conflicting arguments in legal reasoning", in: *Artificial Intelligence and Law* 4 (3-4), 331–368.

— (2004): "The Three Faces of Defeasibility in the Law", in: *Ratio Juris* 17, 118–139.

Raz, Joseph (1972): "Legal Principles and the Limits of Law", in: *Yale Law Journal* 81, 823–854.

— (1975/1999): *Practical Reasons and Norms*, Oxford, New York: Oxford University Press.

— (2001): "Two Views of the Nature of the Theory of Law. A Partial Comparison", in: Jules Coleman (ed.), *Hart's Postscript: Essays on the Postscript to The Concept of Law,* Oxford, New York: Oxford University Press, 1–37.

Redondo, Maria Cristina (2005): "Legal Reasons. Between Universalism and Particularism", in: *Journal of Moral Philosophy* 2 (1), 47–68.

— (2013): "Reasons for Action and Defeasibility", in: Jordi Ferrer Beltrán; Giovanni Battista Ratti (eds.), *Logics of Legal Requirements. Essays on Legal Defeasibility,* Oxford: Oxford University Press, 309–326.

Rissland, Edwina L. (1990): "Artificial Intelligence and Law: Stepping Stones to a Model of Legal Reasoning", in: *The Yale Law Journal* 99 (8), 1957–1981.

Rodríguez, Jorge L. (2000): "Axiological Gaps and Normative Relevance", in: *Archiv für Rechts- und Sozialphilosophie* 86, 151–167.

— (2013): "Against Defeasibility of Legal Rules", in: Jordi Ferrer Beltrán; Giovanni Battista Ratti (eds.), *Logics of Legal Requirements. Essays on Legal Defeasibility,* Oxford: Oxford University Press, 89–107.

Royakkers, L. M. M. (2000): "Henry Prakken, logical tools for modelling legal argument: A study of defeasible reasoning in law", in: *Journal of Logic, Language and Information* 9 (3), 379–387.

Sachs, Stephen E. (2012): "Constitutional Backdrops", in: *George Washington Law Review* Vol. 80, 1813–1888.

Sartor, Giovanni (1993): "Defeasibility in Legal Reasoning", in: *Rechtstheorie,* 281–316.

— (1994): "A Formal Logic for Legal Argumentation", in: *Ratio Juris* 7, 212–226.

— (1998): "Modelling Reasoning with Precedents in a Formal Dialogue Game", in: *Artificial Intelligence and Law* 6, 231–238.

— (2008): "Syllogism and Defeasibility: A Comment on Neil Mac Cormick's Rhetoric and the Rule of Law", in: *Northern Ireland Legal Quarterly* 59, 20–31.

— (2013): "Defeasibility in Legal Reasoning", in: Jordi Ferrer Beltrán; Giovanni Battista Ratti (eds.), *Logics of Legal Requirements. Essays on Legal Defeasibility,* Oxford: Oxford University Press, 108–136.

Schauer, Frederick (1988): "On the supposed Defeasibility of Legal Rules", in: M.D.A. Freeman (ed.), *Current Legal Problems, vol. 51. Legal Theory at the end of the Millennium*, Oxford; New York: Oxford University Press, 223–240.

— (1991): "Exceptions", in: *The University of Chicago Law Review* 58, 871–904.

— (1991): *Playing by the Rules. A Philosophical Examination of Rule-Based Decision-Making in Law and Life*, Oxford: Clarendon Press.

— (2008): "A Critical Guide to Vehicles in The Park", in: *New York University Law Review* 83, 1109–1134.

— (2013): "Is Defeasibility an Essential Property of Law?", in: Jordi Ferrer Beltrán; Giovanni Battista Ratti (eds.), *Logics of Legal Requirements. Essays on Legal Defeasibility*, Oxford: Oxford University Press, 77–88.

Shapiro, Scott J. (2011): *Legality*, Cambridge, Mass.: Harvard University Press.

Sieckmann, Jan-R. (2003): "Why non-monotonic logic is inadequate to represent balancing arguments" in: *Artificial Intelligence and Law* 11 (2-3), 211–219.

Sinclair Jr., Kent (1971): "Legal Reasoning: In Search of an Adequate Theory of Argument", in: *California Law Review* 59 (3), 821–858.

Soeteman, Arend (Ed.) (2001): *Pluralism and law*, Dordrecht; Boston: Kluwer Academic Publishers.

Stelmach, Jerzy; Brożek, Bartosz (2006): *Methods of Legal Reasoning*, Dordrecht: Springer (Law and Philosophy Library, v. 78).

Stone, Martin (1995): "Focusing the Law. What Legal Interpretation is not", in: Andrei Marmor (ed.), *Law and Interpretation. Essays in Legal Philosophy*, Oxford, New York: Clarendon Press, 31–97.

Sunstein, Cass R. (1996): *Legal Reasoning and Political Conflict*, New York: Oxford University Press.

Susskind, Richard E. (1987): *Expert Systems in Law*, New York: Oxford University Press.

Tur, Richard H. S. (2001): "Defeasibilism", in: *Oxford Journal of Legal Studies* 21 (2), 355–368.

— (2013): "Defeasibility and Adjudication", in: Jordi Ferrer Beltrán; Giovanni Battista Ratti (eds.), *Logics of Legal Requirements. Essays on Legal Defeasibility*, Oxford: Oxford University Press, 362–376.

Verheij, Bart (2000): "Henry Prakken (1997). Logical tools for modelling legal argument. A study of defeasible reasoning in law", in: *Artificial Intelligence and Law* 8 (1), 35–65.

Verheij, Bart (2003): "Dialectical argumentation with argumentation schemes: An approach to legal logic", in: *Artificial Intelligence and Law* 11 (2-3), 167–195.

Walton, Douglas N. (2005): *Argumentation methods for artificial intelligence in law. With 28 figures*, Berlin; New York: Springer.

Wang, Peng-Hsiang (2003): *Defeasibility in der juristischen Begründung,* Baden-Baden: Nomos.

Waluchow J., Wilfrid (2013): "Defeasibility and Legal Positivism", in: Jordi Ferrer Beltrán; Giovanni Battista Ratti (eds.), *Logics of Legal Requirements. Essays on Legal Defeasibility,* Oxford: Oxford University Press, 254–267.

Willaschek, Marcus (2011): "Der Begriff der Willensfreiheit im deutschen Strafrecht", in: Carl Friedrich Gethmann; J. Carl Bottek; Susanne Hiekel (eds.), *Lebenswelt und Wissenschaft. XXI. Deutscher Kongreß für Philosophie 15. – 19. September 2008 an der Universität Duisburg – Essen. Kolloquienbeiträge,* Hamburg: Felix Meiner Verlag, 1185–1203.

3. *Free will, responsibility and philosophy of action*

Austin, J.L. (1956): "A Plea for Excuses", in: *Proceedings of the Aristotelian Society* 57, 1–30.

Ciocchetti, Christopher (2003): "The Responsibility of the Psychopathic Offender", in: *Philosophy, Psychiatry & Psychology* 10 (2), 175–183.

Fischer, John Martin; Ravizza, Mark (1998): *Responsibility and Control,* Cambridge University Press.

Maier, Andreas (2006): *Die Zuschreibung von Verantwortung,* Master-Thesis, Frankfurt am Main. Available online at http://publikationen.ub.uni-frankfurt.de/volltexte/2007/4061/.

Stoljar, S. (1959): "Ascriptive and Prescriptive Responsibility", in: *Mind* 68, 350–360.

Strawson, Peter (1963/2003): "Freedom and Resentment", in: Gary Watson (ed.) *Free Will,* 2. ed., Oxford; New York: Oxford University Press, 72–94.

Wallace, R. Jay (1994): *Responsibility and the Moral Sentiments,* Cambridge: Harvard University Press.

Walsh, V C. "Ascriptions and Appraisals", in: *Journal of Philosophy* 55, 1062– 1072.

Willaschek, Marcus (2002): "DNS – Doch nicht schuldig? Zum Zusammenhang zwischen genetischer Disposition und persönlicher Verantwortung", in: *Jahrbuch für Wissenschaft und Ethik,* 7, 243–257.

— (2003): "Freiheit als Bedingung für Verantwortung. Ein kurzes Argument für den Kompatibilismus", in: S. Mischer, Michael Quante, Christian Suhm (eds.), *Auf Freigang. Metaphysische und ethische Annäherung an die menschliche Freiheit,* Münster, 199–205.

— (2010): "Non-Relativist Contextualism about Free Will", in: *European Journal of Philosophy,* 18 (4), 567–587.

Wilson, P. Eddy (1996): "Sanity and Responsibility", in: *Philosophy, Psychiatry & Psychology* 3 (4), 293–302.

4. *Philosophy of science*

Aliseda, Atocha (2003): "Mathematical Reasoning vs. Abductive Reasoning: A Structural Approach", in: *Synthese* 134 (1/2), 25–44.
Armstrong, David M. (1983): *What is a law of nature?* New York: Cambridge University Press.
Fales, Evan (1978): "Theoretical Simplicity and Defeasibility", in: *Philosophy of Science* 45 (2), 273–288.
Müller, Olaf L. (2000): "Kantische Antworten auf die moderne Physik oder sollen wir Kants Apriori mit Michael Friedman relativieren", in: *Philosophia Naturalis*, 37 Heft 1, 97–130.
Pollock, John L. (1986): "The Paradox of the Preface", in: *Philosophy of Science* 53 (2), 246–258.
— (1992): "The Theory of Nomic Probability", in: *Synthese* 90 (2), 263–299.
— (2002): "Causal Probability", in: *Synthese* 132 (1/2), 143–185.
Ruttkamp, Emma; Heidema, Johannes (2005): "Reviewing reduction in a preferential model-theoretic context", in: *International Studies in the Philosophy of Science* 19 (2), 123–146.
Schurz, Gerhard (2001): "Normische Gesetzeshypothesen und die wissenschaftsphilosophische Bedeutung des nichtmonotonen Schliessens", in: *Journal for General Philosophy of Science* 32 (1), 65–107.
Spohn, Wolfgang (2002): "Laws, ceteris paribus conditions, and the dynamics of belief", in: *Erkenntnis* 57 (3), 373–394.
— (2004): "Laws Are Persistent Inductives Schemes", in: Friedrich Stadler (ed.), *Induction and Deduction in the Sciences*, Dordrecht; Boston: Kluwer, 135–150.
Stadler, Friedrich (Ed.) (2004): *Induction and Deduction in the Sciences,* Dordrecht; Boston: Kluwer.
Suárez, Mauricio (2010): "Experimental realism defended. How inference to the most likely cause might be sound", in: Bovens, Luc; Hoefer, Carl; Hartmann, Stephan (eds.), *Nancy Cartwright's philosophy of science,* London: Routledge (Routledge studies in the philosophy of science), 137–163.
Tohmé, Fernando; Delrieux, Claudio; Otávio, Bueno (2011): "Defeasible Reasoning + Partial Models: A Formal Framework for the Methodology of Research Programs", in: *Foundations of Science* 16 (1), 47–65.

5. *Metaphysics and philosophy of religion*

Alston, William P. (1991): *Perceiving God: The Epistemology of Religious Experience*, Ithaca: Cornell Uni. Press.

Audi, Robert (2008): "Belief, Faith, and Acceptance", in: *International Journal for Philosophy of Religion* 63 (1/3), 87–102.

Bonevac, Daniel (2001): "Defeasibly Sufficient Reason", in: *The Proceedings of the Twentieth World Congress of Philosophy*, 1–10.

Koons, Robert C. (1997): "A New Look at the Cosmological Argument", in: *American Philosophical Quarterly* 34 (2), 193–211.

Koons, Robert C. (2000): *"Realism Regained: An Exact Theory of Causation, Teleology and the Mind*, New York: Oxford University Press.

— (2001): "Defeasible Reasoning, Special Pleading and the Cosmological Argument: Reply to Oppy", in: *Faith and Philosophy* 18, 192–203.

Plantinga, Alvin; Wolterstorff, Nicholas (1983): *Faith and rationality: reason and belief in god*, Norte Dame: University of Norte Dame Press.

6. *Epistemology*

Achinstein, Peter (1965): "Defeasible Problems", in: *Journal of Philosophy* 62, 629–632.

Ackerman, Terrence F. (1974): "Defeasibility Modified", in: *Philosophical Studies: An International Journal for Philosophy in the Analytic Tradition* 26 (5/6), 431–435.

Adler, Jonathan Eric (1983): "A Note on Defeasibility and Skepticism", in: *Philosophia: Philosophical Quarterly of Israel* 12, 299–305.

Almeder, Robert (1973): "Defeasibility and Scepticism", in: *Australasian Journal of Philosophy* 51, 238–244.

Almeida, Claudio (2012): "Epistemic closure, skepticism and defeasibility", in: *Synthese* 188 (2), 197–215.

Angere, Staffan (2007): "The Defeasible Nature of Coherentist Justification", in: *Synthese* 157 (3), 321–335.

Annis, David (1973): "Knowledge and Defeasibility", in: *Philosophical Studies: An International Journal for Philosophy in the Analytic Tradition* 24 (3), 199–203.

— (1978): "A Contextualist Theory of Epistemic Justification", in: *American Philosophical Quarterly* 15, 213–219.

— (1981): "Swain's Causal Theory of Knowledge", in: *Southern Journal of Philosophy* 19, 149–156.

Arrington, Robert (1979): "Criteria and Entailment", in: *Ratio* 21, 62–72.

Audi, Robert (1983): "Foundationalism, Epistemic Dependence, and Defeasibility", in: *Synthese* 55 (1), 119–139.

— (1995): "Deductive Closure, Defeasibility and Scepticism: A Reply to Feldman," in: *The Philosophical Quarterly* 45 (181), 494–499.

Axtell, Guy (2007): "Two for the Show: Anti-luck and virtue epistemologies in consonance", in: *Synthese* 158, 363–383.
Bach, Kent (1985): "A Rationale for Reliabilism", in: *The Monist* 68 (2), 246–263.
Belzer, Marvin (1986): "Reasoning with Defeasible Principles", in: *Synthese* 66 (1), 135–158.
Bishop, Michael A. (2000): "In Praise of Epistemic Irresponsibility: How Lazy and Ignorant Can You Be?", in: *Synthese* 122 (1/2), 179–208.
Boghossian, Paul; Williamson Timothy (2003): "Blind Reasoning", in: *Proceedings of the Aristotelian Society*, Suppl. Vol. 77, 225–293.
Brown, Jessica (2004): "Non-Inferential Justification and Epistemic Circularity", in: *Analysis* 64 (4), 339–348.
Burge, Tyler (2003): "Percepetual Entitlement", in: *Philosophy and Phenomenological Research* 67 (3), 503–548.
Byrne, Alex; Logue, Heather (Eds.) (2009): *Disjunctivism. Contemporary Readings*, Cambridge, Mass: Mit Press (MIT readers in contemporary philosophy).
Casullo, Albert (1988): "Revisability, Reliabilism, and A priori Knowledge", in: *Philosophy and Phenomenological Research* 49 (2), 187–213.
— (2003): *A priori Justification*, Oxford; New York: Oxford University Press.
— (2009): "Analyzing a Priori Knowledge", in: *Philosophical Studies* 142 (1), 77–90.
Chisholm, Roderick M. (1957): *Perceiving*, Princeton: Princeton University Press.
— (1966): *Theory of Knowledge*, Englewood Cliffs: Prentice Hall.
Cohen, Stewart (1981): "Defeasibility and Background Beliefs", in: *Philosophical Studies* 39 (3), 263–273.
Cohen, Stewart (1986): "Knowledge and Context", in: *The Journal of Philosophy* 83 (10), 574–583.
— (1987): "Knowledge, Context, and Social Standards", in: *Synthese* 73 (1), 3–26.
— (2010): "Bootstrapping, defeasible reasoning, and a priori justification", in: *Philosophical Perspectives* 24 (1), 141–159.
Colin P., Ruloff (2000): "Some Remarks on Bonjour on Warrant, Proper Function, and Defeasibility", in: *Revista Internacional de Epistemologia* 4, 215–228.
Crane, Tim (1992): *The Contents of Experience: Essays on Perception*, Cambridge; New York: Cambridge University Press.
Dancy, Jonathan (1995): "Arguments from Illusion", in: *Philosophical Quarterly* 45, (181), 421–438.
Dancy, Jonathan (ed.) (1988): *Perceptual Knowledge*, Oxford: Oxford University Press.
De Almeida, Claudio (2007): "Closure, Defeasibility and Conclusive Reasons", in: *Acta Analytica* 22, 301–319.

DeRose, Keith (1995): "Solving the Skeptical Problem", in: *Philosophical Review*, 104 (1), 1–52.

Edidin, Aron (1983): "A Priori Knowledge for Fallibilists", in: *Philosophical Studies* 46, 189–197.

Field, Hartry (1998): "Epistemological Nonfactualism and the a Prioricity of Logic", in*: Philosophical Studies* 92, 1–24.

— (2005): "Recent Debates about the A priori", in: Tamar Szabo (ed.), *Oxford Studies in Epistemology* 1, 69–88.

Geirsson, H. (2005): "Conceivability and Defeasible Modal Justification", in: *Philosophical Studies: An International Journal for Philosophy in the Analytic Tradition* 122 (3), 279–304.

Gendler, Tamar S.; Hawthorne, John (Eds.) (2006): *Perceptual Experience*, Oxford: Clarendon Press.

Gillies, Anthony S. (2004): "New Foundations for Epistemic Change", in: *Synthese* 138 (1), 1–48.

Grundmann, Thomas (2004): "Inferential Contextualism, Epistemological Realism and Skepticism", in*: Erkenntnis* 61, 345 – 352.

— (2009): "Reliabilism and the problem of defeaters", in: *Grazer Philosophische Studien* 79 (1), 65–76.

Henderson, David (2013): "Entitlement in Gutting's Epistemology of Philosophy: Comments on What Philosophers Know", in: *Southern Journal of Philosophy* 51 (1), 121–132.

Huemer, Michael (2001): "The Problem of Defeasible Justification", in: *Erkenntnis* 54 (3), 375–397.

Janvid, Mikael (2008): "Defeaters and Rising Standards of Justification", in: *Acta Analytica* 23 (1), 45–54.

— (2008): "The Experiential Defeasibility and Overdetermination of a Priori Justification", in: *Journal of Philosophical Research* (33), 271–278.

— (2009): "The Value of Lesser Goods: The Epistemic Value of Entitlement, in: *Acta Analytica* 24 (4), 263–274.

Kitcher, Philip (1980): "A priori Knowledge", in: *The Philosophical Review* 89, 3–23.

Kitcher, Philip (1983): *The Nature of Mathematical Knowledge,* New York: Oxford University Press.

Klein, Peter D. (1979): "Comments and Criticism: Misleading 'Misleading Defeaters'", in: *Journal of Philosophy* 76, 382–386.

Klein, Peter D. (1980): "Misleading Evidence and the Restoration of Justification", in: *Philosophical Studies* 37, 81–89.

— (1976): "Knowledge, Causality, and Defeasibility", in: *The Journal of Philosophy* 73 (20), 792–812.

Korb, Kevin B. (1992): "The Collapse of Collective Defeat: Lessons from the Lottery Paradox", in: *PSA: Proceedings of the Biennial Meeting of the Philosophy of Science Association* 1992, 230–236.
Levy, Steven R. (1977): "Defeasibility Theories of Knowledge", in: *Canadian Journal of Philosophy* 7, 115–123.
— (1978): "Misleading Defeaters", in: *Journal of Philosophy* 75, 739–742.
Lewis, David (1996): "Elusive Knowledge", in: *Australasian Journal of Philosophy*, 74 (4), 549–56.
Martin, M. F. (2001): "Epistemic Openess and Perceptual Defeasibility", in: *Philosophy and Phenomenological Research* 63 (2), 441–448.
McDowell, John (1998): "Criteria, Defeasibility and Knowledge", in: John McDowell (ed.), *Meaning, Knowledge and Reality*, Cambridge, Mass.: Harvard University Press, 369–394.
Naylor, Andrew (1982): "Defeasibility and Memory Knowledge", in: *Mind* 91 (363), 432–437.
Neta, Ram (2004): "Perceptual evidence and the new dogmatism", in: *Philosophical Studies* 119 (1–2), 199–214.
— (2009): "Defeating the Dogma of Defeasibility", in: Patrick Greenough; Duncan Pritchard (eds.), *Williamson on Knowledge*, Oxford; New York: Oxford University Press, 161–183.
Olin, Doris (1976): "Knowledge and defeasible justification", in: *Philosophical Studies* 30 (2), 129–136.
Pastin, Mark (1979): "A Decision Procedure for Epistemology?", in: *Philosophical Studies* 35 (3), 257–268.
Pollock, John L. (1967): "Criteria and Knowledge of the Material World", in: *The Philosophical Review*, 28–60.
— (1970): "The Structure of Epistemic Justification", in: *American Philosophical Quarterly* 4, 62–78.
— (1974): *Knowledge and Justification*, Princeton; London: Princeton University Press.
— (1983): "Epistemology and Probability", in: *Synthese* 55 (2), 231–252.
— (1987): "Epistemic Norms", in: *Synthese* 71 (1), 61–95.
Pollock, John L.; Cruz, Joseph (1999): *Contemporary Theories of Knowledge*, 2. ed., Rowman & Littlefield Publishers.
Pollock, John L.; Gillies, Anthony S. (2000): "Belief revision and epistemology" in: *Synthese* 122 (1–2), 69–92.
Prichard, Duncan (2004): "The Epistemology of Testimony", in: *Philosophical Issues* (Nous Supplement) 14, 326–348.
Pryor, James (2000): "The skeptic and the dogmatist", in: *Noûs* 34 (4), 517–549.
Pust, Joel (2002): "Kitcher on tradition-independent a priori warrant", in: *Philosophical Quarterly* 52 (208), 373–376.

Ram, Neta (2004): "Perceptual Evidence and the New Dogmatism", in: *Philosophical Studies* 119 (1-2), 199–214.

Reid, Thomas (1997) [1764]: *An Inquiry into the Human Mind: On the Principles of Common Sense*, (ed.) Derek Brooks, University Park.

Reiser, Andrew (2008): "Weighing Pragmatic and Evidential Reasons for Belief", in: *Philosophical Studies* 138, 17–27.

Scaduto-Horn, Deborah (1982): "A problem for Defeasibility Theories", in: *Journal of Philosophy* 79, 40–45.

Schantz, Richard (2005): Direct Realism, Disjunctivism, and the Common Sensory Content", in: M.E. Reicher; J.C. Marek (eds.), *Experience and Analysis. Akten des 27. internationalen Wittgensteins-Symposiums 2004*, Wien, 321–330.

Snowdon, Paul (1981): "Perception, Vision and Causation", in: *Proceedings of the Aristotelian Society*, 175–192.

— (1990): "The Objects of Perceptual Experience", in: *Proceedings of the Aristotelian Society*, Vol. 64, 121–150.

— (1992): "How to interpret 'Direct Perception'", in: Tim Crane (ed.), *The Contents of Experience*, Cambridge; New York: Cambridge University Press, 48–78.

— (2005): "The Formulation of Disjunctivism. A Response to Fish", in: *Proceedings of the Aristotelian Society*, 129–141.

Spohn, Wolfgang (1998): "How to understand the foundations of empirical belief in a coherentist way", in: *Proceedings of the Aristotelian Society* 98 (1), 22–40.

— (2002): "A brief comparison of Pollock's defeasible reasoning and ranking functions", in: *Synthese* 131 (1), 39–56.

Stevenson, Leslie (1993): "Why believe what people say?", in: *Synthese* 94 (3), 429–451.

Summerfield, Donna (1991): "Modest a Priori Knowledge", in: *Philosophy and Phenomenological Research* 51, 39–66.

Swain, Marshall (1974): "Epistemic Defeasibility", in: *American Philosophical Quarterly* 11, 15–25.

— (1981): *Reasons and Knowledge*, Ithaca: Cornell University Press.

Thurow, Jushua (2006): "Experientially Defeasible a Priori Justification", in: *The Philosophical Quarterly* 56 (225), 596–602.

Vahid, Hamid (1999): "A Priori Knowledge, Experience and Defeasibility", in: *International Journal of Philosophical Studies* 7 (2), 173–188.

Waismann, Friedrich (1945): "Verifiability", in: *Proceedings of the Aristotelian Society*, Suppl. Vol. 19, 119–150.

Walton, Douglas N. (2005): "Pragmatic and Idealized Models of Knowledge and Ignorance", in: *American Philosophical Quarterly* 42 (1), 59–69.

— (2006): "Rules for reasoning from knowledge and lack of knowledge", in: *Philosophia* 34 (3), 355–376.

Willaschek, Marcus (1998): "Skeptical Challenge and the Burden of Proof", in: M. Quante; A. Wüstenhube (eds.), *Pragmatic Idealism. Critical Discussions of Nicholas Rescher's System of Pragmatic Idealism,* Amsterdam, 203–224

— (2000): "Wissen, Zweifel, Kontext. Eine kontextualistische Zurückweisung des Skeptizismus", in: *Zeitschrift für philosophische Forschung* 54, 151–172.

— (2007): "Contextualism about Knowledge and Justification by Default", in: *Grazer Philosophische Studien* 74, 251–27.

Williams, Michael (1991): *Unnatural Doubts: Epistemological Realism and the Basis of Skepticism,* Princeton University Press.

— (2001): *Problems of Knowledge,* Oxford: Oxford University Press.

Wittgenstein, Ludwig (1984): "Über Gewissheit", in: *Ludwig Wittgenstein. Werkausgabe, Bd. 8,* Frankfurt am Main: Suhrkamp, 113–258.

Wolterstorff, Nicholas (2005): "Obligation, Entitlement, and Rationality", in: Matthias Steup (ed.), *Contemporary Debates in Epistemology,* Malden: Blackwell, 326–338.

Wright, Crispin (1984): "Second Thoughts about Criteria", in: *Synthese* 58, 383–406.

— (2004): "On Epistemic Entitlement: Warrant for Nothing (and Foundations for Free)?", in: *Proceedings of the Aristotelian Society,* SuVol. 78, 167–212.

7. *Philosophy of language and linguistics*

Asher, Nicholas (1992): "A Truth Conditional Default Semantics for the Progressive", in: *Linguistics and Philosophy* 15, 469–508.

Avron, Polakow (1982): "Radical Defeasibility and Rigid Designation", in: *Theoria: A Swedish Journal of Philosophy* 48, 78–89.

Bouma, Gosse (1961): *Nonmonotonicity and categorial unification grammar,* Groningen: Rijksuniversiteit Groningen.

Brandom, Robert (1998): *Making it explicit. Reasoning, representing, and discursive commitment,* Cambridge, Mass.: Harvard University Press.

— (2000): *Articulating Reasons. An introduction to inferentialism,* Cambridge, Mass.: Harvard. University Press.

Chellas, Brian (1974): "Conditional obligation", in: Søren Stenlund (ed.), *Logical Theory and Semantic Analysis,* D. Reidel Publishing Company, 23–33.

Hinzen, Wolfram (2000): "Anti-Realist Semantics", in: *Erkenntnis* 52 (3), 281–311.

Lascarides, Alex; Asher, Nicholas (1993): "Temporal Interpretation, Discourse Relations and Commonsense Entailment", in: *Linguistics and Philosophy* 16 (5), 437–493.

Lascarides, Alex; Briscoe, Ted; Asher, Nicholas; Copestake, Ann (1996): "Order Independent and Persistent Typed Default Unification", in: *Linguistics and Philosophy* 19 (1), 1–90.

Lascarides, Alex; Copestake, Ann (1998): "Pragmatics and Word Meaning", in: *Journal of Linguistics* 34 (2), 387–414.
Maier, Frederick; Nute, Donald (2010): "Well-founded semantics for defeasible logic", in: *Synthese* 176 (2), 243–274.
Polakow, Avron (1982): "Radical defeasibility and rigid designation", in: *Theoria* 48 (2), 78–89.
Porello, Daniele (2012): "Incompatibility Semantics from Agreement", in: *Philosophia* 40 (1), 99–19.
Spenader, Jennifer; Maier, Emar (2004): "Unifying contrast and denial", in: Jonathan Ginzburg; Enric Vallduví (eds.), *Proceedings of Catalog'04: The 8th Workshop on the Semantics and Pragmatics of Dialogue.*

8. *Formal logic and formal epistemology*

Alchourrón, Carlos Eduardo; Gärdenfors, Peter; Makinson, David (1982): "On the logic of theory change: contraction functions and their associated revision functions", in: *Theoria* 48, 14–37.
Allott, Nicholas; Uchida, Hiroyuki (2009): "Classical logic, conditionals and nonmonotonic reasoning", in: *Behavioral and Brain Sciences* 32 (1), 85.
Amati, Giambattista; Carlucci-Aiello, Luigia; Pirri, Fiora (1997): "Intuitionistic autoepistemic logic", in: *Studia Logica* 59 (1), 103–120.
Amati, Gianni; Aiello, Luigia Carlucci; Pirri, Fiora (1994): "Defaults as restrictions on classical Hilbert-style proofs", in: *Journal of Logic, Language and Information* 3 (4), 303–326.
Anderson, Alan; Belnap, Nuel; Dunn, J. Michael (1992): *Entailment: The Logic of Relevance and Necessity*, Volume 2, Princeton University Press.
Antonelli, G. Aldo (2005)*: Grounded Consequence for Defeasible Logic*, New York: Cambridge University Press.
Antoniou, Grigoris (1997): *Nonmonotonic reasoning*, Cambridge, Mass: MIT Press (Artificial Intelligence).
Arló-Costa, Horacio; Parikh, Rohit (2005): "Conditional Probability and Defeasible Inference", in: *Journal of Philosophical Logic* 34, 97–119.
Arló-Costa, Horacio; Scott, Shapiro (1992): "Maps Between Conditional Logic and Non-monotonic Logic", in: B. Nebel; C. Rich; W. Swartout (eds.), *Principles of Knowledge Representation and Reasoning: Proceedings of the Third International Conference*, San Mateo, California, 553–565.
Asher, Nicholas; Mao, Y. (2001): "Negated Defaults in Commonsense Entailment", in: *Bulletin of the Section of Logic* 30, 4–60.
Avron, Arnon; Arieli, Ofer (1998): "General Patterns for Nonmonotonic Reasoning: From Basic Entailments to Plausible Relations", in: *Logic Journal of the IGPL* 8 (2), 119–148.

Balduccini, Marcello; Son, Tran Cao (2011): *Logic Programming, Knowledge Representation, and Nonmonotonic Reasoning. Essays Dedicated to Michael Gelfond on the Occasion of His 65th Birthday*, Berlin, Heidelberg: Springer.

Bamber, Donald (2000): "Entailment with near surety of scaled assertions of high conditional probability", in: *Journal of Philosophical Logic* 29 (1), 1–74.

Batens, Diderik (2001): "A dynamic characterization of the pure logic of relevant implication", in: *Journal of Philosophical Logic* 30 (3), 267–280.

Berzati, Dritan (2007): Nonmonotonic reasoning. A unifying framework, Hauppauge, New York: Nova Science Publishers.

Betz, Gregor (2008): "Evaluating dialectical structures with bayesian methods", in: *Synthese* 163 (1), 25–44.

Bochman, Alexander (2000): "Belief contraction as nonmonotonic inference", in: *Journal of Symbolic Logic* 65 (2), 605–626.

— (2001): *A Logical Theory of Nonmonotonic Inference and Belief Change*, Berlin: Springer.

Bodanza, Gustavo A.; Tohmé, Fernando A. (2005): "Local Logics, Non-Monotonicity and Defeasible Argumentation", in: *Journal of Logic, Language, and Information* 14 (1), 1–12.

Bonavec, Daniel (2003): *Deduction: Introductory Symbolic Logic*, 2. ed., Malden, Mass.: Blackwell.

Brewka, Gerhard (2001): "Representing meta-knowledge in Poole-systems", in: *Studia Logica* 67 (2), 153–165.

Brewka, Gerhard; Janke, K. P.; Schmitt, P. H. (Eds.) (1993): *Nonmonotonic and inductive logic. Second international workshop, Reinhardsbrunn Castle, Germany, December 2-6, 1991: Proceedings*, Berlin: Springer-Verlag (Lecture notes in artificial intelligence, 659).

Buchsbaum, Arthur; Pequeno, Tarcisio; Pequeno, Marcelino (2007): "A Logical Expression of Reasoning", in: *Synthese* 154 (3), 431–466.

Cavedon, Lawrence (1998): "Default reasoning as situated monotonic inference", in: *Minds and Machines* 8 (4), 509–531.

Dix, J.; Fuhrbach, Ulrich; Nerode, Anil (Eds.) (1997): *Logic programming and nonmonotonic reasoning. 4th International Conference, LPNMR '97, Dagstuhl Castle, Germany, July 1997: proceedings*, Berlin; New York: Springer (Lecture notes in artificial intelligence, 1265).

Dix, Jürgen; Jantke, K. P.; Schmitt, P. H. (1991): *Nonmonotonic and inductive logic. 1st international workshop, Karlsruhe, Germany, December 4-7, 1990, proceedings*, Berlin; New York: Springer-Verlag (Lecture notes in artificial intelligence, 543).

Dix, Jürgen; Pereira, Luís Moniz; Przymusinski, Teodor C. (1995): *International Conference on Logic Programming: Non-monotonic extensions of logic program-*

ming. ICLP '94 workshop, Santa Margherita Ligure, Italy, June 17, 1994, selected papers, Berlin; New York: Springer (Lecture notes in artificial intelligence, 927).

Dix, Jürgen; Makinson, David (1992): "The relationship between KLM and MAK models for nonmonotonic inference operations", in: *Journal of Logic, Language and Information* 1 (2), 131–140.

Eiter, Thomas; Faber, Wolfgang; Truszczyński, Mirosław (Eds.) (2001): *Logic programming and nonmonotonic reasoning. 6th international conference, LPNMR 2001, Vienna, Austria, September 17–19, 2001: proceedings*, Berlin; New York: Springer (Lecture notes in artificial intelligence, 2173).

Engelfriet, Joeri; Treur, Jan (1998): "An interpretation of default logic in minimal temporal epistemic logic", in: *Journal of Logic, Language and Information* 7 (3), 369–388.

Freund, Michael (1993): "Injective Models and Injunctive Relations", in: *Journal of Logic and Computation* 3, 231–347.

Freund, Michael; Lehmann, Daniel (1994): "Nonmonotonic reasoning: From finitary relations to infinitary inference operations", in: *Studia Logica* 53 (2), 161–201.

Fuhrmann, André (1997): *An Essay on Contraction*, Stanford, California: CSLI Publications.

— (1998): "Nonmonotonic Logic", in: Edward Craig (ed.), *Routledge Encyclopedia of Philosophy*, Vol. 7, London; New York: Routledge, 30–35.

Fuhrmann, André; Levi, Isaac (1994): "Undercutting and the Ramsey test for conditionals", in: *Synthese* 101 (2), 157–169.

Fuhrmann, André; Rott, Hans (Eds.) (1996): *Logic, Action, and Information. Essays on Logic in Philosophy and Artificial Intelligence,* Berlin; New York: De Gruyter.

Gabbay, M.; Woods, J. (2008): "Resource-origins of nonmonotonicity", in: *Studia Logica* 88 (1), 85–112.

Gabbay, M.; Garcez, Artur S. d'Avila(2009): "Logical modes of attack in argumentation networks", in: *Studia Logica* 93 (2-3), 199–230.

Gabbay, M.; Schlechta, Karl (2009): "Reactive preferential structures and nonmonotonic consequence", in: *Review of Symbolic Logic* 2 (2), 414–450.

Gärdenfors Peter (1978): "Conditionals and Changes of Belief", in: *Acta Fennica* 30, 381–404.

— (1986): "Belief Revisions and the Ramsey test of conditionals", in: *Philosophical Review* 95, 81–93.

Gelfond, Michael; Leone, Nicola; Pfeifer, Gerald (Eds.) (1999): *Logic programming and nonmonotonic reasoning. 5th international conference, LPNMR '99, El Paso, Texas, USA, December 2-4, 1999*: proceedings, Berlin; New York: Springer (Lecture notes in computer science, 1730).

Ginsberg, Matthew L. (1987): *Readings in nonmonotonic reasoning*, Los Altos, California: Morgan Kaufmann Publishers.

Goldszmidt, M.; Pearl, J. (1992): "Rank-Based Systems. A Simple Approach to Belief Revision, Belief Update, and Reasoning about Evidence and Action", in: *Proceedings of the Third International Conference on Principles of Knowledge Representation and Reasoning*, San Mateo, California: Morgan Kaufmann Publishers, 661–684.

Gomolinska, Anna (1997): "A nonmonotonic modal formalization of the logic of acceptance and rejection", in: *Studia Logica* 58 (1), 113–127.

— (1998): "On the logic of acceptance and rejection", in: *Studia Logica* 60 (2), 233–251.

Governatori, Guido; Palmirani, Monica; Riveret, Régis; Rotolo, Antonio; Sartor, Giovanni (2006): "Norm Modifications in Defeasible Logic", in: *Proceedings of Jurix 2006*, Amsterdam: IOS, 13–22.

Hahn, Ulrike; Oaksford, Mike (2006): "A Bayesian Approach to Informal Argument Fallacies", in: *Synthese* 152 (2), 207–236.

Harper, W. L. (1975): "Rational Belief Change, Popper Functions and Counterfactionals", in: *Synthese* 30 (1/2), 221–262.

Jago, Mark (2009): "Epistemic logic for rule-based agents", in: *Journal of Logic, Language and Information* 18 (1), 131–158.

Jurjus, Herman; Swart, Harrie de (2001): "Implication with Possible Exceptions", in: *The Journal of Symbolic Logic* 66 (2), 517–535.

Kern-Isberner, Gabriele (2001): *Conditionals in nonmonotonic reasoning and belief revision: Considering conditionals as agents*, Berlin; New York: Springer (Lecture notes in artificial intelligence, 2087).

Kyburg Jr., Henry E. (1992): "The Scope of Bayesian Reasoning", in: *PSA: Proceedings of the Biennial Meeting of the Philosophy of Science Association* 1992, 139–152.

Lang, Jérôme; Marquis, Pierre (2001): "Removing Inconsistencies in Assumption-Based Theories through Knowledge-Gathering Actions", in: *Studia Logica* 67 (2), 179–214.

Levi, Isaac (1996): *For the Sake of the Argument: Ramsey Test Conditionals, Inductive Inference, and Nonmonotonic Reasoning*, Cambridge; New York: Cambridge University Press.

Liberatore, Paolo (2007): "Consistency Defaults", in: *Studia Logica* 86 (1), 89–110.

Lifschitz, Vladimir (1988): "Circumscriptive theories: a logic-based framework for knowledge representation", in: *Journal of Philosophical Logic* 17, 391–441.

— (1989): "Benchmark Problems for Formal Nonmonotonic Reasoning"; in: M. Reinfrank; J. de Kleer; M. L. Ginsberg; E. Sandewel (eds.), *Non-Monotonic Reasoning*, Berlin: Springer, 202–219.

Lifschitz, Vladimir; Niemelä, Ilkka (Eds.) (2004): *Logic programming and non-monotonic reasoning. 7th international conference, LPNMR 2004, Fort Lauderdale, Fla., January 6-8, 2004: proceedings*, Berlin; New York: Springer (Lecture notes in artificial intelligence, 2923).

Lomuscio, Alessio; Sergot, Marek (2003): "Deontic Interpreted Systems", in: *Studia Logica* 75 (1), 63–92.

Lukasiewicz, Thomas (2005): "Nonmonotonic Probabilistic Reasoning under Variable-Strength Inheritance with Overriding", in: *Synthese* 146, 153–169.

Makinson, David (1993): "Five faces of minimality", in: *Studia Logica* 52 (3), 339–379.

— (2005): *Bridges from Classical to Nonmonotonic Logic*, London: King's College Publications.

Makinson David; Gärdenfors, Peter (1991): "Relations between the logic of theory change and Nonmonotonic Logic", in: André Fuhrmann; M. Morreau (eds.), *The Logic of Theory Change: Workshop, Konstanz, FRG, October 13-15, 1989, proceedings*, Berlin: Springer (Lecture notes in computer science, 465.), 185–206.

Makinson, David; Kourousias, George (2006): "Respecting Relevance in Belief Change", in: *Análisis Filosófico* 26(1), 53-61.

Marek, Wiktor; Truszczyński, Mirek (1993): *Nonmonotonic Logic: Context-dependent Reasoning*, Berlin: Springer Verlag.

McCarthy, John M. (2006): What Artificial Intelligence Needs From Symbolic Logic (preprint). Available online at Stanford University, http://www-formal.stanford.edu/jmc/slides/asl/asl-sli.pdf.

McCarthy, John M.; Buvac, Sasa (1997): Formalizing context: Expanded notes (preprint). Available online at http://cogprints.org/419/.

Milnikel, Robert (2003): "Embedding modal nonmonotonic logics into default logic", in: *Studia Logica* 75 (3), 377–382.

Mizumoto, Masaharu (2011): *A Theory of Knowledge and Belief Change - Formal and Experimental Perspectives*, Hokkaido University Press.

Moore, Robert C. (1985): "Semantic Considerations on Nonmonotonic Logic", in: *Artificial Intelligence* 25, 75–94.

Morado, Raymundo (1992): "Models for Belief Revision", in: *Philosophical Issues* 2, 227–247.

Morgan, Charles G. (2000): "The nature of nonmonotonic reasoning", in: *Minds and Machines* 10 (3), 321–360.

Morreau, Michael (1998): "Review of Isaac Levi, For the Sake of the Argument: Ramsey Test Conditionals, Inductive Inference and Nonmonotonic Reasoning", in: *Journal of Philosophy* 95 (10), 540–546.

Nayak, A. C. (1994): "Iterated Belief Change based on epistemic entrenchment", in: *Erkenntnis* 41, 353–390.

Niebergall, Karl-Georg (1999): "Nonmonotonicity in (the metamathematics of) arithmetic", in: *Erkenntnis* 50 (2-3), 309–332.
Nute, Donald; Maier, Frederick (2010): "Well-founded semantics for defeasible logic", in: *Synthese* 176 (2), 243–274.
Paris, J.; Vencovská, A. (1998): "Proof Systems for Probabilistic Uncertain Reasoning", in: *The Journal of Symbolic Logic* 63 (3), 1007–1039.
Pearce, David; Valverde, Agustín (2005): "A first order nonmonotonic extension of constructive logic", in: *Studia Logica* 80 (2-3), 321–346.
Pérez, Ramón Pino; Uzcátegui, Carlos (2000): "On representation theorems for nonmonotonic consequence relations", in: *Journal of Symbolic Logic* 65 (3), 1321–1337.
Politzer, Guy; Bonnefon, Jean-francois (2006): "Two varieties of conditionals and two kinds of defeaters help reveal two fundamental types of reasoning", in: *Mind and Language* 21 (4), 484–503.
Prakken, Henry (1995): "Argumentation with defeasible conditionals: a preliminary report (extended abstract)", in: *Proceedings: Second Dutch/ German Workshop on Nonmonotonic Reasoning*, 152–159.
— (2001): "Relating Protocols for Dynamic Dispute with Logics for Defeasible Argumentation", in: *Synthese* 127 (1/2), 187–219.
— (2002): "Intuitions and the modeling of defeasible reasoning: some case studies", in: *Proceedings of the Ninth International Workshop on Nonmonotonic Reasoning Toulouse 2002*, 91–99.
Primiero, Giuseppe (2012): "A contextual type theory with judgemental modalities for reasoning from open assumptions", in: *Logique and Analyse* 220, 579–600.
Reiter, Raymond (1980): "A logic for default reasoning", in: *Artificial Intelligence* 13, 81–137.
Rosati, Riccardo (1999): "Reasoning about minimal knowledge in nonmonotonic modal logics", in: *Journal of Logic, Language and Information* 8 (2), 187–203.
Rott, Hans (1989): "Conditionals and Theory Change: Revisions, Expansions and Additions", in: *Synthese* 81, 91–113.
Rott, Hans (1991): *Reduktion und Revision. Aspekte des nichtmonotonen Theorienwandels*, Frankfurt am Main; New York: P. Lang.
— (2001): *Change, Choice and Inference: A Study of Belief Revision and Nonmonotonic Reasoning*, Oxford; New York: Clarendon Press.
— (2004): "A counterexample to six fundamental principles of belief formation", in: *Synthese* 139 (2), 225–240.
— (2008): "A new psychologism in logic? Reflections from the point of view of belief revision", in: *Studia Logica* 88 (1), 113–136.
— (2011): "Reapproaching Ramsey: Conditionals and Iterated Belief Change in the Spirit of AGM", in: *Journal of Philosophical Logic* 40 (2), 155–191.

Rott, Hans (2012): "Bounded Revision: Two-Dimensional Belief Change Between Conservative and Moderate Revision", in: *Journal of Philosophical Logic* 41 (1), 173–200.

Schlechta, Karl (1997): *Nonmonotonic logics. Basic concepts, results, and techniques*, Berlin; New York: Springer (Lecture notes in artificial intelligence, 1187).

— (2000): "New techniques and completeness results for preferential structures", in: *Journal of Symbolic Logic* 65 (2), 719–746.

Schöter, Andreas (1996): "Evidential Bilattice Logic and Lexical Inference", in: *Journal of Logic, Language, and Information* 5 (1), 65–105.

Schurz, Gerhard (1996): "The Role of Negation in Nonmonotonic Logic and Defeasible Reasoning", in: *Negation: A Notion in Focus,* New York: De Gruyter, 197–231.

Servi, Gisèle Fischer (1992): "Nonmonotonic consequence based on intuitionistic logic", in: *Journal of Symbolic Logic* 57 (4), 1176–1197.

Shoham, Yoav (1987): "A Semantical Approach to Nonmonotonic Logic", in: John McDermott (ed.), *Proceedings of the Tenth International Conference on Artificial Intelligence*, Los Altos, Calfornia: Morgan Kaufmann, 227–250.

— (1988): "Efficient reasoning about rich temporal domains", in: *Journal of Philosophical Logic* 17 (4), 443–474.

Spohn, Wolfgang (1988): "Ordinal Conditional Functions", in: W. L. Harper; B. Syrms (eds.), *Causation, Decision, Belief Change and Statistics, Volume III*, Dordrecht: Kluwer.

Stachniak, Zbigniew (1995): "Nonmonotonic theories and their axiomatic varieties", in: *Journal of Logic, Language and Information* 4 (4), 317–334.

Stalnaker, R. (1994): "Nonmonotonic consequence relations", in: *Fundamenta Informaticae* 2, 7-21.

Stenning, Keith; van Lambalgen, Michiel (2009): "'Nonmonotonic' does not mean 'probabilistic'", in: *Behavioral and Brain Sciences* 32 (1), 102–103.

Taber, John A. (2004): "Is Indian logic nonmonotonic?", in: *Philosophy East and West* 54 (2), 143–170.

Tan, Yao Hua (1992): *Non-monotonic reasoning. Logical architecture and philosophical applications*, Amsterdam: Drukkerij Elinkwijk.

— (1997): "Is Default Logic a Reinvention of Inductive-Statistical Reasoning?", in: *Synthese* 110 (3), 357–379.

Val, Alvaro Del; Shoham, Yoav (1994): "Deriving Properties of Belief Update from Theories of Action", in: *Journal of Logic, Language, and Information* 3 (2), 81–119.

van der Hoek, Wiebe (2000): "Nonmonotonic reasoning, Grigoris Antoniou", in: *Journal of Logic, Language and Information* 9 (1), 125–128.

van der Hoek, Wiebe; Meyer, John-Jules; Treur, Jan (1998): "Temporalizing epistemic default logic", in: *Journal of Logic, Language and Information* 7 (3), 341–367.
van Ditmarsch, Hans; Labuschagne, Willem (2007): "My Beliefs about Your Beliefs: A Case Study in Theory of Mind and Epistemic Logic", in: *Synthese* 155 (2), 191–209.
van Eijk, Rogier (1999): "Partiality, modality, and nonmonotonicity", in: *Journal of Logic, Language and Information* 8 (2), 251–254.
Wainer, Jacques (2007): "Modeling generalized implicatures using non-monotonic logics", in: *Journal of Logic, Language and Information* 16 (2), 196–216.
Wheeler, Gregory (2008): "Applied Logic without Psychologism," in: *Studia Logica* 88 (1), 137–156.
White, Graham (2008): "Causality, Modality, and Explanation", in: *Notre Dame Journal of Formal Logic* 49 (3), 313–343.
Wobcke, Wayne (1995): "Belief Revision, Conditional Logic and Nonmonotonic Reasoning", in: *Norte Dame Journal of Formal Logic* 36, 55–103.

9. *Philosophy of logic, informal logic, argumentation theory*

Abraham, M.; Gabbay, Dov M.; Schild, U. (2009): "Analysis of the Talmudic Argumentum a Fortiori Inference Rule (Kal Vachomer) using Matrix Abduction", in: *Studia Logica* 92 (3), 281–364.
Adams, Ernest W. (1975): *The Logic of Conditionals*, Dordrecht: Reidel.
Antonelli, G. Aldo (2010): "Non-monotonic Logic", in: Edward N. Zalta (ed.), *The Stanford Encyclopedia of Philosophy.* Available online at Stanford University, http://plato.stanford.edu/entries/logic-nonmonotonic/.
Asher, Nicholas; Morreau Michael: (1991): "Commonsense Entailment: A Modal Nonmonotonic Theory of Reasoning", in: *Lecture Notes in Computer Science*, 478, 1–30.
Blutner, Reinhard (2004): "Nonmonotonic inferences and neural networks", in: *Synthese* 142 (2), 143–174.
Bonavec, Daniel (2003): "Pragma-dialectics and Beyond", in: *Argumentation* 17 (14), 451–459.
Frankish, Keith (2006: "Non-monotonic inference", in: K. Brown (ed.), *Encyclopedia of Language and Linguistics*, 2. ed., Oxford: Elsevier, 672–675.
Franklin, James (2013): "Arguments Whose Strength Depends on Continuous Variation", in: *Informal Logic*, 33–56.
Godden, David; Walton, Douglas N. (2007): "A theory of presumption for everyday argumentation", in: *Pragmatics and Cognition* 15 (2), 313–346.
Green, Nancy (2010): "Representation of Argumentation in Text with Rhetorical Structure Theory", in: *Argumentation* 24 (2), 181–196.

Harman, Gilbert (1984): "Logic and Reasoning", in: *Synthese* 60 (1), 107–127.

Hawthorne, James (1996): "On the logic of nonmonotonic conditionals and conditional probabilities", in: *Journal of Philosophical Logic* 25 (2), 185–218.

— (2007): "Nonmonotonic Conditionals that Behave Like Conditional Probabilities Above a Threshold", in: *Journal of Applied Logic* 5 (4), 625–637.

Horty, John F. (2001): "Nonmonotonic logic", in: Lou Goble (ed.), *The Blackwell Guide to Philosophical Logic*, Malden Mass.: Blackwell Publisher, 336–361.

— (2007): "Defaults with priorities", in: *Journal of Philosophical Logic* 36, 367–413.

Jon Cogburn (2002): "Logical Revision Re-Revisited: On the Wright/Salerno Case for Intuitionism", in: *Philosophical Studies* 110 (3), 231–248.

Koons, Robert C. (2013): "Defeasible reasoning", in: Edward N. Zalta (ed.), *The Stanford Encyclopedia of Philosophy.* Stanford University, available online at http://plato.stanford.edu/entries/reasoning-defeasible/.

Leitgeb, Hannes (2004): *Inference on the Low Level: An Investigation Into Deduction, Nonmonotonic Reasoning, and the Philosophy of Cognition*; Dordrecht: Kluwer Academic Publishers.

Macagno, Fabrizio; Walton, Douglas N. (2009): "Enthymemes, Argumentation Schemes, and Topics", in: *Logique et Analyse* Vol. 205, 39–56.

McNamara, Paul; Henry Prakken (Eds.) (1999): *Norms, Logics and Information Systems. New Studies in Deontic Logic and Computer Science,* Amsterdam: IOS Press.

Molnar, George (1967): "Defeasible Propositions", in: *Australasian Journal of Philosophy* 45 (2), 185–197.

Nute, Donald (1988): "Conditional Logic", in: M. Gabbay; F. Guenther (eds.), *Handbook of Philosophical Logic, Volume II: Extensions of Classical Logic*, Dordrecht: D. Reidel, 387–439.

Nute, Donald (1988): "Defeasible Reasoning: a philosophical analysis in Prolog", in: James Fetzer (ed.), *Aspects of Artificial Intelligence*, Boston: Kluwer Academic Publishers (Studies in Cognitive Science), 251–288.

— (1989). "General and special defeasible theories", in: *Proceedings of the Tübingen Workshop on Semantic Nets and Nonmonotonic Reasoning, Vol. I.* SNS Bericht 89-48, University of Tübingen, 183–197.

Nute, Donald (1994): "Basic defeasible logic", in: L. Fariñas del Cerro; M. Penttonen (eds.), *Intensional Logics for Programming*, Oxford University Press, 125–154.

— (1997): "Introduction", in: Donald Nute; Yu Xiaochang (eds.), *Defeasible Deontic Logic: Essays in Nonmonotonic Normative Reasoning*, Dordrecht: Kluwer Acadmic Publishers, 1–16.

Nute, Donald; Xiaochang Yu (Eds.) (1997): *Defeasible Deontic Logic: Essays in Nonmonotonic Normative Reasoning*, Dordrecht: Kluwer Academic Publishers.

Oaksford, Mike; Hahn Ulrike (2006): "Non-Monotonicity and Informal Reasoning: Comment on Ferguson", in: *Argumentation* (20 (2), 245–251.

Parikh, Rohit (2005): "Conditional Probability and Defeasible Inference", in: *Journal of Philosophical Logic* 34 (1), 97–119.

Parsons, Simon (2001): *Qualitative methods for reasoning under uncertainty*, Cambridge, Mass: MIT Press.

Pelletier, Francis Jeffry; Elio Renée (1996): "On reasoning with default rules and exceptions", in: *Proceedings of the 18th Conference of the Cognitive Science Society*, 131–141.

Pelletier, Francis Jeffry; Elio, Renée (2005): "The case for psychologism in default and inheritance reasoning", in: *Synthese* 146 (1-2), 7–35.

Pollock, John L. (1987): "Defeasible Reasoning", in: *Cognitive Science* 11, 481–518.

— (1988): "Interest-Driven Reasoning", in: *Synthese* 74 (3), 369–390.

Pollock, John L. (1991): "How to Use Probabilities in Reasoning", in: *Philosophical Studies* 64 (1), 65–85.

— (1991): "Self-defeating arguments", in: *Minds and Machines* 1 (4), 367–392.

— (2001): "Defeasible Reasoning with Variable Degrees of Justification", in: *Artificial Intelligence* 133, 233–282.

— (2008): "Defeasible Reasoning", in: Jonathan E. Adler; Lance J. Rips (eds.), *Reasoning. Studies in Human Inference and its Foundations*, Cambridge: Cambridge University Press, 451–471.

— (2009): "A recursive semantics for defeasible reasoning", in: I. Rahwan (ed.), *Argumentation in Artificial Intelligence*, Dordrecht, New York: Springer, 173–199.

— (2010): "Reasoning defeasibly about probabilities", in: Joseph Keim Campbell, Michael O'Rourke, Harry S. Silverstein (eds.), *Knowledge and Skepticism*, Cambridge, Mass.: MIT Press, 219–261.

— (2011): "Defeasible Reasoning and Degrees of Justification", in: *Argument and Computation* 1 (1), 7–22.

Prakken, Henry; G. Vreeswijk (2002), "Logics for defeasible argumentation", in: M. Gabbay; F. Guenther (eds.), *Handbook of Philosophical Logic, Vol. 4*, 2. ed., Kluwer Academic Publishers, 219–31.

Prakken, Henry; McNamara, Paul (Eds.) (1998): *Norms, Logics and Information Systems*, Amsterdam: IOS Press.

Rescher, Nicholas (2006): *Presumption and the practices of tentative cognition*, Cambridge; New York: Cambridge University Press.

Rott, Hans (2011): "Odd Choices: On the Rationality of Some Alleged Anomalies of Decision and Inference", in: *Topoi* 30 (1), 59–69.
Sartor, Giovanni; Prakken, Henry (1996): "A System for Defeasible Argumentation with Defeasible Priorities", in: M. Gabbay et al (eds.), *Proceedings of the International Conference on Formal and Applied Practical Reasoning,* 510–24.
Toulmin, Stephen (1958/ 2003): *The Uses of Argument*, Cambridge: Cambridge University Press.
van Fraassen, Bas (1972): "The logic of conditional obligation", in: *The Journal of Philosophical Logic* 72, 417–438.
von Wright, G. H. (1996): "Conditionality", in: G. H. Von Wright (ed.), *Six Essays in Philosophical Logic, Acta Philosophica Fennica 60,* Helsinki: Societas Philosophica Fennica, 17–32.
Walton, Douglas N.; Reed, C. A. (2005): "Argumentation schemes and enthymemes", in: *Synthese* 145 (3), 339–370.
Walton, Douglas N. (2011): "Defeasible reasoning and informal fallacies", in: *Synthese* 179 (3), 377–407.
Walton, Douglas N. (2011): "Reasoning about knowledge using defeasible logic", in: *Argument and Computation* 2 (2-3), 131–155.
Wansing, Heinrich *(1996): Negation: A Notion in Focus,* New York: De Gruyter.
Wheeler, Gregory; Kyburg, Henry E.; Teng, Choh Man (2007): "Conditionals and consequences", in: *Journal of Applied Logic* 5 (4), 638–650.

10. *Philosophy of mind and philosophy of cognitive science*

Adler, Jonathan Eric; Rips, Lance J. (2008): Reasoning*: Studies of Human Inference and its Foundations,* Cambridge; New York, Cambridge University Press.
Ågotnes, Thomas; Walther, Dirk (2009): "A Logic of Strategic Ability under Bounded Memory", in: *Journal of Logic, Language, and Information* 18 (1), 55–77.
Antonelli, G. Aldo (1997): "Defeasible Reasoning as a Cognitive Model", in: Krister Segerberg (ed.), *The Parikh Project. Seven papers in honour of Rohit,* Uppsala Prints and Preprints in Philosophy, 18, Uppsala, Department of Philosophy, Uppsala University.
Austin, John L. (1964): "Other Minds", in: *Proceedings of the Aristotelian Society,* Suppl. Vol. 20, 148–187.
Baker, Lynne Rudder (2007): "Social externalism and first-person authority", in: *Erkenntnis* 67 (2), 287–300.
Belnap, Nuel; Perloff, Michael; Xu, Ming (2001): *Facing the Future: Agents and Choices in Our Indeterministic World,* Oxford: Oxford University Press.

Ford, Marilyn (2005): "Human nonmonotonic reasoning: The importance of seeing the logical strength of arguments", in: *Synthese* 146 (1-2), 71–92.
Horgan, T.; Tienson J. (1996): *Connectionism and the Philosophy of Psychology*, Cambridge, Mass.: MIT Press.
István, S. N. Berkeley (1997): "Taming type-2 tigers: A nonmonotonic strategy", in: *Behavioral and Brain Sciences* 20 (1), 66–67.
Mulligan, Kevin (1999): "Justification, rule-breaking and the mind", in: *Proceedings of the Aristotelian Society* 99 (2), 123–139.
O'Brien, Gerard (1998): "Connectionism, analogicity and mental content", in: *Acta Analytica* 22, 111–131.
Pfeifer, Niki; Kleiter, Gernot D. (2006): "Is human reasoning about nonmonotonic conditionals probabilistically coherent?", in: *Proceedings of the 7th Workshop on Uncertainty Processing*, 138–150.
— (2002): "Experiments on nonmonotonic reasoning. The coherence of human probability judgments", in: Hannes Leitgeb, Gerhard Schurz (eds.), *Pre-Proceedings of the 1st Salzburg Workshop on Paradigms of Cognition*, Universität Salzburg, Institut für Philosophie.
— (2003): "Nonmonotonicity and human probabilistic reasoning", in: *Proceedings of the 6th Workshop on Uncertainty Processing*, 221–234.
— (2005): "Coherence and nonmonotonicity in human reasoning", in: *Synthese* 146 (1-2), 93–109.
Pollock, John L. (1992): "Rationality, Function, and Content", in: *Philosophical Studies* 65 (1/2), 129–151.
Silverberg, Arnold (1996): "Psychological laws and nonmonotonic logic", in: *Erkenntnis* 44 (2), 199–224.

11. *Artificial intelligence and computer science*

Antonelli, G. Aldo (1999): "A directly cautious theory of defeasible consequence for default logic via the notion of a general extension", in: *Artificial Intelligence* 109, 71–109.
— (1997): "Defeasible inheritance over cyclic networks", in: *Artificial Intelligence* 91, 1–23.
Apt, Krzysztof; Blair, Howard, Walker Adrian (1988): "Towards a theory of declarative knowledge", in: Jack Minker (ed.), *Foundations of Deductive Databases and Logic Programming*, Los Altos, California: Morgan Kaufmann Publishers Inc., 89–148.
Artosi, Alberto; Governatori Guido; Sartor Giovanni: "Towards a Computational Treatment of Deontic Defeasibility", in: *Deontic Logic Agency and Normative Systems,* Berlin: Springer Verlag, 27–46.

Asher, Nicholas; Lascarides, Alex (2003): *Logics of Conversation*, Cambridge: Cambridge University Press.
Avron, Arnon; Iddo, Lev (2001): "A Formula-Preferential Base for Paraconsistent and Plausible Reasoning Systems", in: *Proceedings of the Workshop on Inconsistency in Data and Knowledge (KRR-4) Int. Joint Conf. on AI.*
Avron, Arnon; Arieli, Ofer (1999): "A Model-Theoretic Approach for Recovering Consistent Data from Inconsistent Knowledge-Bases", in: *Journal of Automated Reasoning* 22 (3), 263–309.
Baader, Franz; Hollunder, Bernhard (1995): "Priorities on defaults with prerequisites, and their applications in treating specificity in terminological default logic", in: *Journal of Automated Reasoning* 15, 41–68.
Baral, Chitta; Brewka, Gerhard; Schlipf, John (2007): *Logic programming and nonmonotonic reasoning. 9th international conference, LPNMR 2007, Tempe, AZ, USA, May 15-17, 2007, proceedings*, Berlin: Springer (Lecture notes in artifical intelligence, 4483).
Bell, John (1988): *Predictive conditionals, nonmonotonicity and reasoning about the future*, University of Essex (doctoral thesis).
Benferhat, Salem; Dubois, Didier; Prade, Henri (1997): "Some Syntactic Approaches to the Handling of Inconsistent Knowledge Bases: A Comparative Study: Part 1: The Flat Case", in: *Studia Logica* 58 (1), 17–45.
Brewka, Gerhard (1989): *Nonmonotonic reasoning: From theoretical foundation towards efficient computation*, Universität Hamburg (doctoral thesis).
— (1991): *Nonmonotonic Reasoning. Logical Foundations of Commonsense*, Cambridge: Cambridge University Press.
— (1994): "Adding priorities and specificity to default logic", in: *Proceedings of the European Workshop on Logics in Artificial Intelligence (JELIA-94)*, Springer Verlag Lecture Notes in Artificial Intelligence, 247–260.
— (1994): "Reasoning about priorities in default logic", in: *Proceedings of the Twelveth National Conference on Artificial Intelligence (AAAI-94)*, AAAI/MIT Press, 940–945.
— (1996): "Well-founded semantics for extended logic programs with dynamic preferences", in: *Journal of Artificial Intelligence Research* 4, 19–36.
Brewka, Gerhard; Eiter, Thomas (2000): "Prioritizing default logic", in: St. Hölldobler (ed.), *Intellectics and Computational Logic: Papers in Honor of Wolfgang Bibel*, Kluwer Academic Publishers, 27–46.
Causey, Robert L. (1991): "The epistemic basis of defeasible reasoning", in: *Minds and Machines* 1 (4), 437–458.
— (2003): "Computational Dialogic Defeasible Reasoning", in: *Argumentation* 17 (4), 421–450.
Colburn, Timothy R. (1991): "Defeasible reasoning and logic programming", in: *Minds and Machines* 1 (4), 417–436.

Colburn, Timothy R. (1991): "Program verification, defeasible reasoning, and two views of computer science", in: *Minds and Machines* 1 (1), 97–116.

— (1995): "Heuristics, justification, and defeasible reasoning", in: *Minds and Machines* 5 (4), 476–487.

Cross, Charles B. (2003): "Nonmonotonic Inconsistency", in: *Artificial Intelligence* 149 (2), 161–178.

Dawson, Michael R. W.; Piercey, C. Darren (2001): "On the subsymbolic nature of a PDP architecture that uses a nonmonotonic activation function", in: *Minds and Machines* 11 (2), 197–218.

Delgrande, James P.; Faber, Wolfgang (2011): *Logic Programming and Nonmonotonic Reasoning. 11th International Conference, LPNMR 2011, Vancouver, Canada, May 16-19, 2011*, Proceedings, Berlin, Heidelberg: Springer.

Delgrande, James P.; Schaub, Torsten (2000): "Expressing preferences in default logic", in: *Artificial Intelligence* 123, 41–87.

— (2000): "The role of default logic in knowledge representation", in: Jack Minker (ed.), *Logic Based Artificial Intelligence*, Norwell MA; Dordrecht: Kluwer Academic Publishers, 107–126.

— (2004): "Reasoning with sets of defaults in default logic", in: *Computational Intelligence* 20, 56–88.

Delgrande, James P.; Schaub, Torsten; Jackson, W. Ken (1994): "Alternative approaches to default logic", in: *Artificial Intelligence* 70, 167–237.

Dix, J.; Pereira, Luís Moniz; Przymusinski, Teodor C. (1997): *Non-monotonic extensions of logic programming. 2nd International Workshop, NMELP '96, Bad Honnef, Germany, September 5-6, 1996: Selected papers*, Berlin; New York: Springer (Lecture notes in artificial intelligence, 1216.).

Doherty, Patrick (1991): *NML3: A non-monotonic formalism with explicit defaults*, Linköping, Sweden: Linköping University, Dept. of Computer and Information Science (Linköping studies in science and technology/ Dissertations, no. 258).

Dung, Phan Minh (1995): "On the acceptability of arguments and its fundamental role in nonmonotonic reasoning, logic programming, and *n*-person games", in: *Artificial Intelligence* 77, 321–357.

Etherington, D. W.; Reiter Raymond (1983): "On Inheritance Hierarchies and Exceptions", in: *Proceedings of the National Conference on Artificial Intelligence*, Los Altos, California: Morgan Kaufmann Publishers, 104–108.

Ferraris, Paolo (2007): "A Logic Programming Characterization of Causal Theories", in: *Proceedings of the Twentieth International Joint Conference on Artificial Intelligence*, San Francisco, California: Morgan Kaufmann Publishers, 366–371.

Ferraris, Paolo; Lee, J.; Lierler, Y.; Lifschitz, V.; Yang, F. (2012): "Representing first-order causal theories by logic programs", in: *Theory and Practice of Logic Programming*, 12(3), 383–412.

Gabbay, M. (1985): "Theoretical foundations for nonmonotonic reasoning in expert systems", in: K. Apt (ed.), *Logics and Models of Concurrent Systems*, Berlin and New York: Springer Verlag, 439–459.

Gabbay, M.; Smets, P. (Eds.) (1998): *Handbook of Defeasible Reasoning and Uncertainty Management Systems*, Vol. 3, Dordrecht; Boston: Kluwer Academic Publishers.

Geffner, Hector (1990): "A Framework for Reasoning with Defaults", in: Henry E. Jr., Kyburg; Ronald P., Loui; Greg N., Carlson (eds.), *Knowledge Representation and Defeasible Reasoning*, Dordrecht, Boston: Kluwer Academic Publishers, 69–87.

Geffner, Hector; Pearl, J. (1992): "Conditional entailment: bridging two approaches to default reasoning", in: *Artificial Intelligence* 53, 209–244.

Goodwin, James W. (1987): *A theory and system for non-monotonic reasoning*, Linköping, Sweden: Linköping University, Dept. of Computer and Information Science (Linköping studies in science and technology /Dissertations, no. 165).

Hanks, Steve; McDermott, Drew (1987): "Nonmonotonic Logic and Temporal Projection", in: *Artificial Intelligence* 33, 379–412.

Henry E., Kyburg Jr.; Ronald P., Loui; Greg N., Carlson (Eds.) (1990): *Knowledge Representation and Defeasible Reasoning*, Boston; Dordrcht: Kluwer Academic Publishers.

Horty, John F. (1994): "Some direct theories of nonmonotonic inheritance", in: D. Gabbay; C. Hogger; J. Robinson (eds.), *Handbook of Logic in Artificial Intelligence and Logic Programming, Volume 3: Nonmonotonic Reasoning and Uncertain Reasoning*, Oxford: Oxford University Press, 111–187.

— (2001): "Argument construction and reinstatement in logics for defeasible reasoning", in: *Artificial Intelligence and Law* 9 (1), 1–28.

— (2002): "Skepticism and floating conclusions", in: *Artificial Intelligence* 135, 55–72.

Horty, John F.; Thomason, Richmond H.; Touretzky, D. S. (1990): "A sceptical theory of inheritance in nonmonotonic semantic networks", in: *Artificial Intelligence* 42, 311–348.

Israel, David (1980): "What's wrong with Non-monotonic Logic?", in: *Proceedings of the First National Conference on Artificial Intelligence*, Palo Alto, California: AAAI, 99–101.

Kautz, H.; Selman, B. (1991): "Hard problems for simple default logic", in: *Artificial Intelligence Journal* 49, 243–279.

Kibble, Roger (2004): "Elements of a Social Semantics for Argumentative Dialogue", in: (eds.) Floriana Crasso, Chris Reed, Giuseppe Carenni, *CMNA IV, 4th Workshop in Computational Models of Natural Argument. European Conference on Artificial Intelligence, 2004.*

Kimbrough, Steven O.; Hua, Hua (1991): "On nonmonotonic reasoning with the method of sweeping presumptions", in: *Minds and Machines* 1 (4), 393-416.

Konolige, Kurt (1994): "Autoepistemic Logic", in: M. Gabbay; C. J. Hogger; J. A. Robbinson (eds.) *Handbook of Logic in Artificial Intelligence and Logic Programming, Volume III: Nonmonotonic Reasoning and Uncertain Reasoning,* Oxford: Clarendon Press.

Konolige, Kurt; Myers, Karen (1989): "Representing defaults with epistemic concepts", in: *Computational Intelligence* 5, 32–44.

Kraus, S.; Lehmann, D.; Magidor M. (1990): "Nonmonotonic Reasoning, Preferential Models and Cumulative Logics", in: *Artificial Intelligence* 44, 167–207.

Kyburg Jr., Henry E.; Loui, Ronald P.; N., Greg N. Carlson (Eds.) (1990): *Knowledge Representation and Defeasible Reasoning,* Dordrecht, Boston: Kluwer Academic Publishers.

Kyburg Jr., Henry E. (2001): "Real logic is Nonmonotonic", in: *Minds and Machines* 11 (4), 577–595.

Lehmann, D.; Magidor, M. (1992): "What does conditional knowledge base entail?", in: *Artificial Intelligence* 55, 1-60.

Levesque, H. (1990): "A study in autoepistemic logic", in: Artificial *Intelligence* 42, 263–309.

Lifschitz, Vladimir (1990): "Frame in the space of situations", in: *Artificial Intelligence* 46, 365–376.

— (1994): "Circumscription", in: M. Gabbay; C. J. Hogger; J. A. Robinson (eds.), *Handbook of Logic in Artificial Intelligence and Logic Programming, Volume 3,* Oxford; New York: Oxford University Press, 297–352.

Lin, F.; Reiter, Raymond (1994): "State constraints revisited", in: *Journal of Logic and Computation* 4, 655–678.

Lindström, Sten; Rabinowicz, Wlodek (1998): "Conditionals and the Ramsey test", in: M. Gabbay, P. Smets (eds.): *Handbook of Defeasible Reasoning and Uncertainty Management Systems, Vol 3.*, Dordecht; Boston: Kluwer Academic Publishers, 147–188.

Loui, Ronald P. (1990): "Defeasible Specification of Utilities", in: Henry E. Kyburg Jr. ; Ronald P. Loui; Greg N. Carlson (eds.), *Knowledge Representation and Defeasible Reasoning,* Dordrecht, Boston: Kluwer Academic Publishers.

Loui, Ronald P. (1991): "Argument and belief: Where we stand in the keynesian tradition", in: *Minds and Machines* 1 (4), 357–365.

Makinson, David (1994): "General Patterns in Nonmonotonic Reasoning", in: M. Gabbay; C. J. Hogger; J. A. Robbinson (eds.), *Handbook of Logic in Artificial Intelligence and Logic Programming, Volume 3: Nonmonotonic Reasoning and Uncertain Reasoning,* Oxford: Clarendon Press.

Makinson, David; Schlechta, Karl (1991): "Floating conclusions and zombie paths: two deep difficulties in the "directly skeptical" approach to defeasible inheritance nets", in: *Artificial Intelligence* 48, 199–209.

McCarthy, John M. (1959): "Programs with common sense", in: D. V. Blake; A. M. Uttley, (eds.), *Proceedings of the Symposium on Mechanization of Thought Processes*, H. M. Stationary Office, 77–84.

— (1977): "Epistemological problems in artificial intelligence", in: *Proceedings of the Fifth International Joint Conference on Artificial Intelligence (IJCAI-77)*, Los Altos, California: Morgan Kaufmann Publishers, 1038–1044.

— (1980): "Circumscription—A Form of Non-Monotonic Reasoning", in: *Artificial Intelligence* 13, 27–39.

— (1986): "Application of Circumscription of Formalizing Common-Sense Knowledge", in: *Artificial Intelligence* 28, 89–111.

McCarthy, John M.; Hayes, Patrick (1969): "Some philosophical problems from the standpoint of artificial intelligence", in: B. Meltzer; D. Michie (eds.), *Machine Intelligence. Volume 4*, Edinburgh: Edinburgh University Press, 464–505.

McDermott, Drew; Doyle, Jon (1982): "Non-Monotonic Logic I", in: *Artificial Intelligence* 13, 41–72.

McDermott, Drew (1982): "Non-monotonic logic II", in: *Journal of the Association for Computing Machinery* 29, 33–57.

McNamara, Paul; Prakken, Henry (Eds.) (1999): *Norms, Logics and Information Systems. New Studies in Deontic Logic and Computer Science,* Amsterdam: IOS Press.

Nute, Donald (1988): "Defeasible reasoning and decision support systems", in: *Decision Support Systems* 4, 97–110.

— (1990): "Defeasible Logic and the Frame Problem", in: Henry E. Kyburg Jr.; Ronald P. Loui; Greg N. Carlson (eds.), *Knowledge Representation and Defeasible Reasoning: Studies in Cognitive Science*, Boston: Kluwer Academic Publishers, 3–21.

— (1999): "Norms Priorities and Defeasibility", in: Paul McNamara; Henry Prakken (eds.), *Norms, Logics and Information Systems*, Amsterdam: IOS Press, 201–218.

Nute, Donald (2003): "Defeasible logic: theory, implementation, and applications", in: Oskar Bartenstein; Ulrich Geske; Markus Hannebauer; Osamu Yoshie (eds.), *Web Knowledge Management and Decision Support: Proceedings of INAP 2001, 14th International Conference on Applications of Prolog (Revised Papers*), Berlin; Heidelberg: Springer, 151–169.

Pais, John (1992): "Faithful representation of nonmonotonic patterns of inference", in: *Minds and Machines* 2 (1), 27–49.

Pearl, Judea (1988): *Probabilistic Reasoning in Intelligent Systems: Networks of Plausible Inference*, San Mateo, California: Morgan Kaufmann.

— (1990): "System Z. A Natural Ordering of Defaults with Tractable Applications to Default Reasoning", in: Rohit Parikh (ed.), *Proceedings of the Third Conference on Theoretical Aspects of Reasoning about Knowledge*, San Mateo, California: Morgan Kaufmann.

Pelletier, Francis Jeffry; Elio, Renée (1994): "On Relevance in Nonmonotonic Reasoning: Some Empirical Studies", in: R. Greiner; D. Subramanian (eds.), *Relevance: AAAI 1994 Fall Symposium Series*, Palo Alto: AAAI Press, 64–67.

— (1993): "Human benchmarks on ai's benchmark problems", in: *Proceedings of the fifteenth Annual Conference of the Cognitive Science Society.*

Pollock, John L. (1988): "The Building of Oscar", in: *Philosophical Perspectives* 2, 315–344.

— (1990): "Philosophy and Artificial Intelligence", in: *Philosophical Perspectives* 4, 461–498.

— (1995): "Practical Reasoning in Oscar", in: *Philosophical Perspectives* 9, 15–48.

— (1995): *Cognitive Carpentry*, Cambridge, Mass.: MIT Press.

— (1997): "Reasoning about Change and Persistence: A Solution to the Frame Problem", in: *Noûs* 31 (2), 143–169.

— (1998): "The logical foundations of goal-regression planning in autonomous agents", in: *Artificial Intelligence*, 106, 267–335.

— (1998): "Perceiving and reasoning about a changing world", in: *Computational Intelligence*, Vol. 14, Number 4, 1998, 498–562.

— (2008): "Oscar: An agent architecture based on defeasible reasoning", in: *Proceedings of the 2008 AAAI Spring Symposium on Architectures for Intelligent Theory-Based Agents*, 55–60.

Prakken, Henry (1993): "An argumentation framework in default logic", in: *Annals of Mathematics and Artificial Intelligence* 9, 91–132.

— (1996): "Dialectical Proof Theory for defeasible argumentation with defeasible priorities (preliminary report)", in: J.-J. Ch. Meyer; P.-Y. Schobbens (eds.), *Formal Model Agents: ESPRIT Project Model Age Final Workshop, Selected Papers*, Springer (*Lecture Notes in AI, 1760.)*, 202–215.

Prakken, Henry (2011): "An abstract framework for argumentation with structured arguments", in: *Argument and Computation* 1 (2), 93–124.

Prakken, Henry; Horty, John F. (2012): "An appreciation of John Pollock's work on the computational study of argument", in: *Argument and Computation* 3 (1), 1–19.

Prendinger, Helmut; Schurz, Gerhard (1996): "Reasoning about Action and Change: A Dynamic Logic Approach", in: *Journal of Logic, Language, and Information* 5 (2), 209–245.

Reiter, Raymond; Criscuolo, Giovanni (1981): "On interacting defaults", in: *Proceedings of the Seventh International Joint Conference on Artificial Intelligence (IJCAI-81)*, 270–276.

Rintanen, Jussi (1998): "Lexicographic priorities in default logic", in: *Artificial Intelligence* 106, 221–265.

Sartor, Giovanni (1992): "Defeasible Arguments from Inconsistent Knowledge Bases: A Logic Programming Approach", in: *Technical Report CIOC-90*, Bologna.

— (1993): "Defeasible Arguments in a Logical Programming Model", in: *Atti dell'ottavo convegno sulla programmazione (GULP)*, Rende, Cosenza: Mediterranean Press.

Sartor, Giovanni; Prakken, Henry (1997): "Argument-based Extended Logic Programming with Defeasible Priorities", in: *Journal of Applied Non-classical Logics* 7, 25–75.

Stein, Lynn (1992): "Resolving ambiguity in nonmonotonic inheritance hierarchies", in: *Artificial Intelligence* 55, 259–310.

Stone, Matthew (1997): "Partial order reasoning for a nonmonotonic theory of action", in: *The 1997 AAAI Workshop on Theories of Action, Planning and Control.* Available online at http://www.cs.rutgers.edu/~mdstone/pubs/aaaiw97.pdf.

Thanassas, Dimitrios (1992): *The Phenomenon of commonsense reasoning: nonmonotonicity, action and information*, New York: Ellis Horwood (Ellis Horwood series in artificial intelligence).

Thomason, Richmond H. (1991): "Logicism, AI, and common sense: John McCarthy's program in philosophical perspective", in: Vladimir Lifschitz (ed.), *Artificial Intelligence and Mathematical Theory of Computation*, London: Academic Press, 449–466.

— (1992): "NETL and subsequent path-based inheritance theories", in: *Computers and Mathematics with Application* 23, 179–204.

— (2012): "Logic and artificial intelligence", in: Edward Zalta (ed.) *The Stanford Encyclopedia of Philosophy*, Stanford University, available online at http://plato.stanford.edu/entries/logic-ai/.

Thomason, Richmond H.; Horty, John F. (1987): "A Clash of Intuitions: The Current State of Nonmonotonic Multiple Inheritance Systems", in: *Proceedings of IJCAI-87*, Milan: Morgan Kaufmann, 476–482.

Tin, Erkan; Akman, Varol (1997): "Situated nonmonotonic temporal reasoning with baby-sit", in: *AI Communications* 10, 1–17. Available online at http://cogprints.org/462/.

Touretzky, David (1984): "Implicit ordering of defaults in inheritance systems", in: *Proceedings of the Fourth National Conference on Artificial Intelligence (AAAI-84)*, Los Altos, California: Morgan Kaufmann Publishers 322–325.

— (1986): *The Mathematics of Inheritance Systems*, Los Altos, California: Morgan Kaufmann Publishers.

Touretzky, David; Thomason, Richmond H.; Horty, John F. (1991): "A skeptic's menagerie: conflictors, preemptors, reinstaters, and zombies in nonmonotonic inheritance", in: *Proceedings of the Twelfth International Joint Conference on Artificial Intelligence (IJCAI-91)*, Los Altos, Calofornia: Morgan Kaufmann Publishers, 478–483.

Zhou, Yuli (1991): *A fixpoint theory of nonmonotonic functions and its applications to logic programs, deductive databases and production rule systems*, Harvard University (doctoral thesis).

www.ingramcontent.com/pod-product-compliance
Lightning Source LLC
Chambersburg PA
CBHW031322230926
51848CB00001B/53
9789042037618